Social Entrepreneurship a

Christine K. Volkmann • Kim Oliver Tokarski
Kati Ernst (Eds.)

Social Entrepreneurship and Social Business

An Introduction and Discussion with Case
Studies

Springer Gabler

Editors
Prof. Dr. Christine K. Volkmann
University of Wuppertal, Germany

Dr. Kati Ernst
University of Wuppertal, Germany

Prof. Dr. Kim Oliver Tokarski
Bern University of Applied Sciences,
Switzerland

ISBN 978-3-8349-2729-3
DOI 10.1007/978-3-8349-7093-0

ISBN 978-3-8349-7093-0 (eBook)

The Deutsche Nationalbibliothek lists this publication in the Deutsche Nationalbibliografie; detailed bibliographic data are available in the Internet at http://dnb.d-nb.de.

Springer Gabler
© Gabler Verlag | Springer Fachmedien Wiesbaden 2012

Cover design: KünkelLopka GmbH, Heidelberg

Printed on acid-free paper

Springer Gabler is a brand of Springer DE. Springer DE is part of Springer Science+Business Media.
www.springer-gabler.de

Editors' Preface

Social entrepreneurship with its innovative concepts and thrilling opportunities has begun to infiltrate many economies in recent years. All around the globe, social entrepreneurs stand up to a wide range of societal challenges, ranging from education, health, environment, enterprise development, rural development, children and youth, financial inclusion to water and waste management. Their efforts have not gone unrecognized by academia. By now, research in the field of social entrepreneurship ranges from, e.g., opportunity recognition, business models, function, traits and behaviour of social entrepreneurs, human resource management, marketing, performance measurement, growth, and scaling to finance in social enterprises, as well as to the impact of social entrepreneurship in general. The importance of the topic is reflected by an increasing number of (journal) articles and books. New research centres were installed and business school courses process the ever increasing knowledge on the topic for the education of students and other interested parties.

This textbook offers its readers a comprehensive overview of the field of social entrepreneurship. In addition to a *theoretical* survey of the current knowledge on the topic it also includes case studies as *practical* examples. We hope that after finishing this book, the reader will have gained a deeper understanding of *The Field* (what is social entrepreneurship and which role does it play in theory and practice), *The People* (who works in the field and how do they join forces to do good), *The Business* (business models, marketing and financing of social enterprises as well as success measurement and scaling concepts) and *The Market* (which are the markets social enterprises interact with, what is their current impact and what are critical reflections on social entrepreneurship).

We wish all readers inspiration, motivation and insight when working through this textbook and hope that the discussion of the theoretical concepts of social entrepreneurship and individual case studies will make their reading pleasurable and contribute to a better understanding of the meaning and application of social entrepreneurship.

The realization of this textbook would not have been possible without the work of many different people. At first we would like to thank all authors for their valuable contributions. Our thanks also go to Miriam Thielemann, Beverly Langsch-Brown and Jacqueline Bürki for their help in proof-reading. Further on we would like to thank Kazem Mochkabadi for his support. Our gratitude also goes to Ulrike Lörcher and Katharina Harsdorf at the publishing house Springer Gabler, for their patience, co-operation and continuous support of this project.

A textbook never seems to be completed and we are of course interested in continuously improving the textbook. We therefore welcome suggestions from students and lecturers as well as from social entrepreneurs or other interested parties from the sphere of social entrepreneurship.

Christine K. Volkmann, Kim Oliver Tokarski & Kati Ernst
Wuppertal & Bern, February 2012

Table of Contents

Part I: The Field

Background, Characteristics and Context of Social Entrepreneurship
Christine K. Volkmann, Kim Oliver Tokarski & Kati Ernst

Social Entrepreneurship: Definitions, Drivers and Challenges
Benjamin Huybrechts & Alex Nicholls

1 Background, Characteristics and Context of Social Entrepreneurship

Christine K. Volkmann

University of Wuppertal
Schumpeter School of Business and Economics

Kim Oliver Tokarski

Bern University of Applied Sciences
Faculty of Business

Kati Ernst

University of Wuppertal
Schumpeter School of Business and Economics

Learning goals
Upon completing this chapter, you should be able to accomplish the following:

■ Understand the evolution and historical background of social entrepreneurship.

■ Understand the role of social entrepreneurship in societies, economies and politics.

■ Get first insights into social entrepreneurship research.

1.1   Introduction

Social entrepreneurship has become a relevant topic in business, society and politics. Public attention has also been aroused through the increasing presence of social entrepreneurs in the media and numerous popular science publications. Here we may mention David Bornstein´s book "How to Change the World: Social Entrepreneurs and the Power of New Ideas" (2004) as well as "The Power of Unreasonable People" by Elkington und Hartigan (Bornstein, 2004, Elkington and Hartigan 2008).[1] In his case-study based publication, Bornstein highlights the power (vision, mission and passion) of individual social entrepreneurs in various historical, economic, legal, political and socio-cultural contexts. Many other recent publications in this field focus on the person of the social entrepreneur rather than on the economic function of social entrepreneurship. Social entrepreneurs act as „change agents and engines" of social and economic progress and bring about positive change in the economy as well as the society through their pro-active and innovative activities. Literature on social entrepreneurship often focuses on role models such as Muhammad Yunus.

Some researchers argue that social entrepreneurship is a phenomenon which is anything but new (Boddice, 2009). For example, Bornstein and Davis (2010, p. 2) state: "Social entrepreneurs have always existed. But in the past they were called visionaries, humanitarians, philanthropists, reformers, saints, or simply great leaders". Maybe social entrepreneurship is as old as mankind itself. Nonetheless, their work today is different because it has achieved a potentially global scale (Nicholls, 2006a). At any rate, the term social entrepreneurship is relatively new. Therefore, it is worthwhile to investigate how this modern-day, worldwide social movement came about and how the concept of social entrepreneurship could be described and explained.

---

[1]   For introductory works in the scientific field of social entrepreneurship see for example: Dees (1998), Introduction to social entrepreneurship academia; Leadbeater (1997), The role of social entrepreneurs in society; and Nicholls (2006b), Academic anthology.

1.2 The Role of Social Entrepreneurship in Societies, Economies and Politics

"Many young people today feel frustrated because they cannot recognize any worthy challenge that excites them within the present capitalist system. When you have grown up with ready access to the consumer goods of the world, earning a lot of money isn't a particularly inspiring goal. Social Business can fill this void."
(Muhammad Yunus, 2007)

In 2006, Muhammad Yunus won the Nobel Peace Prize and the idea of social business and social entrepreneurship reverberated around the globe. While working with the poor in Bangladesh, Yunus recognized that many desired to stand on their own feet, for example, by founding their own small business. To do this they needed capital, mostly small amounts, to buy a sewing machine or similar basic tools. Yet, banks were not willing to give the poor loans. They found the risk too high, as no income existed to date, and there was no security available. The bureaucratic processing of these credits also resulted in more costs than the microloans could cover.

The Grameen Bank, founded by Yunus, created an innovative way to make microloans feasible. The bank developed an administration and collection process led by "lending circles", formed by a number of borrowers in each community. Within this circle, borrowers monitor each other and check that each one of them pays back their loans timely and correctly. Defaults make the community as a whole lose credibility. Like this, debtors are motivated to comply with their payment commitments, as they do not want to let down their social network. By involving the community, both the administrative work and a payback security are ensured. These lending circles lead to payback rates higher than those of many large-scale banks. In a social entrepreneurial sense, through this innovative action, social goals are achieved through business. On the one hand, the poor have access to the microloans they need to establish a source of regular income and to look after themselves. On the other hand, like any other bank, the Grameen Bank collects interest, thereby earning revenue. Thus, it acts as a business and in doing so helps a social cause. This is social entrepreneurship.

On this note, Bill Gates spoke at the 2008 World Economic Forum in Davos: "If we can spend the early decades of the twenty-first century finding approaches that meet the needs of the poor in ways that generate profits and recognition for business, we have found a sustainable way to reduce poverty in the world" (Bill Gates, as cited by Kinsley, 2009, p. 16).

The Grameen Bank and numerous other early social entrepreneurial initiatives have their roots in emerging market countries, for instance: Aravind Eye Clinic (www.aravind.org), Fabio Rosa's Agroelectric System of Appropriate Technology (STA), Hippo Roller (www.hipporoller.org), KickStart water pumps (www.kickstart.org), one laptop per child (one.laptop.org), world bike (worldbike.org), BoGo Light (www.bogolight.com), Center for Digital Inclusion (www.cdiglobal.org). But Western societies have followed. For example, in 2003, the association "startsocial" began supporting social initiatives in Germany. In 2006, Ashoka appointed seven social entrepreneurs as the first German Ashoka Fellows. All over the world the relevance of social entrepreneurship in business, society and politics is growing further. While Seelos and Mair (2009) reported that in 2006, a Google search for "social entrepreneurship" resulted in over 1 million hits, six years later, in 2012, it results in about 4 million.

There are both supply and demand side catalysts that contribute to this increasing importance of social entrepreneurship (Nicholls, 2006a):

- **Supply side**
  - increase in per capita wealth
  - better education levels
  - improved communication

- **Demand side**
  - rising crises in environment and health
  - rising economic inequality
  - institutionalization of professional NGOs
  - inefficiencies in public service delivery

The relevance of SE depends on the economic characteristics and conditions in the individual countries but also on the legal, political, socio-cultural, technological and ecological framework. With regard to the degree of welfare there are significant differences around the globe, especially between the developed countries on the one hand and the developing countries on the other. Even among the Western developed nations differences can be noted with regard to the extent of the allocation of public goods by the government. Germany, for example, is a relatively well-developed welfare state in comparison to Great Britain. At the same time, a great heterogeneity and complexity of social problems and challenges form the specific characteristics of social entrepreneurship. Geographically, the business and growth models of social enterprises can range from a local or regional level to an international or even global level. Socio-economic change can take place in an evolutionary or in a revolutionary way. Social entrepreneurship may develop in various contexts such as poverty, economic inequality, (drug-related) crime, crises, climate changes or corruption in the private economy or the state.

From an ecosystem perspective, social entrepreneurship can be categorized into the dimensions *social orientation, market orientation, innovation* and *opportunity (recognition & exploitation)*. Essential elements of the social entrepreneurship framework are *society, economy, politics, culture* (including *ethics, norms & values*) and the regulatory framework. Furthermore, several types of *stakeholders (e.g. employees, suppliers, media, investors, competitors, customers, non-governmental or non-profit organizations, state and public)* are key elements of the system. The social entrepreneurial ecosystem reduces a *structural disequilibrium, creates value, solves a social problem, assumes risks, deals with asymmetric information, allocates resources, creates new jobs* and *generates tax revenues*.

The dimensions and key elements of the social entrepreneurial ecosystem are summarized in **Figure 1.1**. It has to be noted that these dimensions and elements of social entrepreneurship are not conclusive.

Figure 1.1   Social entrepreneurial ecosystem

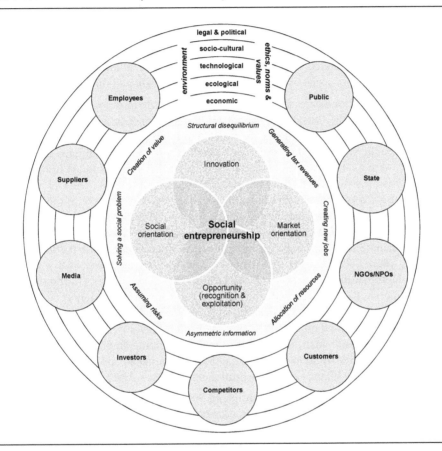

There has been a long way to establish social entrepreneurship in society, and there are still challenges to meet. For example, the fact that social entrepreneurship levels are low is, actually, a challenge for German society, as the country may be missing out on an innovative way to support its citizens. *Entrepreneurship*, in general, is an improvement for society, leading to innovations, fostering employment and resulting in economic growth (e.g., Drucker, 1985; Schumpeter, 1936). "In an entrepreneurial society individuals face a tremendous challenge, a challenge they need to exploit as an opportunity: the need to continuous learning and relearning" (Drucker, 1985, p. 263)..."the emergence of the entrepreneurial society may be a major turning point in history"(....p. 265).

In this sense, social entrepreneurship as a form of entrepreneurial activity can be consid-ered beneficial to society as a whole. Additionally, social entrepreneurship targets social needs unmet by government or business. For example, in 2012, looking back on a welfare state which has offered assistance since the late 19th century, the German government has come to realize that it cannot financially maintain its ample support system. First steps have been taken to reduce unemployment benefits and welfare, and the extent of public healthcare is being reduced. Additionally, the role of the Christian church is diminishing, as fewer citizens pay church taxes and, hence, less money reaches the social causes the churches traditionally address. Overall, large gaps are appearing in the network of social needs which are not catered to by the state or church. This situation in Germany makes innovative solutions for social problems equally more relevant and difficult.

Social entrepreneurship means acting within markets to help a societal cause. This appears when markets fail: either businesses cannot fulfill existing needs, because they cannot be catered to profitably, or governments are not able to fulfill them, as they have low priority in terms of public support (Mair and Marti, 2009). These institutional gaps appear more frequently and to a larger extent in today's societies, as they are embedded in the vast and complex, dynamic structures that are the global markets (Faltin, 2008). The UN millennium development goals (www.un.org/millenniumgoals) are a good example of the large prob-lems the world battles today, e.g., attempting to fight poverty globally. Traditionally, Non-profit Organizations (NPOs) have acted within these institutional voids left by businesses and government (Sud et al., 2009). Yet nowadays, the situation for NPOs has become more challenging (Bull, 2008). On the one hand, competition has increased in this field, with numerous NPOs battling over scarce financial resources (Dees, 1996). On the other hand, the call of money has also reached philanthropy, and investors or donors are expecting more for the funds they put into a social cause (Sud, VanSandt and Baugous, 2009). Frances (2008) describes the situation of NPOs as a fake safety haven which is comfortable and complacent, yet doesn't manage to create thought-changing impact. Hence, traditional NPOs often cannot live up to expectations, and new sustainable and scalable solutions are needed to successfully fill the existing institutional gaps (Dees, 1996).

This is where social entrepreneurship jumps in. Social enterprises attempt to target unful-filled social needs with (more or less) market-based approaches, aiming for sustainable solutions. They do so by creating additional value (social value creation). By moving re-sources to areas of more efficient use, they create value which can be translated into reve-nue (Mair and Marti, 2006). For example, the Spanish dairy company La Fageda (www.fageda.com) employs mentally challenged people to produce their high quality yoghurts, offering them the employment this group of people is often denied. In an eco-nomic sense, the employees are placed in a situation of higher productivity, involving them in economic value creation. Social enterprises also internalize externalities which the mar-ket normally ignores, further increasing the output of social value (Santos, 2009). On top of this, some additional value is created by offering consumers socially aware products, for which they are prepared to pay a price above market value. For example, consumers are willing to pay more for Fair Trade chocolate (see e.g. the GEPA-case in the chapter by Blank in this book) or socially oriented print media like the Big Issue in the UK (see case study in this chapter). These different additional value sources lead to increased sustainability of the venture, making it more attractive for donors and/or investors. Hence, the multiple forms of social value creation are a core function of social enterprises (Auerswald, 2009). By doing this, social entrepreneurship, in its historical establishment through the course of time, fills gaps left unattended by other institutions. Hence the development of social entrepreneurship in the individual countries depends on the gaps and positions which the respective established agents (E, SE, and the government) left open in their distribution of goods.

However, quasi-entrepreneurial activities, which addressed social needs, also took place long before in history. The origins of social entrepreneurship can be found in the establishment of the private sector. Coming from a situation of oppression by feudal lords, churches or slavery, the Enlightenment movement of the 17th century paved the ground for the creation of the private sector, and hence the introduction of the enterprise (Bornstein and Davis, 2010). Over the next decades, laws and practices were introduced which protected individual's ideas and property and led to a thriving private sector. As these laws were first established in the USA, its entrepreneurial sector stood in the forefront to flourish substantially on a broad scale. Together with the progression of the business sector, the state regressed in its responsibilities, leaving institutional gaps and welcoming NPOs and philanthropists into the field (Shaw and Carter, 2007). In Europe, the UK followed suit and was amongst the pioneers to introduce entrepreneurship into the social realm, as in the case of the Victorian private hospitals (Shaw and Carter, 2007). For many years, the coexistence of government, business and NPOs covered a large amount of the occurring social needs.

Here, the organisation Ashoka, founded by Bill Drayton in 1980, a former McKinsey management consultant, played its part (www.ashoka.org; Defourney and Nyssens, 2008). Having travelled India, watching new social enterprises appear, Drayton recognized the value of such sustainable endeavours (Bornstein and Davis, 2010). Subsequently, he founded the first support institution specifically for social entrepreneurs, Ashoka. This organization aims at identifying social entrepreneurs early on and offering them a wide range of assistance, e.g., business consulting, to pursue their goal. With Ashoka's global set-up and their public relations work, the term "social entrepreneur" spread worldwide. Alongside the pioneers and initial support institutions, global developments further aided the creation of social enterprises. Bornstein and Davis (2010) name numerous supporting factors, largely the fall of totalitarian regimes due to a higher level of education and knowledge in societies caused by liberation movements, such as striving for independence for women, and international media such as the internet, especially social media (sites), which helps people worldwide understand the opportunities they have as an individual.

Established on a worldwide level, social entrepreneurship has run through several developmental steps. Various additional support institutions have established themselves, for example the Schwab Foundation and the Skoll Foundation joining Ashoka on a global level. All around the globe national support organizations have also emerged such as the Canadian Centre for Social Entrepreneurship or the Social Entrepreneurship Foundation SEF-Swiss. In Germany, "Bertelsmann Foundation" and "BMW Foundation Herbert Quandt" are examples of organizations which are active in the field of Social Entrepreneurship. Within Europe, Italian cooperatives in the 1980s marked the beginning of wide-scale social entrepreneurship (Defourney and Nyssens, 2008).

Since the 2000s, the UK has established itself as the strongest social entrepreneurial region in Europe (Defourney and Nyssens, 2008). The Global Entrepreneurship Monitor reports levels as high as 6.6% of the UK population participating in social enterprises (Harding, 2004). Bornstein and Davis (2010) even believe that the preoccupation with social entrepreneurship has already reached its third generation. In their view, it started with social entrepreneurship 1.0 which identified social entrepreneurs, described their function and developed support systems, followed by social entrepreneurship 2.0 that focused on the organizational excellence of social enterprises, to social entrepreneurship 3.0 today that looks at the change-making potential of all people.

Also, academia has picked up these themes within social entrepreneurship subsequently. Overall, it represents an interesting topic in particular because social entrepreneurship features different interdisciplinary angels relating to its social, cultural, psychological and economic significance. This plurality of perspectives in studying social entrepreneurship led to initial publications aimed at building a common understanding of what social entrepreneurship is (and what it is not) as well as what social entrepreneurs represent and do. This thrust of research into social entrepreneurship is still evolving as discussed in the next section.

1.3   The Story of Social Entrepreneurship in Academia

The idea of social value creation through business has its academic roots in the 20th century. However, up to the end of the 1990s academic attention was paid to Social Entrepreneurship only sporadically and only a few papers were published (e.g. Parker, 1954; Eppstein, 1964; Hage and Aiken 1970).

In 1973, Davis wrote an article on the different opinions towards business assuming social responsibilities (Davis, 1973). On the one hand, researchers such as Milton Friedman (1962) feared that social responsibility in business would disrupt the very basis of the capitalistic market: "few trends could so thoroughly undermine the very foundations of our free society as the acceptance by corporate officials of a social responsibility other than to make as much money for their stockholders as possible" (cited by Davis, 1973, p. 312; cf. also the chapter by Beckmann). On the other hand, researchers such as Paul A. Samuelson saw it as a core responsibility of business to create social value. Researchers have moved a long way since then, with activities such as Corporate Social Responsibility (CSR) having long taken their place in the business realm. In the context of Non-Profit Organization (NPO) management Dennis R. Young compared "nonprofit entrepreneurs" to managers, focusing on their innovative actions (Young, 1986, as reported by Light, 2005, p. 2). However, Social Entrepreneurship is systematically distinguished from CSR, NPO or Non-Governmental Organization (NGO) management by several criteria and approaches (cf. in more detail chapter 1.4). In the 1980s, academia was still doubtful about the subject of social entrepreneurship. For example, Dees is said to have suggested a social entrepreneurship course to

Harvard Business School which he was "cautioned not to do" (Eakin, 2003). The actual research field of social entrepreneurship subsequently started its growth in the late nineties. Dees' paper on "The Meaning of *Social Entrepreneurship*" (1998) attracted special attention in this phase (see also Waddoch and Post 1991; Leadbeater, 1997). Ever since, there has been a dynamically growing scientific interest in the field of social entrepreneurship. Schools introduced their first social entrepreneurship courses and research networks, such as the EMES European Research Network, engaged in the topic (Defourney and Nyssens, 2008).

Academia is obviously embracing the topic, and research as well as teaching programs on social entrepreneurship are growing fast (Nicholls, 2010; Perrini, 2006). For example, numerous special journals on the topic have emerged over the past few years (e.g. Stanford Social Innovation Review, 2003; Social Enterprise Journal, 2004; Journal of Social Entrepreneurship, 2010; Journal of Social Entrepreneurship and Innovation, 2011). In addition, special issues of journals have emerged (e.g. International Journal of Entrepreneurial Behaviour & Research, 2008, Entrepreneurship Theory and Practice, 2010) and edited volumes and monographic books have been published. New social entrepreneurship conferences are being launched (e.g. Skoll World Forum on Social Entrepreneurship, NY-Stern Conference on Social Entrepreneurship). The managers of tomorrow are taking social entrepreneurship classes at top business schools (e.g., Columbia Business School in New York, IESE in Barcelona; also see Tracey and Phillips, 2007; www.aacsb.edu offers an overview of available courses). Furthermore universities are appointing professorships specifically to this research field (e.g., the Leuphana University Lüneburg, Rotterdam School of Management, University of Nottingham, Copenhagen Business School, University of Oxford, Vlerick Leuven Gent Management School, IESE Business School, University of Geneva, School for Social Entrepreneurs, University of Cambridge, Universidad de Los Andes, Asian Institute of Management, Tata Institute of Social Sciences, University of Calgary, Leonard N. Stern School of Business, Portland State University, Duke University, Babson College, Stanford Graduate School of Business, Harvard Business School). Nonetheless, it is widely agreed that the theoretical examination of this phenomenon is in its infancy – and researchers point out the small number of publications and accessible empirical studies on the topic (e.g., Certo and Miller, 2008; Desa, 2007; Mair and Marti, 2006; Peattie and Morley, 2008; Robinson, Mair and Hockerts 2009).

Researchers and educators are positioning themselves as thought leaders of the field and taking ownership in moving it forwards, such as Alex Nicholls (University of Oxford: Saïd Business School), Gregory Dees (Duke University: The Fuqua School of Business), Johanna Mair (University of Navarra: IESE Business School) or Paul C. Light (NYU: Robert F. Wagner Graduate School of Public Service), to name but a few. Besides the broad phenomena, elements of social entrepreneurship are also now being studied in detail.

Additionally, researchers and educators are assisting in the development of practitioner guides to help social entrepreneurs further improve their businesses (Brinckerhoff, 2000; Dees, Emerson and Economy, 2001, 2002; Durieux and Stebbins, 2010).

Hence, while traction is currently high, the field should be treated as the young area that it is and take its time to develop sound theories to build upon (Harding, 2004). In this sense, and moving back to Bornstein and Davis' vision of social entrepreneurship 3.0, the field of social entrepreneurship research has not even fully grasped social entrepreneurship 1.0, the comprehension of what social entrepreneurship is and how it functions. There is currently no established theory (as criticized by Harding, 2004; Light, 2011; Weerawardena & Mort, 2006) or presence of large-scale quantitative studies (as criticized by Hockerts, 2006; Light, 2011). A large part of the field is based on anecdotal cases and is, therefore, phenomenon-driven (as criticized by Mair and Marti, 2006; Nicholls and Cho, 2006).² However, this is fairly typical for a relatively new, evolving field of research in the social sciences. And while it is mandatory to build further large-scale empirical evidence on social entrepreneurship, the field still should preserve its interdisciplinary, multi-facetted origin and core. This seems necessary since social entrepreneurial behavior will almost always involve social and economic action in a rich cultural context. This nature of social entrepreneurship also makes it an interesting, fascinating, and important topic to learn about and to study in depth.

1.4 Concepts and Typologies of Social Entrepreneurship

1.4.1 Social Entrepreneurship and Social Entrepreneur

In the previous chapter, we showed that social entrepreneurship has developed into a dynamically evolving field of research and teaching since the late 1990s. However, literature in this context is still widely based on a variety of definitions and conceptual approaches (see also chapter two of Huybrechts and Nicholls in this book). Up to date there still is no consistent or standard definition of the term. This may result from the fact that the respective research topics have emerged from different disciplines (e.g. economics, entrepreneurship, sociology, psychology). The definitions range from a very narrow to a very wide understanding (for a detailed overview on social entrepreneurship definitions, see e.g. Dacin, Dacin and Matear, 2010; Zahra et al., 2009). The lack of conceptual accordance leads to a lack of clear rules for the description and explanation of the concept. This chapter will present selected conceptual approaches in order to illustrate their variety. In spite of the fact that definitions and approaches are heterogeneous, there is a consensus with regard to the objectives of social entrepreneurship and social entrepreneurs. According to this, social entrepreneurship aims for the exploitation of opportunities and for social change rather than for maximum profit in the traditional sense. In this sense social entrepreneurship re-

---

²   For a selection of case studies, see Alvord, Brown and Letts (2004); Bhawe, Jain and Gupta (2007); Bornstein (2004); Corner and Ho (2010); Elkington and Hartigan (2008); Faltin (2009); Mair and Marti (2009); Spear (2006), Thompson, Alvy and Lees (2000); Thompson and Dorothy (2006) as well as Waddock and Post (1991).

fers "to an ability to leverage resources that address social problems" (Dacin, Dacin and Matear, 2010, p. 38). According to a definition by Mair and Marti (2006, p. 37), social entrepreneurship "is primarily intended to explore and exploit opportunities to create social value by stimulating social change or meeting social needs". In the context of a general entrepreneurship definition there is a critical debate if the separate term "social entrepreneurship" is actually necessary. This approach is, e.g., reflected by Schramm (2010) who holds the opinion that "all entrepreneurship is social", because it generates economic and social value (jobs and tax revenues).

In a differentiated analysis of Schumpeter's thoughts, Swedberg (2006) proposed that according to Schumpeter social entrepreneurship could be defined as a form of dynamic behaviour in a non-economic societal area. Deducing the social entrepreneurship concept from Schumpeter's general theory of entrepreneurship thus offers a basis for further differentiation and analysis of the concept according to a deductive analytic approach (Volkmann and Tokarski, 2010). **Figure 1.2** suggests a potential basic classification in this field.

Figure 1.2   Economic Change and Social Entrepreneurship

	Economy	Society
Dynamic or entrepreneurial change	Development	*Social Entrepreneurship*
Static or non-entrepreneurial change	Adaption	Social Evolution

Own illustration based on Swedberg (2006)

Schumpeter himself mentioned that economic development includes social change, which shows that he, too, took the relation and interaction between economy and society into account (Swedberg, 2006).

In general, social entrepreneurship can be seen as a form of entrepreneurship. Likewise, social entrepreneurs "are one species in the genus entrepreneur" (Dees, 1998, p. 2). In the view of Dacin, Dacin and Matear (2010) social entrepreneurship is related to or embedded in other forms of entrepreneurship. They distinguish four types of entrepreneurs/entrepreneurship; one of them is a social entrepreneur/social entrepreneurship:

■ **conventional entrepreneurship/conventional entrepreneur**, as an agent who enables or enacts a vision based on new ideas in order to create successful innovations. The predominant organizational form is profit oriented whilst the primary motive (aim) is economic.

- **institutional entrepreneurship/institutional entrepreneur,** as an agent who mobilizes resources to influence or change institutional rules in order to support or change an existing institution, or to establish a new one. The predominant organizational form is profit oriented whilst the primary motive (aim) is institutional reform respectively development.

- **cultural entrepreneurship/cultural entrepreneur,** as an individual who identifies an opportunity and acts upon it in order to create social, cultural, or economic value. The predominant organizational form is either non-profit or profit-oriented whilst the primary motive (aim) is cultural diffusion respectively enlightenment.

- **social entrepreneurship/social entrepreneur,** as an actor who applies business principles to solving social problems. The predominant organizational form is non-profit or profit-oriented whilst the primary motive (aim) is social change respectively well-being.

In a detailed literature analysis, Dacin, Dacin and Matear (2010) found that the existing definitions of social entrepreneurship focus on four key factors: the *characteristics of individual social entrepreneurs,* their *scope of activity,* the *processes and resources used by social entrepreneurs,* and the *primary mission and outcomes associated with the social entrepreneur which are creating social value* (see **Figure 1.3**).

Figure 1.3   Four key factors of social entrepreneurship definitions

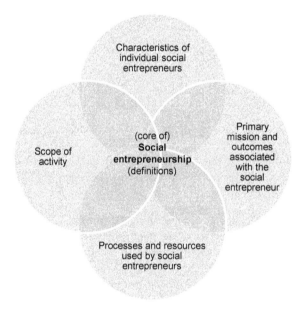

Own illustration inspired by the textual approach of Dacin, Dacin and Matear (2010)

While in the view of researchers, approaches with the focus on the characteristics of individual social entrepreneurs are not very promising for definition and differentiation purposes (see e.g. Gartner, 1988), recent research concentrates especially on the development of social entrepreneurship concepts which comprise the scope of activity, the processes and (innovative) use of resources as well as the mission and outcomes of social entrepreneurs (social entrepreneurship). The terms and topics which are covered by these concepts range from social entrepreneurial activities versus social activism, not-for-profit versus for-profit, social outcome versus economic outcome to social wealth creation versus economic wealth creation. In contrast to the representatives of such extreme positions there are also researchers who have adopted a more differentiated perspective and have developed more comprehensive and integrated definitions and concepts.

One example of such an economically broader perspective is the definition by Zahra et al. (2009, p. 522) who suggest that "any definition, measurement or evaluation of social entrepreneurship should reflect both social and economic considerations." Therefore they propose a standard to evaluate those opportunities and organizational processes related to social entrepreneurship which should be reflected by a broader term called "total wealth", which has tangible outcomes (e.g., products, clients served, or funds generated) and intangible outcomes (e.g., wealth, happiness and general well-being).

Definition of Total Wealth:
- Total Wealth (TW) = Economic Wealth (EW) + Social Wealth (SW)

    - EW = Economic Value (EV)
    ../. Economic Costs (EC)
    ../. Opportunity Costs (OC);

    - SW = Social Value (SV)
    ../. Social Costs (SC)

- As a result the Total Wealth can be calculated as follows:

    - TW = EV + SV – (EC + OC + SC).

The „total wealth" calculated in this way illustrates the range of possible combinations between the extremes "economic wealth" on the one hand and "social wealth" on the other which may occur in entrepreneurial entities. For a practical application of the total wealth calculation, however, it will be necessary to assess the economic and/or social value as well as the relevant economic costs (e.g. environmental pollution) and/or social costs (e.g. social discord). Since entrepreneurial entities are usually characterized by a scarcity of resources, the calculation must also take opportunity costs into account. Used in this way, the total wealth standard may be useful for scholars and practitioners to evaluate both economic and social opportunities and ventures (Zahra et al., 2009).

Social entrepreneurs can be regarded as driving forces of social and economic change in several contexts. They recognize or discover and exploit new opportunities; they enter a process of innovation, adaptation and learning. They generate social and economic wealth.

Zahra et al. (2009) developed an economic-theory based approach in which they distinguish between three different types of entrepreneurs/entrepreneurship: the *social bricoleur* (Hayek, 1945), the *social constructionist* (Kirzner, 1973) and the *social engineer* (Schumpeter, 1934). The three types are distinguished by the way in which social entrepreneurs recognize opportunities, define mission and goals, acquire and use resources, address social problems and widen their geographical scope (see own **Table 1.1** based on Zahra et al., 2009). Social bricoleurs address social needs and problems at a local level. In contrast to other types of social entrepreneurs they can tap the scarce resources only at a local level and use them to address social issues in their communities. Their actions are ruled by their unique local and tacit knowledge. According to Kirzner's theory, social constructionists have to be alert to opportunities in social contexts. For example, they might take action in cases of market or government failure. Wherever gaps occur in social systems or structures which are not or only insufficiently bridged by existing companies, government organizations or NPOs, social entrepreneurs may discover their entrepreneurial opportunities. In contrast to social bricoleurs, social constructionists aim for a more extensive and scalable solution for social issues. The third type, social engineers, tackles complex national, transnational and global social problems in a systematic way. According to Schumpeter, social engineers do not only bring about incremental social improvements but fundamental, revolutionary social changes. They operate on a large scale and scope and their activities thus have a high social and economic impact.

Table 1.1 Typology of social entrepreneurship/social entrepreneurs

Type	Social Bricoleur	Social Constructionists	Social Engineer
Theory	Hayek	Kirzner	Schumpeter
What they do?	Perceive and act upon opportunities to address a local social needs they are motivated and have the expertise and resources to address.	Build and operate alternative structures to provide goods and services addressing social needs that governments, agencies, and businesses cannot.	Creation of newer, more effective social systems designed to replace existing ones when they are ill-suited to address significant social needs.
Scale, scope and timing	Small scale, local in scope—often episodic in nature.	Small to large scale, local to international in scope, designed to be institutionalized to address an ongoing social need.	Very large scale that is national to international in scope and which seeks to build lasting structures that will challenge existing order.
Why they are necessary?	Knowledge about social needs and the abilities to address them are widely scattered. Many social needs are non-discernable or easily misunderstood from afar, requiring local agents to detect and address them.	Laws, regulation, political acceptability, inefficiencies and/or lack of will prevent existing governmental and business organizations from addressing many important social needs effectively.	Some social needs are not amenable to amelioration within existing social structures. Entrenched incumbents can thwart actions to address social needs that undermine their own interests and source of power.
Social Significance	Collectively, their actions help maintain social harmony in the face of social problems	They mend the social fabric where it is torn, address acute social needs within existing broader social structures, and help maintain social harmony.	They seek to rip apart existing social structures and replace them with new ones. They represent an important force for social change in the face of entrenched incumbents.
Effect on Social Equilibrium	Atomistic actions by local social entrepreneurs move us closer to a theoretical "social equilibrium."	Addressing gaps in the provision of socially significant goods and service creates new "social equilibriums."	Fractures existing social equilibrium and seeks to replace it with a more socially efficient one
Source of Discretion	Being on the spot with the skills to address local problems not on others' "radars." Local scope means they have limited resource requirements and are fairly autonomous. Small scale and local scope allows for quick response times.	They address needs left un- addressed and have limited/no competition. They may even be welcomed and be seen as a "release valve" preventing negative publicity/social problems that may adversely affect existing governmental and business organizations.	Popular support to the extent that existing social structures and incumbents are incapable of addressing important social needs.
Limits to Discretion	Not much aside from local laws and regulations. However, the limited resources and expertise they possess limit their ability to address other needs or expand geographically.	Need to acquire financial and human resources necessary to fulfill mission and institutionalize as a going concern. Funder demands oversight. Professional volunteers and employees are needed to operate organization.	Seen as fundamentally illegitimate by established parties that see them as a threat, which brings scrutiny and attempts to undermine the ability of the social engineers to bring about change. The perceived illegitimacy will inhibit the ability to raise financial and human resources from traditional sources. As a consequence, they may become captive of the parties that supply it with needed resources.

Another strategic approach which is based on economic theories was developed by Santos (2009). Depending on the question whether or not profit is maximized, entrepreneurship is either classified in the category "value creation" or "value appropriation". The latter means in this context that entrepreneurs will be able to keep a large part of the value they generate. Accordingly, while social entrepreneurship is assumed to create a high social value, it does not offer much potential for value appropriation. In a capitalist economic system commercial entrepreneurs who pursue a profit-oriented strategy would consequently squeeze social entrepreneurs out of the market because the former have more capital at their disposal. Santos also distinguishes several stakeholders (government, business, charity, commercial entrepreneurship, social activism and social entrepreneurship) who represent different roles in the economic system, pursue different institutional goals and differ in their logic of action (see **Table 1.2**). According to this categorization social entrepreneurs are mainly active in less profitable contexts in which positive external effects can be generated (cf. in more detail also the chapter by Berg/Grünhagen in this book). The mitigation of negative external effects is the task of social activists. The dominant logic of action is assumed to be control in managers, innovation in commercial entrepreneurs and empowerment in social entrepreneurs respectively.

While social entrepreneurship is the term most commonly used in the field of study, it relates to the terms of social entrepreneur – the person engaging in social entrepreneurship, and also social enterprise – the venture run by the social entrepreneur. As these terms refer to the same phenomenon, they are all applied in the course of this theoretical excursion. They all relate to the same core at different levels of analysis (Hockerts, 2006; Peredo and McLean, 2006). Therefore, the next step will be to address the construct of the social enterprise at the organizational level.

Table 1.2   Institutional actors in modern capitalist economies

Stakeholders	Distinct role in economic system	Dominant institutional goal	Dominant logic of action
Governments	Centralized mechanism through which the infrastructure of the economic system is created and enforced (and public goods provisioned)	Defend public interest	Regulation
Business	Distributed mechanism through which society's resources and skills are allocated to the most valued activities	Create sustainable advantage	Control
Charity	Distributed mechanism through which economic outcomes are made more equitable despite uneven resource endowments	Support disadvantaged populations	Goodwill
Commercial entrepreneurship	Distributed mechanism through which neglected opportunities for profit are explored	Appropriate value for stakeholders	Innovation
Social activism	Distributed mechanism through which behaviors that bring negative externalities are selected out	Change social system	Political action
Social Entrepreneurship	Distributed mechanism through which neglected positive externalities are internalized in the economic system	Deliver sustainable solution	Empowerment

Own table based on Santos (2009)

1.4.2   Social Enterprise

In analogy to the terms Social Entrepreneurship and Social Entrepreneur, numerous approaches have attempted to classify the term social enterprises (e.g. Dees, Emerson and Economy 2001; John, 2006; Alter, 2007; Neck, Brush and Allen 2009).

For example, Dees, Emerson and Economy (2001) suggest that social enterprises can be differentiated and located on a diametrically opposed scale between *purely philanthropic* (non-profit enterprises, which aim at generating a high social return) and *purely commercial* (for-profit enterprises striving for a maximum financial return). *Hybrid models* exist between these two extremes (see **Figure 1.4**).

Figure 1.4   Social enterprise spectrum

	continuum of options		
	purely philanthropic	**hybrids**	**purely commercial**
general motives, methods, and goals	• appeal to goodwill • mission-driven • social value creation	• mixed motives • balance of mission and market • social and economic value	• appeal to self-interest • market-driven • economic value creation
key stakeholders			
beneficiaries	pay nothing	subsidized rates and/or mix of full payers and those who pay nothing	pay full market rates
capital	donations and grants	below market capital and/or mix of full payers and those who pay nothing	market capital rate
workforce	volunteers	below market wages and/or mix of volunteers and fully paid staff	market rate compensation
suppliers	make in-kind donations	special discounts and/or mix of in-kind and full price	charge market prices

Own illustration based on Dees, Emerson and Economy (2001)

Depending on these three categories (purely philanthropic, hybrid, purely commercial) there are different benefits and returns for stakeholders who commit resources to a social enterprise:

- **purely philanthropic:**
  The general motive of this category of enterprises is that they are mission-driven. Their methods and aims entail the appeal to good-will and the creation of social values. Beneficiaries (customers) do pay nothing for their product or service offers. The capital required to build a philanthropic enterprise is commonly raised by donations and grants. The workforce consists of volunteers. Suppliers make in-kind donations.

- **hybrid:**
  Enterprises in this domain have mixed motives. Their methods and aims embrace a balance of social mission and market orientation in order to create both social and economic value. Beneficiaries (customers) do pay subsidized rates for the goods or services or there is a mix of full payers and those who pay nothing. Financial funds are raised at below market capital rates. Their workforce is paid below market wages and/or there is a mix of volunteers and fully paid staff. Suppliers typically offer special discounts and/or there is a mix of in-kind contributions and full prices.

- **purely commercial:**
  These enterprises are completely market-driven. Their methods and aims are the appeal to self-interest, including the creation of economic values. Customers will pay fair market prices. Investors provide capital at market rates. The workforce receives market salaries and suppliers charge full market prices.

In addition, Alter (2007) proposed a differentiation in which the spectrum of social enterprises ranges from (traditional) non-profit enterprises to (traditional) for-profit enterprises including a hybrid category in between (see also the chapter by Mair and Sharma in this book).

The hybrid category can be further differentiated into four sub-categories (non-profit enterprises with income-generating activities, social enterprises, socially responsible businesses and enterprises practicing social responsibility). To the left side of the spectrum among the hybrids are those non-profit enterprises (non-profit enterprises with income-generating activities, social enterprises) whose business activities generate profits to fund their social mission and report back to their stakeholders. To the right side of the hybrid spectrum there are for-profit enterprises (socially responsible businesses and enterprises practicing social responsibility) which create social value but are mainly driven by profits and are accountable to shareholders. **Figure 1.5** shows a combination of two separate illustrations by Alter (2007).

Figure 1.5   Social enterprise typology and dual value creation

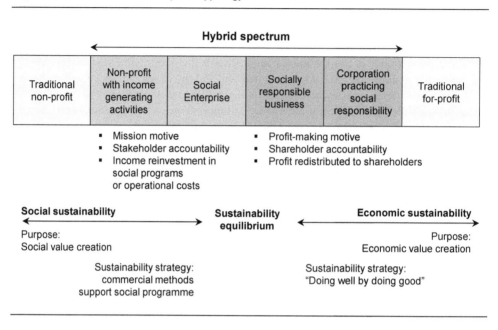

Own illustration based on Alter (2007)

Boyd et al. (2008) note that this model is useful so as to highlight differences and tradeoffs among hybrid organizations. However, for research purposes the category of hybrid organizations cannot be differentiated along a single dimension. Profit and mission motives are relatively independent organizational dimensions. There are hybrid organizations which are strongly driven by both profit and mission, and thus challenge the notion of tradeoffs between mission and profit motives.

Despite the criticism regarding the usefulness for research purposes the model shows the mindset for a social enterprise typology and dual value creation. It generates a better understanding than a mere overview on the topic of the classification of social enterprises.

Another distinction of social enterprises can be made according to the overlapping areas of government, (voluntary) associations and business from an institutional perspective. Ridley-Duff (2008) proposes a model from a stakeholder perspective and governance philosophy/perspective, which balances the disciplines of social responsibility, participative governance and market success (see **Figure 1.6**).

Figure 1.6   Social enterprises and institutional perspectives

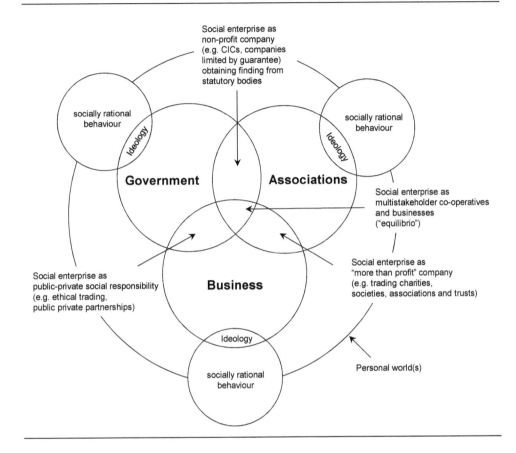

Own modified illustration based on Ridley-Duff (2008)

Ridley-Duff (2008, p. 305) argues that "instead of viewing 'social enterprise' as a subset of the social economy, it can be viewed as a range of business practices that proactively build economic and social capital across the affected stakeholder groups. As such, it regains an ideological character (and basis) that moves the definition away from "profit"-based categorizations towards an understanding of social entrepreneurship as the development of alternative business structures (and practices) that support socially rational objectives."

In particular, the global economic crisis which began in 2008 and left governments with rapidly growing deficits and overstretched budgets may result in increased demands for social enterprises to provide substitute products for (previously) public goods and services (e.g. social casework). For example, social entrepreneurs may be able to claim that there are products and services required which are neither (or no longer) adequately provided by the state nor by pure for-profit businesses in the market. Such negligence by the public and the market may create a demand to be addressed by social enterprises. To address such gaps and the supply of goods and services, social enterprises will need external resources so as to pursue their mission and establish their place in society alongside social, economic, and political considerations. This need to obtain resources and support from stakeholders and society as a whole shows that the establishment of a social enterprise is far from trivial and deserves further attention in terms of managerial challenges and policy-making. The facets and issues involved will be discussed throughout this book.

1.5   Case Study

The magazine The Big Issue is a weekly entertainment, news and culture magazine styled like a commercial magazine which is sold on the streets of many British cities by homeless people. It was launched in 1991 by Gordon Roddick and A. John Bird. Roddick and Bird believed that the key to solving the problem of homelessness lay in helping people to help themselves. The aim is to provide work for them so they can earn their own income. So vendors buy an amount of magazines with their own money and sell them at their own risk (profit or loss).This is intended to raise their awareness for their own situation and poverty and their willingness to take over control of their lives again. Another (indirect) aim is to call attention to social grievances.

The magazine is positioned through the quality of the thematic content. It is not just de-signed as a means to the end of collecting donations. The magazine is sold on the streets exclusively and not in shops or newspaper kiosks. So customers are in direct contact with the vendor when buying a magazine.

The price of the magazine (currently) is 2.50 GBP (3.00 Euros or 4.00 US-Dollars approxi-mately). The street vendors buy the magazine for 1.25 GBP from The Big Issue Company Ltd. and sell it at a price of 2.50 GBP to the customers on the streets. Each (certified) new vendor receives short instructions, respectively training, for the sale of the magazine and (five) free copies (in London ten). Copies which are not sold cannot be returned and no money is refunded. Any further turnover of the magazine, for example from advertise-ments, is realized directly by The Big Issue Company Ltd.

The organization behind The Big Issue is divided into two parts: On the one hand, there is The Big Issue Company Ltd., which produces the magazine and sells it to a street vendor network. On the other hand, there is The Big Issue Foundation (established in 1995), a non-profit foundation which aims at helping the street vendors regain control of their lives. The Big Issue Foundation offers counseling services and references in the areas *health* (e.g., ac-cess to health care), *finance* (e.g., help gaining ID; opening a bank union account), *housing* (e.g., access to temporary and permanent housing) as well as *personal aspirations* (e.g., access to training and employment opportunities).

The Big Issue organization is supported by the government only to a minimum extent. The whole organization depends almost exclusively on selling the issue, advertisements, (vol-untary) donations and volunteering. Without the generosity of the individual or company buyers and donors as well as charitable organizations the magazine and the counseling services could not be provided.

Currently the organization supports 2,800 homeless and vulnerably housed people all over Great Britain. Every week 125,000 copies of The Big Issue are circulated and read by 522,000 people (NRS Jan-Dec 2010). The Big Issue vendors earned more than £5million to release them from dependence.

The Big Issue states that the magazine "has become synonymous with challenging, independent journalism, and renowned for securing exclusive interviews with the most elusive of superstars. The Big Issue is a media phenomenon and one of the world's leading social enterprises with a business model which has inspired hundreds of imitations; from Johannesburg to Tokyo, Sydney to Addis Ababa, Perth to Sao Paolo, Seoul to Nairobi, The Big Issue is leading a global self-help revolution." (The Big Issue)

The Development of this case study, data and information based on/retrieved from www.bigissue.com and www.bigissue.org.uk)

Questions:

1. Would you call Gordon Roddick and A. John Bird social entrepreneurs?

2. What problems does The Big Issue address?
   Is this a (good) example of social entrepreneurship?

3. What kind of value is created?

4. What do you think: Is The Big Issue a social enterprise?

5. How do you (critically) judge the concept(s) and organizational structure(s) of The Big Issue?

Further Questions (related to the other chapters of the textbook)

Let's assume that the managing director of The Big Issue Company Ltd. is not happy with the present business model and the company's development. He hires you to (further) develop the business model in order to create a company that can support itself almost alone. In this context, the following tasks and questions will have to be dealt with (You can make realistic assumptions to support your answers.):

6. Outline the current business model of The Big Issue in a short survey
   (use a model you know as a basis for your argumentation).

7. For the further development of the business model you are expected to make suggestions for a growth strategy. Present a short sketch for a growth-oriented (re-) positioning of The Big Issue.

Use your social entrepreneurship knowledge to find holistic but well-structured arguments on the basis of the (current) business model.

8. What would you (have to) change in order to reduce the dependence on donations?
   Sometimes this may involve questions with regard to products and innovations.

9. In general: How do you want to earn your money? What is the value proposition?
   Who are your customers? How can you address them?

1.6   Further Reading

[1] Bornstein, D. and Davis, S. (2010), *Social entrepreneurship: what everyone needs to know*, Oxford Univ. Press, Oxford.
[2] Dacin, P.A., Dacin, M.T. and Matear, M. (2010), "Social Entrepreneurship: Why We Don't Need a New Theory and How We Move Forward From Here", in *Academy of Management Perspectives*, vol. 24, no. 3, pp. 37-57.
[3] Dees, J.G. (2010), Creating Large-Scale Change: Not 'Can' But 'How', What Matters, McKinsey & Company, New York.
[4] Nicholls, A. (ed.) (2006), *Social Entrepreneurship. New Models of Sustainable Social Change*, Oxford University Press, Oxford.
[5] Nicholls, A. (2010), "The Legitimacy of Social Entrepreneurship: Reflexive Isomorphism in a Pre-Paradigmatic Field", in Entrepreneurship Theory and Practice, vol. 34, issue 4, pp. 611-633.
[6] Zahra, S.A., Gedajlovic, E., Neubaum, D.O. and Shulman, J.M (2009), "A typology of social entrepreneurs: Motives, search processes and ethical challenges", in *Journal of Business Venturing*, vol. 24, no. 5, pp. 519–532.

1.7   Bibliography

[1] Alter, S.K. (2007), "Social Enterprise Typology", Virtue Ventures, online: http://www.4lenses.org/setypology/print.
[2] Alvord, S. H., Brown, L.D. and Letts, C.W. (2004), "Social entrepreneurship and societal transformation", in *Journal of Applied Behavioral Science*, vol. 40, no. 3, pp. 260-282.
[3] Auerswald, P. (2009), "Entrepreneurship and Social Value", in *Stanford Social Innovation Review*, vol. 7, no. 2, pp. 50-55.
[4] Bhawe, N., Jain, T.K. and Gupta, V.K. (2007), The entrepreneurship of the good samaritan: a qualitative study to understand how opportunities are perceived in social entrepreneurship, Paper presented at the BCERC.
[5] Boddice, R. (2009), "Forgotten antecedents: entrepreneurship, ideology and history", in Ziegler, R. (ed.), *An Introduction to Social Entrepreneurship - Voices, Preconditions, Contexts*, Edward Elgar, Cheltenham, pp. 133-152.
[6] Bornstein, D. (2004), *How to Change the World: Social Entrepreneurs and the power of New Ideas*, Oxford University Press, Oxford.
[7] Bornstein, D. and Davis, S. (2010), *Social entrepreneurship: what everyone needs to know*, Oxford Univ. Press, Oxford.
[8] Boyd, B., Henning, N., Reyna, E., Wang, D. and Welch, M. (2008), *Hybrid Organizations: Innovations toward Sustainability*, University of Michigan, Michigan.
[9] Brinckerhoff, P.C. (2000), *Social entrepreneurship - The art of mission-based venture development*, John Wiley & Sons, New York.
[10] Certo, S.T. and Miller, T. (2008), "Social entrepreneurship: Key issues and concepts", in *Business Horizons*, vol. 51, no. 4, pp. 267-271.
[11] Corner, P.D. and Ho, M. (2010), "How opportunities develop in social entrepreneurship", in: *Entrepreneurship: Theory & Practice*, vol. 34, no. 4, pp. 635-659.
[12] Dacin, P.A., Dacin, M.T. and Matear, M. (2010), "Social Entrepreneurship: Why We Don't Need a New Theory and How We Move Forward From Here", in *Academy of Management Perspectives*, vol. 24, no. 3, pp. 37-57.
[13] Davis, K. (1973), "The case for and against business assumption of social responsibilities", in *The Academy of Management Journal*, vol. 16, no. 2, pp. 312-322.
[14] Dees, J.G. (1996), *The Social Enterprise Spectrum: from Philanthropy to Commerce*, Harvard Business School Press, Harvard.

[15] Dees, J.G. (1998), "The meaning of "social entrepreneurship", online: http://www.fntc.info/files/documents/The%20meaning%20of%20Social%20Entreneurship.pdf.

[16] Dees, J.G., Emerson, J. and Economy, P. (2001), *Enterprising nonprofits: a toolkit for social entrepreneurs*, Wiley, New York.

[17] Dees, J.G., Emerson, J., and Economy, P. (2002), *Strategic toolkit for social entrepreneurs - Enhancing the performance of your enterprising nonprofit*, Wiley, New York.

[18] Defourny, J. and Nyssens, M. (2008), *Social Enterprise in Europe: Recent Trends And Developments*, WP no. 08/01, European Research Network.

[19] Desa, G. (2007), "Social entrepreneurship: snapshots of a research field in emergence", online: http://www.cbs.dk/content/download/64150/877865/file/Social%20Entrepreneurship%20-%20Snapshots%20of%20a%20Research%20Field%20in%20Emergence%20(G.%20Desa%20revised).doc, accessed date 3/17/2009.

[20] Drucker, P.F. (1985), *Innovation and Entrepreneurship: Practice and Principles*, Harpercollins, New York.

[21] Durieux, M.B. and Stebbins, R.A. (2010), *Social entrepreneurship for dummies*, Wiley Publishing, Hoboken.

[22] Eakin, E. (2003), "How to save the world? Treat it like a business", *New York Times*, online: http://www.collegesummit.org/images/uploads/PP-How_to_Save_The_World-Treat_it_Like_a_Business.pdf, accessed date: 10/29/2009.

[23] Elkington, J. and Hardigan, P (2008), *The Power of Unreasonable People*, Harvard Business Press, Cambridge.

[24] Epstein, S. (1964), "Social Structure and Entrepreneurship", in *International Journal of Comparative Sociology*, vol. 5, no. 2, pp. 162-165.

[25] Faltin, G. (2008), "Social Entrepreneurship – Definitionen, Inhalte, Perspektiven", in Braun, G. and French, M. (eds.), *Social Entrepreneurship: unternehmerische Ideen für eine bessere Gesellschaft*, HIE-RO, Rostock, pp. 25–46.

[26] Faltin, G. (2009), "Teekampagne - "Citizen entrepreneurship" for a meaningful life", online: http://labor.entrepreneurship.de/downloads/Citizen_E-Ship.pdf, accessed date: 6/8/2009.

[27] Frances, N. (2008), *The end of charity: time for social enterprise*, Allen & Unwin, Crows Nest.

[28] Friedman, M. (1962), *Capitalism and freedom*, University of Chicago Press, Chicago.

[29] Gartner, W.B. (1988), "Who is an entrepreneur? Is the wrong question", in *American Journal of Small Business*, vol. 12, no. 4, pp. 11-32.

[30] Hage, J. and Eiken, M.T. (1970), *Social Change in Complex Organizations*, New York, Random House.

[31] Harding, R. (2004), "Social enterprise: the new economic engine?", in *Business Strategy Review*, vol. 15, no.4, pp. 39-43.

[32] Hayek, F.A. (1945), "The use of knowledge in society", in *American Economic Review*, vol. 35, no. 4, pp. 519-530.

[33] Hockerts, K. (2006), "Entrepreneurial opportunity in social purpose business ventures", in Mair, J., Robinson J.A. and Hockerts, K. (eds.), *Social entrepreneurship*, Palgrave Macmillan, New York, pp. 142-154.

[34] John, R. (2006), *Venture Philanthropy – The Evolution of High Engagement Philanthropy in Europe*, Skoll Center for Social Entrepreneurship, Said Business School, University of Oxford, Oxford.

[35] Kinsley, M. (2009), *Creative capitalism*, Simon & Schuster, London.

[36] Kirzner, I.M. (1973), *Competition and Entrepreneurship*, University of Chicago Press, Chicago.

[37] Leadbeater, C. (1997), *The rise of the social entrepreneur*, Demos, London.

[38] Light, P.C. (2005), *Searching for social entrepreneurs: who they might be, where they might be found, what they do*, Paper presented at the Association for Research on Nonprofit and Voluntary Associations.

[39] Light, P.C. (2011), *Driving social change - How to solve the world's toughest problems*, Wiley, Hoboken.

[40] Mair, J. and Marti, I. (2006), "Social entrepreneurship research: A source of explanation, prediction, and delight", in *Journal of World Business*, vol. 41, no. 1, pp. 36-44.

[41] Mair, J. and Martí, I. (2009), "Entrepreneurship in and around institutional voids: A case study from Bangladesh", in *Journal of Business Venturing*, vol. 24, no.5, pp. 419-435.

[42] Michael Bull, (2008), "Challenging tensions: critical, theoretical and empirical perspectives on

social enterprise", in *International Journal of Entrepreneurial Behaviour & Research*, vol. 14, no. 5, pp. 268-275.

[43] Neck, H., Brush, C. and Allen, E. (2009), "The landscape of social entrepreneurship", in *Business Horizons*, vol. 52, no. 1, pp. 13-19.

[44] Nicholls, A. (2006a), "Introduction", in: Nicholls, A. (ed.), *Social Entrepreneurship. New Models of Sustainable Social Change*, Oxford University Press, Oxford, pp. 1-35.

[45] Nicholls, A. (2006b) (ed.), *Social Entrepreneurship. New Models of Sustainable Social Change*, Oxford University Press, Oxford.

[46] Nicholls, A. and Cho, A.H. (2006), "Social entrepreneurship: the structuration of a field", in Nicholls, A. (ed.), *Social entrepreneurship - New models of sustainable social change*, Oxford University Press, New York, pp. 99-118.

[47] Parker, W.N. (1954), "Entrepreneurial Opportunities and Response in the German Economy," in *Explorations in Entrepreneurial History*, vol. 7, no.1, pp. 26-36.

[48] Peattie, K. and Morley, A. (2008), "Eight paradoxes of the social enterprise research agenda", in *Social Enterprise Journal*, vol. 4, no. 2, pp. 91-107.

[49] Peredo, A.M. and McLean, M. (2006), "Social entrepreneurship: a critical review of the concept", in *Journal of World Business*, vol. 41, no. 1, pp. 56-65.

[50] Perrini, F. (2006). "Social entrepreneurship domain: setting boundries", in Perrini, F. (ed.), *The new social entrepreneurship: what awaits social entrepreneurship ventures?*, MPG Books, Bodmin, pp. 1-25.

[51] Ridley-Duff, R. (2008),"Social enterprise as a socially rational business", in *International Journal of Entrepreneurial Behaviour& Research*, vol. 14, no. 5, pp. 291-312.

[52] Robinson, J.A., Mair, J., and Hockerts, K. (2009), "Introduction", in Robinson, J.A.,Mair, J. and Hockerts, K. (eds.), *International perspectives on social entrepreneurship,*).Palgrave Macmillan, , Houndsmill, pp. 1-6.

[53] Santos, F.M. (2009), *A positive theory of social entrepreneurship*, ISEAD faculty & research – working paper, Fontainebleau, ISEAD.

[54] Schramm, C. (2010), "All Entrepreneurship Is Social: Let's not overlook what traditional entrepreneurs contribute to society", in *Stanford Social Innovation Review*, Spring 2010, pp. 21-22.

[55] Schumpeter, A.J. (1936), "Review: The General Theory of Employment, Interest and Money. John Maynard Keynes", in *Journal of the American Statistical Association*, vol. 31, no. 196, pp. 791-795.

[56] Schumpeter, J.A. (1934), *The theory of economic development*, Harvard University Press, Cambridge.

[57] Seelos, C. and Mair, J. (2009), "Hope for Sustainable Development: How Social Entrepreneurs Make it Happen", in Ziegler, R. (ed.), *An Introduction to Social Entrepreneurship: Voices, Preconditions and Contexts*, Edward Elgar, Cheltenham.

[58] Shaw, E. and Carter, S. (2007), "Social entrepreneurship: Theoretical antecedents and empirical analysis of entrepreneurial processes and outcomes", *in Journal of Small Business and Enterprise Development*, vol. 14, no. 3, pp. 418-434.

[59] Spear, R. (2006), "Social entrepreneurship: a different model?", in: *International Journal of Social Economics*, vol. 33, no. 5/6, pp. 399-410.

[60] Sud, M., VanSandt, C.V. and Baugous, A.M. (2009), "Social Entrepreneurship: The Role of Institutions", in *Journal of Business Ethics*, vol. 85, pp. 201–216.

[61] Swedberg, R. (2006), "Social entrepreneurship, the view of young Schumpeter", in Steyaert, C. and Hjorth, D. (eds.), *Entrepreneurship as social change. A third movements in entrepreneurship book*, Elgar, Cheltenham, pp. 21-34.

[62] Thompson, J. and Dorothy, B. (2006), "The diverse world of social enterprise: a collection of social enterprise stories", in *International Journal of Social Economics*, vol. 33, no. 5/6, pp. 361-375.

[63] Thompson, J., Alvy, G. and Lees, A. (2000), "Social entrepreneurship – A new look at the people and the potential", in *Management Decision*, vol. 38, no. 5, pp. 328-338.

[64] Volkmann, C. and Tokarski, K.O. (2010), "Soziale Innovationen und Social Entrepreneurship", in Baumann, W., Braukmann, U. and Matthes, W. (eds.), *Innovation und Internationalisierung*, Gabler, Wiesbaden, pp. 151-170.

[65] Waddock, S.A. and Post, J.E. (1991), "Social entrepreneurs and catalytic change", in *Public Administration Review*, vol. 51, no. 5, pp. 393-401.

[66] Weerawardena, J. and Mort, G.S. (2006), "Investigating social entrepreneurship: a multidimensional model", in *Journal of World Business*, vol. 41, no. 1, pp. 21-35.

[67] Young, D.R. (1986), "Entrepreneurship and the behavior of nonprofit organizations: Elements of a Theory", in Rose-Ackerman, S. (ed.), *The economics of nonprofit institutions: studies in structure and policy*, Oxford University Press, New York, pp. 161-184.

[68] Zahra, S.A., Gedajlovic, E., Neubaum, D.O. and Shulman, J.M (2009), "A typology of social entrepreneurs: Motives, search processes and ethical challenges", in *Journal of Business Venturing*, vol. 24, no. 5, pp. 519–532.

2 Social Entrepreneurship: Definitions, Drivers and Challenges

Benjamin Huybrechts

University of Liege
HEC Management School
Centre for Social Economy

Alex Nicholls

University of Oxford
Saïd Business School
Skoll Centre for Social Entrepreneurship

Learning goals
Upon completing this chapter, you should be able to accomplish the following:

- Explain the three pillars of social entrepreneurship.

- Explain how social entrepreneurship can be differentiated from other related concepts such as the third sector (or the social economy), social business, social innovation and corporate social responsibility.

- List and describe some of the drivers of social responsibility and apply/adapt them to your own context.

- Explain why measuring social entrepreneurship is difficult; provide some figures/evidence from initiatives you know of.

- Identify and characterize socially entrepreneurial initiatives in terms of definitions, drivers, size and key challenges.

2.1   Introduction

Social entrepreneurship has become a fashionable construct in recent years. Often evidenced by success stories across the world in diverse fields (health, education, finance, culture, etc.), the concept has become increasingly evident in commercial markets, academic discourses and policy making (Boschee, 2006; Light, 2008; Nicholls, 2006b). Besides transforming extant markets, social entrepreneurship has also been instrumental in creating new markets and market niches, with initiatives such as fair trade (Huybrechts forthcoming; Nicholls, 2010a) and microfinance (Armendáriz de Aghion and Morduch, 2005; Battilana and Dorado, 2010). The latter field has regularly been cited as a flagship of social entrepreneurship, especially since the Nobel Peace Prize was awarded to the Grameen Bank and its founder Mohammad Yunus.

Nearly absent in academic research until the end of the 1990s, social entrepreneurship and social enterprise have become an important research area since then (Dacin et al., 2010; Fayolle and Matlay, 2010; Short et al., 2009), with a growing number of articles and books devoted to the issue (in an Internet search through EBSCO and Google Scholar in March 2011, 75 articles and 23 books comprising the term "social entrepreneurship" were identified.). Special issues of several journals have focused on social entrepreneurship and at least two journals have been created especially to deal with this and closely related issues: The Social Enterprise Journal (Emerald) and The Journal of Social Entrepreneurship (Routledge).

Despite widespread acknowledgement that social entrepreneurship and social enterprise remain highly contextual –and, therefore, contestable– notions which can be interpreted in various ways depending on the ideology and the goals of the institutions championing them (Dart, 2004; Dey and Steyaert, 2010; Nicholls, 2010c), there are common features upon which most scholars and commentators can agree. This chapter aims to capture the essence of what social entrepreneurship is and also of what it is not. The chapter is structured as follows. The following section examines the concept of social entrepreneurship and reviews a number of definitions in order to highlight common features. Then, social entrepreneurship is compared with, and differentiated from, related –but distinctive– concepts. After this, the fourth section looks at the origins and drivers of social entrepreneurship in an historical perspective. Finally, this chapter concludes by suggesting a number of challenges for practice, policy and research in this field.

2.2   Social Entrepreneurship Defined

Establishing an agreed definition of social entrepreneurship has not proved to be an easy task. The main difficulty is that social entrepreneurship is a contextual and contingent set of activities, subject to interpretive analysis and measurement (Bacq and Janssen, 2011; Nicholls, 2010c; see also Dey's chapter in this book). This is unusual in the field of entrepreneurship, but less so in areas of the social sciences more concerned with societal issues. The literature on the subject uses three different terms which, at first sight, might seem linked in a very simple way: "social entrepreneurship" is the dynamic process through which specific types of individuals deserving the name of "social entrepreneurs" create and develop organizations that may be defined as "social enterprises" (Defourny and Nyssens, 2008b; Mair and Marti, 2006). However, the use of one term or the other is often linked to a different focus and/or understanding of the phenomenon depending on context and perspective. In this chapter, "social entrepreneurship" will be used to designate a broader range of socially innovative initiatives in a spectrum from for-profit to voluntary organizations. "Social enterprises" are a subset of such activities in which commercial models are used as the vehicle by which social objects are achieved (Nicholls, 2006b; Thompson, 2008).

The study of social entrepreneurship has developed quite differently in the 'Anglo-sphere' of the UK and US compared with continental Europe. In the former, the focus has been on the commercialization of the not-for-profit sector and on private initiatives that can deliver public welfare goods. In the latter, the focus has been much more on collective entrepreneurship and analyses at the organizational level (Defourny and Nyssens, 2008a; Kerlin, 2006; 2008). However, in more recent years, these regional differences seem to have been blurring as better dialogues have evolved between the two traditions facilitated by a new set of academic events such as the Social Entrepreneurship Research Colloquium (Bacq and Janssen, 2011; Defourny and Nyssens, 2008a; Hulgard, 2008; Kerlin, 2006).

In reality, the diversity of discourses that characterize the definitional debates around social entrepreneurship reflect the internal logics of a broad range of influential, resource holding actors who are actively involved in shaping the field, rather than any attempts at capturing the 'reality' of the field itself (Dart, 2004; Dey and Steyaert, 2010; Nicholls, 2010c). Thus, for civil society actors, social entrepreneurship may represent a driver of systemic social change (Nicholls, 2006), a space for new hybrid partnerships (Austin et al., 2006a), or a model of political transformation and empowerment (Alvord et al., 2004). For government, social entrepreneurship (particularly in the form of social enterprises) can be one of the solutions to state failures in welfare provision (Leadbeater, 1996; Nyssens, 2006). Finally, for business, social entrepreneurship can offer a new market opportunity (Karamchandani et al., 2009) or a natural development from socially responsible investment (Freireich and Fulton, 2009).

In Kuhnian terms, the lack of a unified definition is characteristic of a field which is still in an early stage of development and has not yet achieved paradigmatic status (Nicholls, 2010c). Dacin et al. (2010) counted 37 definitions of social entrepreneurship or social entrepreneurs. Bacq and Janssen (2011) noted 17 different definitions of "social entrepreneurs",

12 definitions of "social entrepreneurship" and 18 definitions of "social enterprise", "social entrepreneurial venture" or "social entrepreneurship organization".

One key debate has concerned how broad or narrow the scope of social entrepreneurship might be (Light, 2008), reflecting Dees' (1998; 2001) call for an equilibrium between inclusiveness (defining social entrepreneurship very broadly) and exclusiveness (defining it very narrowly). An extreme response to this apparent confusion over definitions has been to suggest –contra empirical evidence– that there is nothing theoretically distinctive about social entrepreneurship when compared to entrepreneurship more generally (Dacin et al., 2010).

Despite continued debates, one of the most commonly used definitions was provided by Dees (1998, revised 2001):

"Social entrepreneurs play the role of change agents in the social sector, by:

- Adopting a mission to create and sustain social value (not just private value),

- Recognizing and relentlessly pursuing new opportunities to serve that mission,

- Engaging in a process of continuous innovation, adaptation, and learning,

- Acting boldly without being limited by resources currently in hand, and

- Exhibiting a heightened sense of accountability to the constituencies served and for the outcomes created" (2001, p. 4)

Subsequent work focussed on the processes of social entrepreneurship. According to Mort et al. (2003, p. 76), social entrepreneurship is "a multidimensional construct involving the expression of entrepreneurially virtuous behaviour to achieve the social mission, a coherent unity of purpose and action in the face of moral complexity, the ability to recognise social value-creating opportunities and key decision-making characteristics of innovativeness, proactiveness and risk-taking". Mair and Marti (2004, p. 3) view social entrepreneurship as "a process consisting of the innovative use and combination of resources to explore and exploit opportunities, that aims at catalysing social change by catering to basic human needs in a sustainable manner". Austin et al. (2006b, p. 2) define social entrepreneurship as an "innovative, social value creating activity that can occur within or across the nonprofit, business, or government sectors". Finally, Zahra et al. (2009, p. 5) suggest that social entrepreneurship encompasses "activities and processes undertaken to discover, define, and exploit opportunities in order to enhance social wealth by creating new ventures or managing existing organizations in an innovative manner".

Despite these ongoing disputes and debates, there remains some broad agreement about a number of key characteristics that set the boundaries of socially entrepreneurial action (Martin and Osberg, 2007; Nicholls, 2006a). All the definitions of social entrepreneurship agree on a central focus on social or environmental outcomes that has primacy over profit maximization or other strategic considerations. A second defining feature is innovation. Innovation can be pursued through new organizational models and processes, through new products and services, or through new thinking about, and framing of, societal challenges. Several social entrepreneurship initiatives combine these different ways of innovating. Finally, many authors emphasize how social entrepreneurs diffuse their socially innovative models via market oriented action that is performance driven, scaling up their initiatives in other contexts through alliances and partnerships, with the idea of reaching broader and more sustainable outcomes. These dimensions map onto what Nicholls and Cho (2006) identify as the main building blocks of social entrepreneurship: *sociality, innovation,* and *market orientation.*

The first dimension, "sociality", refers to the social and environmental focus of social entrepreneurship. Such a focus may be identified through the creation of public goods and positive externalities. Six fields or domains are natural settings for social entrepreneurship initiatives:

- welfare and health services (such as the Aravind eye hospitals in India)

- education and training (such as the Committee to Democratize Information Technology in Brazil)

- economic development (such as work integration social enterprises, or WISEs, in Europe)

- disaster relief and international aid (such as Keystone's innovative "Farmer Voice" project)

- social justice and political change (including race and gender empowerment, such as SEWA, the Self-Employed Women's Association in Pakistan)

- environmental planning and management (such as the Marine Stewardship Council).

But sociality may also lie in the organizational processes themselves. Indeed, socially innovative solutions have been pioneered by social entrepreneurs in terms of employment practices (WISEs employing low-skilled workers), supply chain management (a good example is Fair Trade), energy usage and recycling (such as citizen-based renewable energy cooperatives), and access to credit and financial services (different types of microfinance). Finally, sociality may be identifiable in the outcomes of the organization which will be focussed on social and/or environmental impact rather than on financial returns. In order to capture these outcomes, the field of social entrepreneurship has pioneered a range of new performance evaluation criteria and methods that take into account these non-financial impacts (Stone and Cutcher-Gershenfeld, 2001).

Regarding the second characteristic of social entrepreneurship, innovation, it is interesting to note that its approach in social entrepreneurship has much in common with models found in commercial entrepreneurship. For example, in some cases, Schumpeter's idea of "creative destruction" processes that change systems and realign markets around new economic equilibriums can also be found in social entrepreneurship initiatives, either through incremental changes at the micro-level or through disruptive interventions at the systems level (Martin and Osberg, 2007).

Third, market orientation is manifest in a variety of ways in social entrepreneurship, most obviously in the for-profit social enterprise form, which operates in commercial markets and generates profits to reinvest in their social mission (Alter, 2006). Defourny (2001) and other authors from the EMES network suggest that social enterprises, unlike traditional NGOs and nonprofits, have a continuous production of goods and/or services and take economic risks – bankruptcy is always a possible outcome. A minimum amount of paid work, i.e., a workforce not only composed of volunteers, is also suggested as an element differentiating social enterprise. Nicholls and Cho (2006) identify other features that extend the market orientation dimension, notably a clear focus on continual performance improvement and metrics, increased accountability, and a relentless focus on achieving their mission that permeates the entire organizational culture.

Based on how social enterprises integrate these building blocks, different typologies of social entrepreneurship have been proposed. In 2000, Fowler suggested three types of social entrepreneurship: 'integrated' (when economic activity in itself produces social outcomes); 're-interpreted' (when an existing not-for-profit increases its earned income); and 'complementary' (where commercial revenues cross-subsidize the social mission of a related not-for-profit). In a similar exercise, Alter (2006) distinguishes social enterprise models based on their mission orientation (from mission-oriented to profit-oriented), on their target group, and on how the social programs and the business activities relate to each other. Alter identifies three core models of social enterprise: embedded (when social programs are inherent in the business activities, as in Fair Trade); integrated (when social programs overlap with business activities, for instance at the Scojo Foundation in India); and external (when business activities are an external source of funding for social programs, typically in health or education not-for-profits).

2.3   What Social Entrepreneurship is Not

Having established the key definitional dimensions of social entrepreneurship, this section will explore alternative notions which differ from social entrepreneurship to a certain extent – though the latter's boundaries are still contested (see Dey further in this book). Four notions of relevance will be discussed below: social entrepreneurship is not a discrete sector; it is not a synonym of social business; it is not a new form of corporate social responsibility; and it is not the only model of social innovation.

2.3.1   Not a Discrete Sector

Much social entrepreneurship has been identified as a boundary blurring form of action between the ideal types of the private, public and civil society sectors. For example, whilst a good deal of social entrepreneurship has its roots in civil society, there has been an evolution towards a stronger market orientation in recent years (Monaci and Caselli, 2005). This links to the notion of the 'social economy' as widely used in continental Europe, Canada and other parts of the world. The social economy encompasses organizations which are located between the public sector and the for-profit business sector. Characteristic of a so-cial economy organization is "to provide services to its members or to a wider community, and not serve as a tool in the service of capital investment [...]. The generation of a surplus is therefore a means to providing a service, not the main driving force behind the economic activity" (Defourny et al., 2000, 16).

However, the social economy is both a broader and a narrower concept than social entre-preneurship. It is broader because it includes organizations which are not necessarily en-trepreneurial and do not necessarily rely on market resources. In fact, the same remark can be made for not-for-profit organizations, which are not all entrepreneurial. On the other hand, the social economy can be seen as narrower than social entrepreneurship because it only includes organizations with specific legal forms: not-for-profits/charities, cooperatives, mutuals and foundations. It thus ignores the social enterprises which have not adopted one of these forms and which do not formally limit profit distribution. Other examples and models of social entrepreneurship incorporated as small and/or family businesses, located in the public sector and in the corporate world, and resulting from partnerships with and between these sectors also blur the association of social entrepreneurship with the civil society and social economy sectors. Moreover, the levels of analysis are clearly diverging. The social economy refers to a field or a sector (the "third sector") in a static way. Social entrepreneurship is not a discrete sector, it is a set of hybrid organizations and processes, which may take place in different institutional spaces between and across existing sectors.

2.3.2   Not a Synonym for Social Business

Although the term "social business" has been used earlier than that of social entrepreneur-ship, its diffusion is more recent and is mainly due to Nobel Peace Prize winner Muham-mad Yunus, founder of the Grameen Bank. Yet, it has not yet received much attention in the academic literature, despite Yunus' own writings (Yunus, 2006; 2007; Yunus et al., 2010).

At first sight, the way in which Yunus describes a social business might seem quite similar to the principles of a social enterprise: "a company that is cause-driven rather than profit-driven, with the potential to act as a change agent for the world" (Yunus, 2007, p. 22). How-ever, when we look at the distinctive features of social business he sets out, it appears that this concept is much more restrictive than social entrepreneurship or social enterprise. First, while social enterprise considers mission-aligned profit distribution, Yunus suggests that such profit distribution is prohibited in a social business: "the investors who support it do not take any profits out of the company" (Yunus 2007, p. 22). Social businesses are thus submitted to the "nondistribution constraint" which is more typical of not-for-profit organ-izations (Hansmann, 1980). But unlike not-for-profits, social businesses are required to raise all their incomes and recover all their costs through the market, and not through philan-thropy or public funding.

Through emphasizing "full cost recovery" as a criterion which distinguishes social business from charity, Yunus ignores the possible hybridization of social and business logics which lies at the heart of many social enterprises (Billis, 2010; Di Domenico et al., 2010; Huybrechts forthcoming). Yunus' emphasis on market income, while finding some echo in certain conceptions of social entrepreneurship, lies at odds with the mixed income models described by a majority of social entrepreneurship scholars (Bacq and Janssen, 2011). Finally, it should be noted that the social business examples cited by Yunus still mainly consist of partnerships between the Grameen Bank and multinational business such as Danone, Veolia and Siemens. One may thus wonder whether the concept Yunus promotes has a broader empirical basis beyond the initiatives specifically framed in this way.

2.3.3   Not a New Form of Corporate Social Responsibility

A third concept that might be confused with social entrepreneurship is corporate social responsibility. According to the European Union (Lisbon strategy), CSR refers to "[a] concept whereby companies integrate social and environmental concerns in their business operations and in their interaction with their stakeholders on a voluntary basis" . In its integration of social aims in the business realm and in the innovative nature of some of its initiatives, CSR might be considered close or even a synonym of social entrepreneurship. Adopting this view, Baron (2007) labels initiators of CSR projects as "social entrepreneurs". Without going as far in the association of the concepts, Austin and his colleagues suggest that social entrepreneurship "is for corporations, too" (Austin et al., 2006a) and labels this as "corporate social entrepreneurship" (Austin and Reficco, 2005).

However, two elements differentiate social entrepreneurship from CSR. First, CSR is not necessarily entrepreneurial nor innovative. CSR may indeed consist of aligning corporate practices with practices and norms which are long established (including law), thereby lacking innovativeness. Secondly, the respective goals of CSR projects and social entrepreneurship fundamentally diverge. In social entrepreneurship, the social mission has primacy and profits are means to reach this mission; it should, thus, be at least partly reinvested in the project rather than mainly appropriated by shareholders. In corporations, however responsible, profit maximization remains the ultimate goal and is directed towards shareholder value appropriation. Hence, beyond the respective positions of profit and social mission, it is the issue of value appropriation that differentiates social entrepreneurship from CSR (Santos, 2009). Of course, such a distinction may not be easy to establish empirically and the question of what proportion of CSR initiatives may be labelled as corporate social entrepreneurship remains open to debate.

2.3.4   Not the Only Model of Social Innovation

Social innovation is another concept which has gained increasing attention recently (Martin and Osberg, 2007; Mulgan et al., 2007; Phills et al., 2008). Drawing on the literature on innovation and on its broad conceptualization by Schumpeter, Nicholls (2010a, p. 247) distinguishes three types of social innovation: "in new product and service development (institutional innovation); in the use of existing goods and services in new –more socially productive– ways (incremental innovation); in reframing normative terms of reference to redefine social problems and suggest new solutions (disruptive innovation)". While much of the literature has focused on innovation as inherent in entrepreneurship and market orientation, the concept of social innovation tends to consider innovation in a much broader way. Social innovation, broadly defined as new solutions to social needs, is not necessarily market-based and can be found in any sector (Mulgan et al., 2007; Phills et al., 2008): public (example of participative budgeting in Porto Alegre and elsewhere, see for instance Novy and Leubolt, 2005), private for-profit (Austin et al., 2006), or non-profit (Gerometta et al., 2005). In such sense, whilst social entrepreneurship and social innovation clearly overlap, a difference lies in the fact that social innovation is not necessarily market oriented, while social entrepreneurship clearly is. Hence, some authors view social innovation as the broader umbrella term under which social entrepreneurship, as well as other novel public and third sector initiatives located outside the market, can be affiliated (Mulgan et al., 2007; Phills et al., 2008).

2.4   The Drivers of Social Entrepreneurship

Whilst interest in social entrepreneurship is growing, it is not a new phenomenon. Examples of organizations demonstrating the three building blocks of social entrepreneurship (sociality, innovation and market orientation) can be found throughout history and across geographical settings. For example, figures as diverse as Robert Owen (one of the fathers of the co-operative movement), Vinoba Bhave (one of Ghandi's disciples) and Jean-Baptiste André Godin (a French entrepreneur who provided extensive and innovative social welfare services to his workers) are typical figures of 19th century social entrepreneurs that conform to the definitions discussed here (Boutillier, 2009; Mulgan et al., 2007).

Nevertheless, the specific identification of certain actors and activities with social entrepreneurship is a recent matter, with the term itself only beginning to emerge in the 1970s. During the 1980s and 1990s field building organizations emerged that focussed exclusively on social entrepreneurship (e.g., Ashoka founded in 1981, the Schwab Foundation 1998, the Skoll Foundation 1999, UnLtd 2002, the Omidyar Network 2004, and the Young Foundation 2006: see Nicholls, 2010c). At the same time, government policy in several countries began to explore the possibilities of the field in terms of welfare provision as well (Dees, 1998; Dees and Elias, 1998; Leadbeater, 1996). The nomination of Muhammad Yunus and the Grameen Bank as Nobel Prize for Peace winners has been seen by many as a turning point in the global recognition of social entrepreneurship (Martin and Osberg, 2007) and social innovation in general (Mulgan et al., 2007).

But beyond the activities of field-building organizations, some major changes in socio-economic, political and cultural contexts across the world have also acted as drivers of the recent acceleration in the growth of socially entrepreneurial discourses and in practices. First, the proliferation of global crises has driven demand for innovative social and environmental action able to respond to the new challenges posed by these so-called 'wicked problems' (Bornstein, 2004). Major challenges include: climate change and environmental degradation; inequality and poverty; lack of access to basic healthcare, clean water and energy; mass migration; international terrorism.

Secondly, the rise of global connectedness has improved the ability of citizens to identify and respond to social and environmental needs. The rise of new social media has also accelerated and intensified the interactions among social entrepreneurs, funders and other stakeholders. The involvement of individuals as social actors can be linked to the development of a "pro-am" culture (Leadbeater, 2006) and the emergence of "new localism" (Murray et al., 2010).

A third major driver has been the redefinition of the role of the state, starting with the rise of neo-conservative politics in the 1980s (Grenier, 2009). In the context of "new public management", these politics encouraged a more managerialist functioning of the state (Osbourne and Gaebler, 1992) and the creation of internal "quasi-markets" within state welfare systems (Bode et al., 2011; Flynn and Williams, 1997; Le Grand, 1991). Not-for-profits were encouraged to compete with each other (and often with for-profit businesses) to contract with the government. Increasingly, discourses of enterprise were decoupled from business and applied not only to the activities of the public sector but also to civil society action more generally (Dart, 2004). Thus, market failures in the provision of welfare services led to new opportunities for social entrepreneurs (in health, education, etc.).

Finally, the combination of the proliferation of not-for-profits and other civil society organizations (Salamon et al., 2003) and several economic recessions, lead to a growing mismatch between the supply and demand of resources to sustain social organizations. This has led civil society organizations to become more entrepreneurial and to diversify their funding by seeking commercial revenues and new partnerships with the state and the business sectors (Kanter and Summers, 1987). As a result, successful social entrepreneurs have managed to reduce their dependence on the state and/or donors via new social enterprise models. However, the negative consequences of depending on market resources have also been pointed out (Battle Anderson and Dees, 2006; Dart, 2004).

2.5   The Size and Scope of the Field of Social Entrepreneurship

Social entrepreneurship is not characterized by a single legal form. Specific legal forms do exist for social entrepreneurship, such as the Social Purpose Company in Belgium, the Community Interest Company (CIC) form in the United Kingdom, Social Cooperatives (Types 1 and 2) in Italy, and L3C organizations in the US. The field, however, also includes a variety of other legal forms (cooperatives, nonprofits, businesses, etc.), some of which are combined in the context of hybrid structures. As a consequence, it has proved to be a significant challenge to derive consistent data on the size and scope of social entrepreneurship across countries.

Nevertheless, attempts have been made to give a snapshot of the field in different contexts, particularly in the UK where there has been a large interest in, and support for, the field. A survey for the UK government estimated the number of social enterprises as 62,000 across the country, contributing £24 billion Gross Value Added to the economy from 2005 to 2007 (Williams and Cowling, 2009). At the international level, the Global Entrepreneurship Monitor (GEM) survey is a valuable source of information. The GEM 2010 survey took, for the first time, a worldwide perspective on social entrepreneurship (Bosma and Levie, 2010). It estimated that an average of 1.9% of the population directly engaged with social entrepreneurship, with important differences depending on the region concerned and its level of economic development.

To build a picture of the scale of social entrepreneurship in specific contexts, it is instructive to look at some of its well-established sub-fields. For example, Dees (2010) provides some impressive figures about the Bangladesh Rural Advancement Committee (BRAC): it runs more than 37,000 schools, with 120,000 workers, 80,000 health volunteers, it offers microfinance products to over eight million poor people, reaching over 100 million people in total. Another success story is the Fair Trade movement, which now generates more than €2.4 billion of sales worldwide and reaches more than seven million people across the world (FLO-I, 2010). Finally, the activities of field builders supporting social entrepreneurs also give an indication of the global outreach of the phenomenon: Ashoka's global Fellowship now exceeds 2,000 members and, since 2001, UnLtd in the UK has supported more than 3,000 people to initiate and scale socially entrepreneurial projects.

2.6   Conclusion and Future Research

This chapter has defined social entrepreneurship as market-oriented initiatives pursuing social aims in an innovative way. Beyond these commonly agreed building blocks, social entrepreneurship remains a contested phenomenon that is understood and promoted in different ways in different contexts. This is partly a product of the inherently hybrid qualities of much social entrepreneurship that blurs the boundaries between previously well distinguished sectors and organizational forms. This chapter has also compared and differentiated social entrepreneurship from other notions with which it is often compared or associated.

Then, in the context of the profusion of initiatives and concepts aiming to reconcile business and social change, several factors have been highlighted to explain the success of social entrepreneurship in terms of its practice, discourses and support. Besides the dynamic promotion of the concept by scholars, foundations and other field building actors, four factors related to the broader environment have been noted: the social, economic and environmental crises providing new challenges and opportunities; the rise of global connectedness, enabling entrepreneurs better to identify opportunities and connect with stakeholders (such as funders) across the globe; the redefinition of the role of the state, with more indirect support for private social action; and the decreasing resources of governments and traditional philanthropy, which have led social entrepreneurs to imagine new resource-raising models. Finally, this chapter has provided some data on the scale and scope of the field of social entrepreneurship. The growth of socially entrepreneurial organizations and the increasing support they have received tends to corroborate the claim that social entrepreneurship is making a difference and holds the potential for broader systemic change.

However, there remains significant work that needs to be done to generate a reliable and consistent data set on social entrepreneurship – this represents the largest and most challenging research task at hand. Elsewhere, there are several other important critiques of social entrepreneurship as it is currently conceived and enacted. Each of these offers a further set of new research opportunities.

In particular, the emphasis on the individual, "hero" social entrepreneur has been criticized as reflecting Western cultural values and as not corresponding to the reality of the field in practice where collective action is of central important (Lounsbury and Strang, 2009; Nicholls, 2010c). Moreover, it seems that local institutions and partnerships are as important for successful social impact as the dynamics of individual entrepreneurs, how motivated and charismatic they may be (Yujuico, 2008). Collective social entrepreneurship developing through partnerships embedded in local institutional contexts can be found in many examples from the cooperative movement, such as the cases of Desjardins (Québec) and Mondragon (Spain). An important reason for this is that enduring social change cannot be the result of social entrepreneurship alone; it necessarily involves political action at various levels from the formal to the informal, as well as partnerships with broader social movements. A research agenda that explores the politics of social entrepreneurship in various socio-cultural contexts and at multiple societal levels from government to grass-roots represents a second major stream of potential future scholarly work.

Next, there continues to be a need for more and better work on tracking the impacts and outcomes associated with social entrepreneurship. Such a programme of work would encompass not only an investigation of the mechanisms by which social impact is measured, but also the broader context of such metrics including a consideration of their governance and accountability implications. It is also a matter of credibility for social entrepreneurs and the people who support and research them not to exaggerate their contribution and locate it in the broader societal context. Learning from socially entrepreneurial failures, including instances of negative social impacts and externalities, is also crucial to strike a balance between enthusiastic optimism and clear-sighted pragmatism.

A final important area for future research is social finance and investment (Nicholls, 2010b). This stream of work would explore how flows of new resources reach socially entrepreneurial organizations and projects. Different aspects of this work would include analyses of what the investor rationales for social investment are, how the market structures of social investment are configured, and what barriers lie in the way of growing and consolidating such capital allocation.

This chapter has suggested that social entrepreneurship represents both a growing field of hybrid action and a catalyst for wider recalibrations of the roles and boundaries of the market, the state and civil society. However, the field is still in a pre-paradigmatic state where definitions remain contested and various actors are promoting self-legitimating accounts of what social entrepreneurship is and is not (Dey and Steyaert, 2010; Nicholls, 2010c). In such a context, scholars can play a useful role in assessing competing claims on the field and presenting theoretically and empirically driven accounts of the reality of practice in context. This chapter has attempted to make a modest contribution to this ongoing process.

2.7   Exercise: Using Case Studies to Discuss Definitional Issues

After reading this chapter, the following exercise is suggested:

1. Collect different examples of socially entrepreneurial initiatives (in your city, region, country or at a global level). Describe them (history, founders, goals, model, etc.).

2. Identify to what extent the three building blocks presented here – sociality, market orientation and innovation – are salient in these initiatives. How can they be traced in the discourses and practices?

3. Examine how these elements can be related to each other. What are the synergies between sociality, market orientation and innovation? What are the possible tensions between social and commercial goals?

4. Among the different cases, what patterns can be distinguished in terms of founders, stakeholders involved, organizational models, resource mixes, scaling up trajectories or other variables?

5. To what extent do contextual factors (culture, religion, socio-economic context, public policy, support structures, etc.) shape the emergence and configuration of the socially entrepreneurial initiatives?

6. How do these initiatives differ from others which you would locate outside the scope of social entrepreneurship?

2.8   Further Reading

[1]   Austin, J., Stevenson, H. and Wei-Skillern, J. (2006b), "Social and Commercial Entrepreneurship: Same, Different, or Both?", in *Entrepreneurship: Theory & Practice*, vol. 30, no. 1, pp. 1-22.

[2]   Bacq, S. and Janssen, F. (2011), "The multiple faces of social entrepreneurship: A review of definitional issues based on geographical and thematic criteria", in *Entrepreneurship & Regional Development: An International Journal*, vol 23, no. 5, pp. 373 – 403

[3]   Dacin, P.A., Dacin, M.T. and Matear, M. (2010), "Social Entrepreneurship: Why We Don't Need a New Theory and How We Move Forward From Here", in *Academy of Management Perspectives*, vol. 24, no. 3, pp. 37-57.

[4]   Dees, J.G. (2001), *The Meaning of "Social Entrepreneurship"*, The Fuqua School of Business, Duke University.

[5]   Mair, J. and Marti, I. (2006), "Social entrepreneurship research: A source of explanation, prediction, and delight", in *Journal of World Business*, vol. 41, no. 1, pp. 36-44.

[6]   Martin, R.L. and Osberg, S. (2007), "Social Entrepreneurship: The Case for Definition", in *Stanford Social Innovation Review*, Spring 2007, pp. 29-39.

[7]   Mort, G.S., Weerawardena, J. and Carnegie, K. (2003), "Social entrepreneurship: Towards conceptualisation", in *International Journal of Nonprofit & Voluntary Sector Marketing*, vol. 8, no. 1, pp. 76.

[8]   Nicholls, A. (2010c), "The Legitimacy of Social Entrepreneurship: Reflexive Isomorphism in a Pre-Paradigmatic Field", in *Entrepreneurship Theory and Practice*, vol. 34, no. 4, pp. 611-633.

2.9   Bibliography

[1]   Alter, S.K. (2006), "Social Enterprise Models and Their Mission and Money Relationships", in Nicholls, A. (Ed.), *Social Entrepreneurship. New Models of Sustainable Social Change*, Oxford University Press, Oxford, pp. 205-232.

[2]   Alvord, S., Brown, L. and Letts, C. (2004), "Social Entrepreneurship and Societal Transformation: an Exploratory Study", in *Journal of Applied Behavioral Science*, vol. 40, no.3, pp. 260-283.

[3]   Armendáriz de Aghion, B. and Morduch, J. (2005), *The Economics of Microfinance*, Massachusetts Institute of Technology Press, London.

[4]   Austin, J., Leonard, H.B., Reficco, E. and Wei-Skillern, J. (2006a), "Social Entrepreneurship: It Is For Corporations, Too", in Nicholls, A (ed.), *Social Entrepreneurship. New Models of Sustainable Social Change*, Oxford University Press, Oxford, pp. 169-204.

[5]   Austin, J. and Reficco, E. (2005), "Corporate Social Entrepreneurship", *Harvard Business School Working Paper*, 09-101.

[6]   Austin, J., Stevenson, H. and Wei-Skillern, J. (2006b), "Social and Commercial Entrepreneurship: Same, Different, or Both?", in *Entrepreneurship: Theory & Practice*, vol. 30, no. 1, pp. 1-22.

[7]   Bacq, S. and Janssen, F. (2011), "The multiple faces of social entrepreneurship: A review of definitional issues based on geographical and thematic criteria", in *Entrepreneurship & Regional Development: An International Journal*, vol.,23, no. 5, pp. 373-403.

[8]   Baron, D.P. (2007), "Corporate Social Responsibility and Social Entrepreneurship", in *Journal of Economics & Management Strategy*, vol. 16, no. 3, pp. 683-717.

[9]   Battilana, J. and Dorado, S. (2010), "Building sustainable hybrid organizations: the case of commercial microfinance organizations", in *Academy of Management Journal*, vol. 53, no. 6, pp. 1419-1440.

[10] Battle Anderson, B. and Dees, J.G. (2006), "Rhetoric, Reality, and Research: Building a Solid Foundation for the Practice of Social Entrepreneurship", in Nicholls, A. (ed.), *Social Entrepreneurship. New Models of Sustainable Social Change*, Oxford University Press, Oxford, pp. 144-168.

[11] Billis, D. (2010), *Hybrid Organizations and the Third Sector. Challenges for Practice, Theory and Policy*, Palgrave-MacMillan, New York.

[12] Bode, I., Gardin, L. and Nyssens, M. (2011), "Quasi-marketization in domiciliary care: Varied patterns, similar problems?", in *International Journal of Sociology and Social Policy*, vol. 31, no. 3, pp. 225-235.

[13] Bornstein, D. (2004), *How To Change The World: Social Entrepreneurs and the Power of New Ideas*, Oxford University Press, Oxford.

[14] Boschee, J. (2006), "Social Entrepreneurship: The Promise and the Perils", in Nicholls, A. (ed.), *Social Entrepreneurship. New Models of Sustainable Social Change*, Oxford University Press, Oxford, pp. 356-390.

[15] Bosma, N. and Levie, J. (2010), "A Global Comparison of Social Entrepreneurship", in GEM (ed.), *Global Entrepreneurship Monitor 2009 Executive Report*, GERA, London, pp. 44-51.

[16] Boutillier, S. (2009), "Aux origines de l'entrepreneuriat social. Les affaires selon Jean-Baptiste André Godin (1817-1888)", in *Innovations*, vol. 30, pp. 115-134.

[17] Dacin, P.A., Dacin, M.T. and Matear, M. (2010), "Social Entrepreneurship: Why We Don't Need a New Theory and How We Move Forward From Here", in *Academy of Management Perspectives*, vol. 24, no. 3, pp. 37-57.

[18] Dart, R. (2004), "The legitimacy of social enterprise", in *Nonprofit Management & Leadership*, vol. 14, no. 4, pp. 411-424.

[19] Dees, J.G. (1998), *The Meaning of "Social Entrepreneurship"*, Graduate School of Business, Stanford University.

[20] Dees, J.G. (2010), *Creating Large-Scale Change: Not 'Can' But 'How'*, What Matters, McKinsey & Company, New York.

[21] Dees, J.G. and Elias, J. (1998), "The challenges of combining social and commercial enterprise", in *Business Ethics Quarterly*, vol. 8, no. 1, pp. 165-178.

[22] Defourny, J. (2001), "From Third Sector to Social Enterprise", in Borzaga, C. and Defourny, J. (eds.), *The Emergence of Social Enterprise*, Routledge, London, pp. 1-28.

[23] Defourny, J., Develtere, P. and Fonteneau, B. (2000), in *Social Economy North and South*, Katholieke Universiteit Leuven, Leuven.

[24] Defourny, J. and Nyssens, M. (2008a), "Conceptions of Social Enterprise in Europe and in the United States. A Comparative Analysis", *8th ISTR International Conference and 2nd EMES-ISTR European Conference: "The Third Sector and Sustainable Social Change: New Frontiers for Research"*, Barcelona.

[25] Defourny, J. and Nyssens, M. (2008b), "Social Enterprise in Europe: Recent Trends and Developments", *EMES Working Paper*, 08:01.

[26] Dey, P. and Steyaert, C. (2010), "The politics of narrating social entrepreneurship", in *Journal of Enterprising Communities: People and Places in the Global Economy*, vol. 4, no. 1, pp. 85-108.

[27] Di Domenico, M., Haugh, H. and Tracey, P. (2010), "Social Bricolage: Theorizing Social Value Creation in Social Enterprises", in *Entrepreneurship: Theory & Practice*, vol. 34, no. 4, pp. 681-703.

[28] Fayolle, A. and Matlay, H. (eds.) (2010), *Handbook of Research on Social Entrepreneurship*, Edward Elgar, Cheltenham.

[29] FLO-I (2010), *Growing Stronger Together. Annual Report 2009-2010*, Fairtrade Labelling Organizations International, Bonn.

[30] Flynn, R. and Williams, G. (eds.) (1997), *Contracting for Health: Quasi-Markets and the NHS*, Oxford University Press, Oxford.

[31] Freireich, J. and Fulton, K. (2009), *Investing For Social and Environmental Impact: A Design for Catalyzing an Emerging Industry*, Monitor Group, New York.

[32] Gardin, L. (2006), "A variety of resource mixes inside social enterprises", in Nyssens, M. (ed.), *Social Enterprise. At the crossroads of market, public policies and civil society*, Routledge, London, pp. 111-136.

[33] Gerometta, J., Häussermann, H. and Longo, G. (2005), "Social innovation and civil society in urban governance: Strategies for an inclusive city", in *Urban Studies*, vol. 42, no. 11, pp. 2007-2021.

[34] Grenier, P. (2009), "Social Entrepreneurship in the UK: From Rhetoric to Reality?", in Zeigler, R.

(ed.), *An Introduction to Social Entrepreneurship: Voices, Preconditions, Contexts*, Edward Elgar, Cheltenham.

[35] Hansmann, H. (1980), "The Role of Non-Profit Enterprise", in *Yale Law Journal*, vol. 89, no. 5, pp. 835-901.

[36] Hulgard, L. (2008), "Discourses of Social Entrepreneurship in USA and Europe: Variations of the same theme?".

[37] Huybrechts, B. (forthcoming), *Fair Trade Social Enterprises. Social Innovation through Hybrid Organizational Models*, Routledge, New York.

[38] Kanter, R.M. and Summers, D. (1987), "Doing Well While Doing Good", in Powell, W.W. (ed.), *The Nonprofit Sector: A Research Handbook*, Yale University Press, New Haven.

[39] Karamchandani, A., Kubzansky, M. and Frandano, P. (2009), *Emerging Markets, Emerging Models*, Monitor Group, New York.

[40] Kerlin, J.A. (2006), "Social Enterprise in the United States and Europe: Understanding and Learning from the Differences", in *Voluntas: International Journal of Voluntary and Nonprofit Organizations*, vol. 17, no. 3, pp. 246-262.

[41] Kerlin, J.A. (2008), "A Comparative Analysis of the Global Emergence of Social Enterprise", *8th ISTR Conference & 2nd EMES-ISTR Conference*, Barcelona.

[42] Le Grand, J. (1991), "Quasi-markets and Social Policy", in *The Economic Journal*, 101:408, pp. 1256-1267.

[43] Leadbeater, C. (1996), *The Rise of the Social Entrepreneur*, Demos, London.

[44] Leadbeater, C. (2006), "The Socially Entrepreneurial City", in Nicholls, A. (ed.), *Social Entrepreneurship. New Models of Sustainable Social Change*, Oxford University Press, Oxford, pp. 233-246.

[45] Light, P. (2008), *The Search For Social Entrepreneurship*, The Brookings Institution, Washington, D.C.

[46] Lounsbury, M. and Strang, D. (2009), "Social Entrepreneurship. Success Stories and Logic Construction", in Hammack, D. and Heydemann, S. (eds.), *Globalization, Philanthropy, and Civil Society*, Indiana University Press, Bloomington.

[47] Mair, J. and Marti, I. (2006), "Social entrepreneurship research: A source of explanation, prediction, and delight", in *Journal of World Business*, vol. 41, no. 1, pp. 36-44.

[48] Martin, R.L. and Osberg, S. (2007), "Social Entrepreneurship: The Case for Definition", in *Stanford Social Innovation Review*, Spring 2007, pp. 29-39.

[49] Monaci, M. and Caselli, M. (2005), "Blurred Discourses: How Market Isomorphism Constrains and Enables Collective Action in Civil Society", in *Global Networks*, vol. 5, no. 1, pp. 49-69.

[50] Mort, G.S., Weerawardena, J. and Carnegie, K. (2003), "Social entrepreneurship: Towards conceptualisation", in *International Journal of Nonprofit & Voluntary Sector Marketing*, vol. 8, no. 1, p. 76.

[51] Mulgan, G., Tucker, S., Ali, R. and Sanders, B. (2007), *Social innovation: what it is, why it matters and how it can be accelerated*, Working Paper, Skoll Centre for Social Entrepreneurship, Oxford.

[52] Murray, R., Caulier-Grice., J. and Mulgan, G. (2010), *The Open Book of Social Innovation*, NESTA and the Young Foundation, London.

[53] Nicholls, A. (2006a), "Introduction", in Nicholls, A. (ed.), *Social Entrepreneurship. New Models of Sustainable Social Change*, Oxford University Press, Oxford, pp. 1-35.

[54] Nicholls, A. (ed.) (2006b), *Social Entrepreneurship. New Models of Sustainable Social Change*, Oxford University Press, Oxford.

[55] Nicholls, A. (2010a), "Fair Trade: Towards an Economics of Virtue", in *Journal of Business Ethics*, vol. 92, no. 0, pp. 241-255.

[56] Nicholls, A. (2010b), "The Institutionalization of Social Investment: The Interplay of Investment Logics and Investor Rationalities", in *Journal of Social Entrepreneurship*, vol. 1, no. 1, pp. 70-100.

[57] Nicholls, A. (2010c), "The Legitimacy of Social Entrepreneurship: Reflexive Isomorphism in a Pre-Paradigmatic Field", in *Entrepreneurship Theory and Practice*, vol. 34, no. 4, pp. 611-633.

[58] Nicholls, A. and Cho, A.H. (2006), "Social Entrepreneurship: The Structuration of a Field", in Nicholls, A. (ed.), *Social Entrepreneurship. New Models of Sustainable Change*, Oxford University Press, Oxford, pp. 99-118.

[59] Novy, A. and Leubolt, B. (2005), "Participatory budgeting in Porto Alegre: Social innovation and the dialectical relationship of state and civil society", in *Urban Studies*, vol. 42, no. 11, pp. 2023-2036.

[60] Nyssens, M. (ed.) (2006), *Social Enterprise. At the crossroads of market, public policies and civil society*, Routledge, London.

[61] Osbourne, D. and Gaebler, T. (1992), *Reinventing Government*, Addison-Wesley, Reading.

[62] Phills, J.A.J., Deiglmeier, K. and Miller, D.T. (2008), "Rediscovering Social Innovation", in *Stanford Social Innovation Review*, Fall 2008, pp. 34-43.

[63] Salamon, L.L., Sokolowski, S.W. and List, R. (2003), *Global Civil Society: An Overview*, Johns Hopkins Center for Civil Society Studies, Baltimore.

[64] Santos, F. (2009), "A Positive Theory of Social Entrepreneurship", *INSEAD Faculty & Research Working Paper*, 2009/23/EFE/ISIC.

[65] Short, J., Moss, T. and Lumpkin, G. (2009), "Research in Social Entrepreneurship: Past Contributions and Future Opportunities", in *Strategic Entrepreneurship Journal*, vol. 3, pp. 161-194.

[66] Stone, M. and Cutcher-Gershenfeld, S. (2001), "Challenges of Measuring Performance in Nonprofit Organizations", in Flynn, P. and Hodgkinson, V. A. (eds.), *Measuring the Impact of the Nonprofit Sector*, Academic/Plenum Publishers, New-York.

[67] Thompson, J.L. (2008), "Social enterprise and social entrepreneurship: where have we reached?: A summary of issues and discussion points", in *Social Enterprise Journal*, vol. 4, no. 2, pp. 149-161.

[68] Williams, M. and Cowling, M. (2009), *Annual Small Business Survey 2007/08*, Department for Business Enterprise and Regulatory Reform, London.

[69] Yujuico, E. (2008), "Connecting the Dots in Social Entrepreneurship through the Capabilities Approach", in *Socio-Economic Review*, vol. 6, no. 3, pp. 493-513.

[70] Yunus, M. (2006), "Social Business Entrepreneurs Are the Solution", in Nicholls, A. (ed.), *Social Entrepreneurship. New Models of Sustainable Social Change*, Oxford University Press, Oxford, pp. 39-44.

[71] Yunus, M. (2007), *Creating a World Without Poverty: Social Business and the Future of Capitalism*, Public Affair, New York.

[72] Yunus, M., Moingeon, B. and Lehmann-Ortega, L. (2010), "Building Social Business Models: Lessons from the Grameen Experience", in *Long Range Planning*, vol. 43, no. 2-3, pp. 308-325.

[73] Zahra, S.A., Gedajlovic, E., Neubaum, D.O. and Shulman, J.M. (2009), "A typology of social entrepreneurs: Motives, search processes and ethical challenges", in *Journal of Business Venturing*, vol. 24, no. 5, pp. 519-532.

Part II: The People

Social Entrepreneurs and their Personality
Kati Ernst

Human Resource Management and Volunteer Motivation
Christiane Blank

Collaborations and Partnerships
Heike Schirmer & Heather Cameron

3   Social Entrepreneurs and their Personality

Kati Ernst

University of Wuppertal
Schumpeter School of Business and Economics

Learning goals

Upon completing this chapter, you should be able to accomplish the following:

- Understand the role of personality in entrepreneurship studies.

- Describe the current knowledge on the personality in social entrepreneurs.

- Name and explain the core elements of the entrepreneurial, and the prosocial personality of a social entrepreneur.

3.1   Introduction

Social entrepreneurial personality
The person of the social entrepreneur is a topic which is often discussed in popular literature in the field. To name examples, Bornstein's (2004) book "How to change the world:
Social entrepreneurs and the power of new ideas" and Elkington and Hartigan's (2008)
book "The power of unreasonable people - How social entrepreneurs create markets that
change the world" both focus on individual entrepreneurs, their stories and their personality. So what can be said about these people who become social entrepreneurs?

Looking into demographics, there doesn't seem to be a clear trend when it comes to social
entrepreneurs. See **Figure 3.1** and **Figure 3.2**. Here, GEM studies can serve as a source of
insight. The GEM is the Global Entrepreneurship Monitor, a research consortium which
produces the largest studies on entrepreneurial activity on a global level. In 2006, the GEM
published a statistical report on levels of social entrepreneurship in the UK, and reported
additional information on who the people are who become social entrepreneurs. These
numbers show that social entrepreneurs are pretty much average people when it comes to
demographics. They have various educational backgrounds – from no formal education to
doctorates – and come from all ethnic groups. And even though there are slightly more
male than female social entrepreneurs, there is no male dominance as in the case of commercial entrepreneurship. So why is it that so much razzmatazz is made about social entrepreneurs?

Figure 3.1   Share of people with respective degree who become social
entrepreneurs

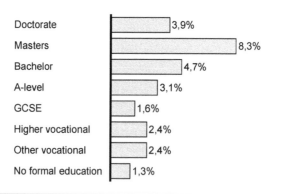

Doctorate   3,9%
Masters   8,3%
Bachelor   4,7%
A-level   3,1%
GCSE   1,6%
Higher vocational 2,4%
Other vocational   2,4%
No formal education 1,3%

Own illustration based on Harding (2006)

Figure 3.2   Share of males or females who choose career path social entrepreneur
                      or entrepreneur

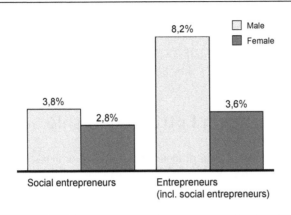

Own illustration based on Harding (2006)

It seems to be the **personality** of the social entrepreneur which has fascinated practitioners
and researchers. On the one hand, a large part of social entrepreneurship literature to date
deals with the overarching category of the 'social entrepreneur' and their personality. This
ranges from anecdotal tales about social entrepreneurs, telling of their extraordinary character (e.g., Bornstein, 2004; Elkington and Hartigan, 2008; Frances, 2008), to lists of attributes, to studies specifically dedicated to gaining further insight on the relevant traits of
social entrepreneurs. Overall, research underlines that social entrepreneurs' personality is
something special and unseen in other areas. And it goes as far as that some authors shape
their entire definition of social entrepreneurship around the person of the social entrepreneur. Some examples can be seen in **Table 3.1** below.

Table 3.1   Definitions of social entrepreneurs or social entrepreneurship

Source	Definition
Bornstein, 2004, p. 1f.	"Transformative forces: people with new ideas to address major problems who are relentless in the pursuit of their visions, people who simply will not take "no" for an answer, who will not give up until they have spread their ideas as far as they possibly can"
Crutchfield and McLeod Grant, 2008, p. 24f.	"[...] they create social value; they relentlessly pursue new opportunities; they act boldly without being constrained by current resources; they innovate and adapt; and they are obsessed with results"
Roberts and Woods, 2005, p. 49	"[Social entrepreneurship is] the construction, evaluation and pursuit of oppor-tunities for transformative social change carried out by visionary, passionately dedicated individuals"

Own table

Being of such interest, there seems to be something that makes a social entrepreneurial personality special. So what needs to be known about the social entrepreneurial personality, and what makes it so different?

Before taking a look into what this may entail, it seems reasonable to introduce a definition. For the course of this chapter *social entrepreneurial personality* is understood as a combination of stable traits common to social entrepreneurs, uncommon within the rest of the population, which cause them to act the way they do.

3.2   Personality in Entrepreneurship Studies

Looking into personality within entrepreneurial studies – to which social entrepreneurship belongs – is not an easy endeavour. For many years there has been a large discussion whether there is such thing as a personality which effects entrepreneurial behaviour.

Since the early days of entrepreneurship research, studies focused on the person of the entrepreneur and character traits, pioneers like Israel Kirzner and Joseph A. Schumpeter placing them in the heart of their entrepreneurship theories. This trend contributed to what is known as the traits approach of entrepreneurship, based on the traits school of personality. The traits school argues that certain behaviour is not solely based on learned reactions but on stable traits of the acting individual. These traits form dispositions to act a certain way and can be understood as propensities to act. Together, they make up a personality. The traits approach puts personality at the core of business entrepreneurship – and largely dominated the field of entrepreneurship research for many years. As research progressed, it became apparent that many studies on the topic only showed weak direct links between personality and entrepreneurship (e.g., Ajzen, 1991; Brockhaus, 1980). Nonetheless, some researchers continued to show enthusiasm for the role of personality in entrepreneurship research, and, in past years, research has shown that there are, in fact, links between personality and entrepreneurship (especially in the following meta-analyses: Collins, Hanges and Locke, 2004; Rauch and Frese, 2007). These recent studies come to the conclusion that previous inconsistent findings on the effect of personality on entrepreneurship were due to unclear definitions, measurement mistakes, or an incorrect selection of traits included in research (Cromie, 2000; Johnson, 1990). They argue the person of the entrepreneur back into the field, then as Johnson states "Individuals are, after all, the energizers of the entrepreneurial process" (Johnson, 1990, p. 48). Also, personality plays a significant role when situations are complex and uncertain, as is the case in entrepreneurship, especially in its initial stages.

Consequently, the personality of the entrepreneur has been increasingly included in recent studies. What has changed is that the role of personality is looked at in a more differentiated manner. On the one hand, the field has gone from looking at what entrepreneurs are like to what aspects of personality *motivate* entrepreneurs. On the other hand, it has also been discussed if personality has no direct but a profound indirect effect on entrepreneurship. Baum and Locke (2004), for example, found that traits indeed had an effect on enterprise growth, yet indirectly through antecedents such as goals. Additionally, the assumption is no longer that the "entrepreneurial" traits are necessary or sufficient for entrepreneurial activity. Rather, they can be seen as facilitators of entrepreneurial activity, as the expected utility of being self-employed is higher for people who have the characteristics which can help successfully establish an enterprise (Bönte and Jarosch, 2010). Overall, it seems to be an interesting question to look at what makes up the personality of people acting entrepreneurially – in this case specifically as social entrepreneurs.

Figure 3.3   Different links between personality and entrepreneurial behaviour

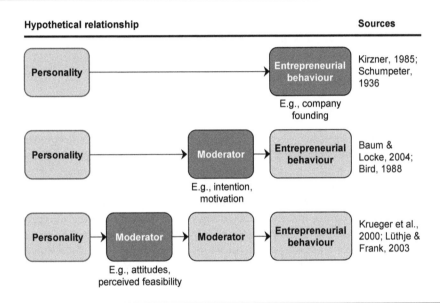

Own illustration

At the same time, it must be mentioned that some sceptical voices are still to be heard, although they rather caution research to be more vigorous in the area than completely annihilate the important role of personality. Especially in social entrepreneurship some authors criticize the 'cult' towards social entrepreneurs' personality in research (e.g., Paul C. Light). Selected studies have even found disapproval of this point of view within practicing organisations (Seanor and Meaton, 2007; Spear, 2006), who focus more on team-level processes and success than that on one individual in the enterprise. Nonetheless, the central role of social entrepreneurs' personality both in practical social entrepreneurial support as well as research on the topic is apparent. As Bill Drayton – the founder of Ashoka – said when asked to define a social entrepreneur: "The core is personality [...]" (Meehan, 2004, p. 11). His organisation, in fact, believes that if you want to know if an idea is successful, you must focus on the person behind it.

3.3 Elements of the Social Entrepreneurial Personality

Authors suggest that the social entrepreneurial personality is a mixture of an *entrepreneurial personality*, on the one hand, and a *socially oriented* one, on the other. After many years of study, in 2011, Paul C. Light, a harsh critic of the personality approach to social entrepreneurship, actually came to the cautious conclusion that social entrepreneurs are not only a breed of business entrepreneurs: they have a businesslike thinking and act similarly to high achievers, but they are different in their deep commitment to a social cause. Simms and Robinson (2005) go a step further and suggest that social entrepreneurs have dual personalities, split between activists and business entrepreneurs. So let's take a deeper look into what constitutes these two parts of the social entrepreneurial personality.

3.3.1 Entrepreneurial Personality

"Social entrepreneurs are one species in the genus entrepreneur" (Dees, 1998, p. 3)

Social entrepreneurs are often seen as a subspecies of the business entrepreneur (e.g., Achleitner, Heister, and Stahl, 2007). Various researchers have found personality traits in social entrepreneurs which are associated with business entrepreneurs. For example, Thompson, Alvy, and Lees (2000) list numerous characteristics shared by social and business entrepreneurs: e.g., ambitious, and able to communicate and recruit resources. Martin and Osberg (2007) recognize that the social entrepreneur, like the business entrepreneur, is inspired by the unsatisfying equilibrium, creatively develops a solution, takes direct action, has the courage to start and the fortitude to continue. Perrini and Vurro (2006) also name various factors in which social entrepreneurs are similar to business entrepreneurs: entrepreneurial aptitude, risk-tolerance, strong desire to control, founding orientation, unhappy with the status quo, building of portfolios of resources, and an aptitude for networking.

Yet, there is a difference between the understanding of what an entrepreneurial character is, especially between society and science. In line with the definition of the social entrepreneurial personality above, this chapter understands *entrepreneurial personality* to be a combination of stable traits common to entrepreneurial actors, uncommon within the rest of the population, which causes them to act the way they do. Further disagreement exists with regard to which exact traits establish such an entrepreneurial personality. Numerous traits have been associated with the entrepreneurial personality, some studies listing over 30 potential characteristics (Cromie, 2000).

The inclusion of a single trait is not enough to capture the complexity of the entire construct of the entrepreneurial personality. Typically, five traits reoccur when speaking of the entrepreneurial personality: *risk-taking propensity, innovativeness, need for achievement, need for independence* and *proactiveness*. Let's review them shortly.

Risk-taking propensity

Risk-taking is especially interesting as entrepreneurship is an area defined by high levels of uncertainty. Entrepreneurs can, therefore, be expected to be risk-bearing people as they choose the risky path of entrepreneurship. This trait is used frequently in entrepreneurship research. Research to date also suggests a high level of risk-taking propensity in social entrepreneurs. While no specific empirical work has been done, anecdotal studies describe the social entrepreneur as risk-friendly (e.g., Frances, 2008; Mort, Weerawardena, and Carnegie, 2003; Peredo and McLean, 2006). The UK GEM report also shows that, on average, social entrepreneurs are less likely to let fear of failure stop them from starting a venture – even though they still show less risk-taking propensity than commercial entrepreneurs. Dees (1998) confirms that social entrepreneurs act boldly in the face of the challenges they meet. Therefore, risk-taking propensity is considered part of the entrepreneurial personality of a social entrepreneur.

Innovativeness

Schumpeter already recognized that the person founding an enterprise must be willing to "reform or revolutionize" (Bönte and Jarosch, 2010, p. 7, quoting Schumpeter 1934). Other early thought leaders in business entrepreneurship, such as Peter F. Drucker highlighted the importance of innovativeness, as the core of entrepreneurial activity. Innovative character traits are also found in social entrepreneurs (e.g., Leadbeater, 1997; Mort et al., 2003; Peredo and McLean, 2006). For example, Dees (1998) attests that they engage in continuous innovation. Therefore, innovativeness is included as part of the entrepreneurial personality of a social entrepreneur.

Need for achievement

In entrepreneurial research, need for achievement can be understood as "a person's need to strive hard to attain success" (Cromie, 2000, p. 16). This trait was also mentioned early on in the field, David C. McClelland even placing it in the centre of entrepreneurial activity. As with the previous traits, anecdotal evidence in social entrepreneurship research points to the relevance of need for achievement. Some of the adjectives used are ambitious (Winkler, 2008), relentless (Frances, 2008), and determined (Leadbeater, 1997). Dees (1998) states that social entrepreneurs relentlessly pursue new opportunities. Therefore, need for achievement is integrated within the entrepreneurial personality of a social entrepreneur.

Need for independence

Studies have shown that entrepreneurs find it hard to work within rules and boundaries (Cromie, 2000). This is associated with a need for independence or autonomy. Similar to the dispute over the existence of a team-less social entrepreneur, acting as an individual hero, some researchers disagree with the idea that social entrepreneurs work independently (e.g., Light, 2011; Seanor and Meaton, 2007). Nonetheless, others say that social entrepreneurs, too, prefer self-determined, independent work (e.g., Barendsen and Gardner, 2004; Winkler, 2008), and are the sole individuals who lead these active organisations (Leadbeater, 1997). Therefore, need for independence is considered an element of the entrepreneurial personality of a social entrepreneur.

Proactiveness

Proactiveness is considered as an entrepreneurial trait, as those willing to shape things are most likely the ones who become entrepreneurs. Again, social entrepreneurial studies hint at the presence of this trait in social entrepreneurs. While Mort, Weerawardena, and Carnegie (2003) specifically describe social entrepreneurs as proactive, Peredo and McLean (2006) circumscribe the trait by stating that they take advantage of opportunities around them. Therefore, proactiveness is added to the construct of the entrepreneurial personality of a social entrepreneur.

To sum up, risk-taking propensity, innovativeness, need for achievement, need for independence and proactiveness are identified as elements of the entrepreneurial personality.

Besides identifying similarities, all the papers comparing social and business entrepreneurs point out the one core difference between the two: the goal of their enterprise. While business entrepreneurs are said to strive for profit, social entrepreneurs focus on their social mission. It is based on this fact, that there may exit a socially oriented personality alongside the entrepreneurial personality in the case of social entrepreneurs.

3.3.2   Prosocial Personality

"[…] Social entrepreneurs are more than another breed of business entrepreneur"
(Light, 2011, p. 44)

Many anecdotal works on social entrepreneurship outline the passion the entrepreneurs develop for their cause, often pointing out the selflessness of their deeds. This commitment towards addressing social injustice is considered a sign of prosocial behaviour and suggests the existence of a prosocial personality. Penner and Finkelstein (1998) define a prosocial personality as "an enduring tendency to think about the welfare and rights of other people, to feel concern and empathy for them, and to act in a way that benefits them" (p. 526).

Many researchers recognize this existence of a social drive in social entrepreneurs. In this sense, Guclu and Dees (2002) write "Social entrepreneurs must have the same commitment and determination as a traditional business entrepreneur, plus a deep passion for the social cause, minus an expectation of significant financial gains" (p. 13).

To further specify what defines this social element, researchers have begun to focus on personality aspects. In a rather abstract manner, Drayton (2002) names "strong ethical fibre" (p. 124) as a necessary ingredient to becoming a social entrepreneur. Further researchers attest that social entrepreneurs have values from early on and show non-egotistical behaviour (e.g., Hemingway, 2005). Others identify specific character traits representing this social aspect in social entrepreneurs' personalities. Mair and Noboa (2006) recognize an additional trait for social entrepreneurs: "[..] many of these attributes may equally apply to business entrepreneurial behaviour, with one exception, receptivity to the feelings of others, or put differently, empathy" (p. 123f.). This concept is also recognized by Bhawe, Jain and Gupta (2007), whose qualitative study shows that social entrepreneurs have a strong empathy for people affected by social problems. Both studies regarding empathy obtain their insight from work on prosocial character traits. This is supported by numerous studies in social psychology, which have shown a link between a prosocial personality and prosocial behaviour such as helping or volunteering (e.g., Bierhoff, 2010; Davis et al., 1999). Hereby, those actions are considered as prosocial behaviour which society sees as generally beneficial. In this sense, social entrepreneurship can be considered prosocial behaviour. Hence, the prosocial personality is a relevant element when looking at social entrepreneurship.

The prosocial personality is made up of the traits moving people to act in a way benefiting other people than themselves. This phenomenon and related behaviour has been treated extensively in general social psychology research to date. One finding has been that there seems to be a prosocial personality, which is consistent over time (Eisenberg et al., 2002). The related characteristics cause a person to act when the distress of others arouses them (Penner et al., 2005). Prosocial personality is associated with helping, social responsibility, care orientation, consideration of others, and sympathy (Eisenberg et al., 2002). In line with the definitions of the social entrepreneurial and entrepreneurial personality above, this chapter understands *prosocial personality* to be a combination of stable traits common to prosocial actors, uncommon within the rest of the population, which cause them to act the way they do.

As in the case of entrepreneurial personality, there is much discussion of what traits make up the prosocial personality, a quest initiated by Louis A. Penner in the 1980s. In general, they are traits which foster helping attitudes. Here, Hans-Werner Bierhoff's concept is adapted and includes the dimensions of empathy and social responsibility in the prosocial personality.

Empathy
Empathy is a central core of all constellations of prosocial personality. The construct comes from social psychology and describes the ability of a person to put oneself in another's shoes. Frequently, it is split into affective and cognitive empathy. Affective empathy means the actual emotional compassion with another, cognitive empathy means the ability to perceive the emotional state of other people. Researchers have seen that empathy supports social entrepreneurial intention formation (Mair and Noboa, 2006). Bhawe, Jain, and Gupta (2007) assume that empathy is necessary to be able to identify opportunities in social entrepreneurship. Therefore, the concept of empathy is included as part of the prosocial personality.

Sense of social responsibility
Sense of social responsibility is the trait which causes a sense of obligation to assist those in distress. Hereby, the inner conviction to help overweighs the costs of doing so. This aspect shows itself in numerous papers on volunteering. When studying volunteers in several countries, Hustinx, Handy, Cnaan, Brudney, Pessi and Yamauchi (2010) discover that the number one motivation to help is that the people find it "important to help others" (p. 363). Within social entrepreneurship research, while the topic of social responsibility has not

been addressed specifically, it seems to be an inherent assumption in line with this choice of career path. As mentioned, authors such as Bornstein (2004) underline the selflessness of social entrepreneurs, and Drayton (2002) highlights their 'ethical fibre'. These aspects indicate the presence of a sense of social responsibility in social entrepreneurs. Therefore, the concept of social responsibility is included as part of the prosocial personality.

3.3.3   The Social Entrepreneurial Personality

In summary, it can be expected that social entrepreneurs have both characteristics considered as typically entrepreneurial, as well as those associated with prosocial behaviour. The summary of the seven identified traits can be seen in the **Figure 3.4** below.

Figure 3.4   The characteristics within the social entrepreneurial personality

---

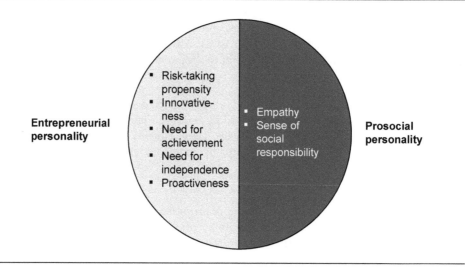

Own illustration

3.4   Case Study

In his successful book, "How to Change the World", David Bornstein takes the time to reflect on Florence Nightingale, who he considers to be a prime example of a social entrepreneur. While Bornstein reflects on large stretches of Nightingale's life, this case study focuses on the early years of her social work, as he described them in his book.

While many young girls enjoyed playing with dolls, even as a child, Nightingale felt drawn towards helping those in need. At a young age, she watched by sick beds and tried to heal hurt animals. Growing older, this wish to help become stronger, and she dreamed of becoming a nurse. Yet, in the England of the 19th century, nursing was not considered a suitable work for a lady from society's upper class. Concerned, Nightingale's father forbade her to choose this profession. Upset by not being able to attend nursing school, Nightingale thought of alternate possibilities to come closer to her ideal. While travelling with her family, she frequently visited clinics, and at home, she read books and reports on hospitals and medicine. Becoming further infatuated with the topic, Nightingale chose to further argue with her parents, and after four years, was finally allowed to take a training course for nursing in Germany.

Entering the profession in a hospital in London, Nightingale became fully devoted to her job, refusing to let anything distract her. For example, she rejected all suitors and took all other means to remain independent, and thereby able to optimally pursue her work. Soon, she received an interesting offer from Istanbul: War was waging, and English soldiers were fighting alongside the Turkish, against the Russians. She did not only agree to take charge of the military hospitals in the region, she also joined together 38 nurses to accompany her. Arriving in the war zone, she encountered chaos. Hygienic circumstances were abysmal, dirt piling in beds and on clothes. The necessary medical supplies were not available, water scarce, and numerous diseases were leading to death rates of close to 50%. At first, army officials refused to work with her, a simply woman from London. Yet soon, their desperation led them to accept her.

Immediately, Nightingale took charge. In her actions, she was described as strict and stern, with great precision and determination. Ordering 200 scrubbing brushes, she instructed her staff to thoroughly clean the wards and ensure clothes and linen were washed. Failing to acquire the necessary medicine and supplies through the standard routes, Nightingale invested the £30,000 collected prior to her trip to buy them, taking over the army's deliverer's job. Likewise, whichever obstacles she encountered, she fought, argued, and negotiated until a solution was found. One after the other, she built new wards, kitchens, laundry services, and introduced booking keeping and strict hygienic standards. Additionally, she made sure that the personal comforts were met for the injured soldiers, introducing recreational space, and consoling those in despair with a soft voice. Within a few moths, the death rate in the hospitals fell to 2%, making her an idol of the soldiers, and later of the English people.

Questions

1. The text offers cues on Florence Nightingale's personality. Please go through the case study and look for traits she may have had.

2. Please match the description of Florence Nightingale's personality with the individual social entrepreneurial personality traits we learned about in this chapter.

3. Which aspects match the suggestions made in the chapter? Which don't? Please discuss the implications of your findings.

3.5   Further Reading

[1] Bornstein, D. (2004), *How to change the world: Social entrepreneurs and the power of new ideas*, Oxford University Press, Oxford, UK.
[2] Elkington, J. and Hartigan, P. (2008). *The power of unreasonable people - How social entrepreneurs create markets that change the world*, Harvard Business School Press, Boston.
[3] Hemingway, C. A. (2005), "Personal values as a catalyst for corporate social entrepreneurship", in *Journal of Business Ethics*, vol. 60, no. 3, pp. 233-249.
[4] Mair, J., Robinson, J.A. and Hockerts, K. (eds.), *Social Entrepreneurship*, Palgrave Macmillan, New York.
[5] Rauch, A. and Frese, M. (2007), "Let's put the person back into entrepreneurship research: a meta-analysis on the relationship between business owners' personality traits, business creation, and success", in *European Journal of Work & Organizational Psychology*, vol. 16, no. 4, pp. 353-385.

3.6   Bibliography

[1] Achleitner, A.-K., Heister, P. and Stahl, E. (2007), "Social Entrepreneurship – Ein Überblick", in Achleitner, A.-K., Pöllath, R. and Stahl, E. (eds.), *Finanzierung von Sozialunternehmern - Konzepte zur finanziellen Unterstützung von Social Entrepreneurs*, Schäffer-Poeschel, Stuttgart, pp. 1-25.
[2] Ajzen, I. (1991), "The theory of planned behavior", in *Organizational Behavior and Human Decision Processes*, vol. 50, no. 2, pp. 179-211.
[3] Barendsen, L., and Gardner, H. (2004), "Is the social entrepreneur a new type of leader?", in *Leader to Leader, 2004(34)*, pp. 43-50.
[4] Baum, J.R., and Locke, E.A. (2004), "The relationship of entrepreneurial traits, skill, and motivation to subsequent venture growth", in *Journal of Applied Psychology*, vol. 89, no. 4, pp. 587-598.
[5] Bhawe, N., Jain, T.K., and Gupta, V.K. (2007), *The entrepreneurship of the good samaritan: a qualitative study to understand how opportunities are perceived in social entrepreneurship*. Paper presented at the BCERC.
[6] Bierhoff, H.-W. (2010), *Psychologie prosozialen Verhaltens - Warum wir anderen helfen*, W. Kohlhammer, Stuttgart.
[7] Bönte, W. and Jarosch, M. (2010), *Mirror, mirror on the wall, who is the most entrepreneurial of them all?* [Schumpeter Discussion Papers - 2010-009]. University of Wuppertal, Schumpeter School of Business and Economics, Wuppertal.
[8] Bornstein, D. (2004), *How to change the world: Social entrepreneurs and the power of new ideas*, Oxford University Press, Oxford, UK.
[9] Brockhaus, R.H., Sr. (1980), "Risk taking propensity of entrepreneurs", in *The Academy of Management Journal*, vol. 23, no. 3, pp. 509-520.
[10] Collins, C.J., Hanges, P.J. and Locke, E.A. (2004), "The relationship of achievement motivation to entrepreneurial behavior: a meta-analysis", in *Human Performance*, vol. 17, no. 1, pp. 95-117.
[11] Cromie, S. (2000), "Assessing entrepreneurial inclinations: some approaches and empirical evidence", in *European Journal of Work & Organizational Psychology*, vol. 9, no. 1, pp. 7-30.
[12] Davis, M.H., Mitchell, K.V., Hall, J.A., Lothert, J., Snapp, T. and Meyer, M. (1999), "Empathy, expectations, and situational preferences: personality influences on the decision to participate in volunteer helping behaviors", in *Journal of Personality*, vol. 67, no. 3, pp. 469-503.
[13] Dees, J.G. (1998), *The meaning of "social entrepreneurship"*, Retrieved March 31, 2009, from http://www.fntc.info/files/documents/The%20meaning%20of%20Social%20Entreneurship.pdf.
[14] Drayton, W. (2002), "The citizen sector: becoming as entrepreneurial and competitive as business", in *California Management Review*, vol. 44, no. 3, pp. 120-132.
[15] Eisenberg, N., Guthrie, I.K., Cumberland, A., Murphy, B.C., Shepard, S.A., Zhao, Q., et al. (2002), "Prosocial development in early adulthood: A longitudal study", in *Journal of Personality and Social Psychology*, vol. 82, no. 6, pp. 993-1006.

[16] Elkington, J. and Hartigan, P. (2008), *The power of unreasonable people - How social entrepreneurs create markets that change the world.* Harvard Business School Press, Boston.

[17] Frances, N. (2008), *The end of charity: time for social enterprise,* Allen & Unwin, Crows Nest.

[18] Guclu, A., Dees, J.G. and Anderson, B.B. (2002), *The process of social entrepreneurship: creating opportunities worthy of serious pursuit.* Retrieved June 8, 2009, from http://www.caseatduke.org/documents/seprocess.pdf.

[19] Harding, R. (2006), *Social Entrepreneurship Monitor,* Global Entrepreneurship Monitor (GEM), London.

[20] Hemingway, C.A. (2005), "Personal values as a catalyst for corporate social entrepreneurship" in *Journal of Business Ethics,* vol. 60, no. 3, pp. 233-249.

[21] Hustinx, L., Handy, F., Cnaan, R.A., Brudney, J.L., Pessi, A.B. and Yamauchi, N. (2010), "Social and cultural origins of motivations to volunteer: a comparison of university students in six countries", in *International Sociology,* vol. 25, no. 3, pp. 349-382.

[22] Johnson, B.R. (1990), "Toward a multidimensional model of entrepreneurship: the case of achievement motivation and the entrepreneur", in *Entrepreneurship: Theory & Practice,* vol. 14, no. 3, pp. 39-54.

[23] Leadbeater, C. (1997), *The rise of the social entrepreneur,* Demos, London.

[24] Light, P. C. (2011), *Driving social change - How to solve the world's toughest problems,* Wiley, Hoboken.

[25] Mair, J. and Noboa, E. (2006), "Social entrepreneurship: how intentions to create a social enterprise get formed", in Mair, J., Robinson, J.A. and Hockerts, K. (eds.), *Social Entrepreneurship,* Palgrave Macmillan, New York, pp. 121-135.

[26] Martin, R.L. and Osberg, S. (2007), "Social entrepreneurship: the case for definition", in *Stanford Social Innovation Review,* (Spring), pp. 28-39.

[27] Meehan, B. (2004), "15 minutes - Bill Drayton", in *Stanford Social Innovation Review,* (Spring), pp. 11-12.

[28] Mort, G.S., Weerawardena, J. and Carnegie, K. (2003), "Social entrepreneurship: towards conceptualisation", in *International Journal of Nonprofit & Voluntary Sector Marketing,* vol. 8, no. 1, pp. 76-88.

[29] Penner, L.A. and Finkelstein, M.A. (1998), "Dispositional and structural determinants of volunteerism", in *Journal of Personality and Social Psychology,* vol. 74, pp. 525–537.

[30] Penner, L.A., Dovidio, J.F., Piliavin, J.A. and Schroeder, D.A. (2005), "Prosocial behavior: multilevel perspectives", in *Annual Review of Psychology,* vol. 56, no. 1, pp. 365-392.

[31] Peredo, A.M. and McLean, M. (2006), "Social entrepreneurship: a critical review of the concept", in *Journal of World Business,* vol. 41, no. 1, pp. 56-65.

[32] Perrini, F. and Vurro, C. (2006), "Social entrepreneurship: innovation and social change across theory and practice", in Mair, J., Robinson J.A. and Hockerts, K. (eds.), *Social entrepreneurship,* Palgrave Macmillan, New York, pp. 57-85.

[33] Rauch, A. and Frese, M. (2007), "Let's put the person back into entrepreneurship research: a meta-analysis on the relationship between business owners' personality traits, business creation, and success", in *European Journal of Work & Organizational Psychology,* vol. 16, no. 4, pp. 353-385.

[34] Seanor, P. and Meaton, J. (2007), "Making sense of social enterprise", in *Social Enterprise Journal,* vol. 3, no. 1, pp. 90-100.

[35] Simms, S.V. K. and Robinson, J.A. (2005), *Activist or entrepreneur? An identity-based model of social entrepreneurship.* Paper presented at the USASBE 2006 Conference.

[36] Spear, R. (2006), "Social entrepreneurship: a different model?", in *International Journal of Social Economics,* vol. 33, no. 5/6, pp. 399-410.

[37] Thompson, J., Alvy, G. and Lees, A. (2000), "Social entrepreneurship – A new look at the people and the potential", in *Management Decision,* vol. 38, no. 5, pp. 328-338.

[38] Winkler, A. (2008), "Gemeinsamkeiten und Unterschiede zwischen Social Entrepreneurs und Business Entrepreneurs", in Braun, G. and French, M. (eds.), *Social Entrepreneurship - Unternehmerische Ideen für eine bessere Gesellschaft,* HIE-RO Institut, Universität Rostock, Rostock. pp. 95-119

4 Human Resource Management and Volunteer Motivation

Christiane Blank

University of Wuppertal
Schumpeter School of Business and Economics

Learning goals
Upon completing this chapter, you should be able to accomplish the following:

- Describe the special characteristics of volunteers.

- Explain the theoretical background and the motivational factors of volunteering.

- Describe procedural measures for the promotion of volunteer work ("volunteer programs").

- Illustrate the theoretical elements in a practical context.

4.1   Introduction

Social enterprises form a topic which challenges us to reclassify known concepts from economics research in general and entrepreneurship research in particular within a new context. Their social orientation and the fact that they are only indirectly profit-oriented distinguish social enterprises from commercial business enterprises (Part I), but nevertheless they also need to survive in the market, and they, too, have organizational structures and hierarchies that we know from classical economics. This chapter will focus on Human Resource Management and on employee motivation and commitment strategies. These topics were comprehensively analyzed in the context of purely profit-oriented companies (Wöhe and Döring, 2005). However, Human Resource Management in social enterprises is subject to some special conditions. Although many social enterprises have paid employees, volunteers form a decisive part of their workforce and play a big part in the performance and continued existence of social enterprises. It can even be assumed that volunteers, along with funding, are the most wanted resource of social enterprises. Dealing with volunteers is therefore a specific aspect of successful social work. Volunteers are not a mere accessory, they do not function casually, and they do not come for free either. In the light of the present demographic development and from an economic point of view, the volunteer must be regarded as a rare and much sought-after resource which several social enterprises are competing for. A company's ability to attract qualified volunteers and to win their lasting loyalty without cutting back on the quality standards of the services offered, will be fundamental for a successful market position in the future (Rosenkranz and Schill, 2009).

Choosing volunteers, creating tasks for them and ensuring their lasting commitment in the absence of formal contracts are important challenges that the management of social enterprises has to face. In this context, the fact that volunteers do not have a work contract is but one of several factors which distinguish volunteers from full-time associates. Cnaan and Cascio (1998) list further important differences:

- Absence of financial motivation
- Limited time
- In most cases contact with several companies
- No existential dependence from the company
- Informal application processes which often result in a test phase
- No obligation to abide by bureaucratic rules and structures
- No personal liability in case of mistakes

Volunteers freely decide to support a company's vision without a financial interest. Therefore, they seem to be ideal co-workers who meet the desires of many entrepreneurs. However, volunteers are often more critical with regard to the organizations they work for because they can choose their work targets and the extent to which they engage themselves. Hence, it is interesting to compare volunteers on the one hand and highly qualified, much sought-after regular workers who can choose the aims and organization for which they want to work on the other (Mayerhofer, 2001).

Based on the insights above, the human resource management of social enterprises has to take into account individual interests when designing tasks and establishing structures for decision, communication and cooperation processes. It is essential for a successful management to analyze the intrinsic motives which drive the volunteers and the expectations they have with regard to their work in order to retain their loyalty even if they sometimes are given less attractive tasks. Only if the individual motives are known it will be possible to keep motivating the volunteers and to earn their lasting commitment to the company. A strong commitment and identification will lead to even greater engagement in the support of the company's interests and aims, to a better acceptance of changes and new developments and to lasting loyalty even if attractive alternatives are offered (Felfe, 2008). Commitment strategies therefore form an important aspect of dealing with volunteers (**Table 4.1**).

The next chapter gives an overview of the different forms of employment in social enterprises, starting with a differentiation between contract-based forms of employment and employment without a contract. Then volunteers themselves are analyzed in chapter 4.3 with regards to their socio-economic status, interpersonal networks, demographic characteristics and personality traits. Chapter 4.4 deals with altruistic and egoistic motives which may result in voluntary work. It covers the theoretical background as well as motivational factors. In the final chapter 4.5 the basic principles from chapter 4.4 are pulled together in a functional context. Referring to the findings on motivational background, implications for volunteer management are derived with a special focus on procedural measures for the promotion of volunteer work ("volunteer program").

Table 4.1   Chances and positive consequences of employee commitment

Level	Employee commitment
Organizations	– Readiness for action – Motivation, Output – No fluctuation or absenteeism
Employees	– Self-respect – Content through satisfaction of need for affiliation – Resource for stress reduction (social support)

Own table based on Felfe (2008)

4.2   Personnel Work in Social Enterprises

In social enterprises a number of different ways of employment exist which – in addition to specific characteristics of volunteer work – form a challenge to human resource management because in most cases several forms of employment have to be managed at the same time (Mroß, 2009). Mroß distinguishes employees who are bound by a (work) contract and employees without a (work) contract. Employees with a work contract work full-time or part-time and earn their living with this work. Others who also have a work contract may include interns or trainees. The second group of employees in social enterprises are those who do not have a legal work contract in the sense of the BGB (Bürgerliches Gesetzbuch). Here, Mroß counts volunteers, conscientious objectors doing alternative civilian service, members of religious orders and young people who are taking a gap year to do voluntary social or ecological work. According to Mroß, this category is solely defined through the lack of a work contract which in some cases is replaced by other legal contracts or laws (**Figure 4.1**).

Figure 4.1   Categories of personnel work

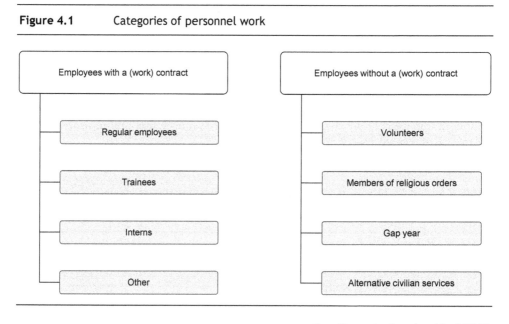

Own illustration based on Mroß (2009)

Mroß' categories are helpful for the definition and distinction of voluntary work which is to be used in the context of this chapter. It is perceived as a work form which is done voluntarily without financial compensation and not as a regular employment, and which is dedicated to social welfare (Strecker, 2002; In this context it has to be noted that for some voluntary work small compensations are paid. However, since these are usually really small, these cases are counted as free of charge, too.) It is not done to earn a living but is performed in addition to a regular employment. For the context of social entrepreneurship, this chapter will focus on voluntary work in operative positions which are designed to create an added social value rather than on voluntary work for an association or as board member of a club. Voluntary work also has to be distinguished from housework, such as caring for the sick or elderly, or neighborly help. This distinction is made assuming that voluntary work has to be done in an organization. Such work is defined as formal voluntary work while the rather informal housework or neighborly help can hardly be statistically surveyed (Holzer, 2005; Strecker, 2002).

4.3   The Person Who Volunteers

Volunteers are not a homogeneous group. They come from all age groups and different social backgrounds. In order to find out who volunteers really are, several factors are taken into account: socio-economic status, interpersonal networks, demographic characteristics and personality traits (Pearce, 1993).

Socio-economic status: „Those with higher income, educational level, occupational status, and family/lineage status and those who own more property are more likely to volunteer, to volunteer for multiple associations and organizations, and to assume leadership roles in their organizations that are those who have fewer of these advantages."(Pearce, 1993, p. 65). These results have been verified by a number of studies in different decades and countries.

Interpersonal Networks: Many studies have led to the result that people who know volunteers are more willing to take up voluntary work themselves (Scott, 1957). Research has shown that most volunteers are recruited through personal contacts. Thus the more friends people have the more likely they are to work as volunteers.

Demographic characteristics: The impact of demographic factors on voluntary commitment is not easy to outline comprehensively. The complexity of the context starts with the relation of age and voluntary commitment. „Volunteering among teenagers increases until about 18 years, then decreases, remaining low until the late twenties, when it rises, researching a peak from age 40 to 55, from which it gradually decreases." (Pearce, 1993, p. 68). Gender-specific influences in general result in more female than male volunteers, but the engagement clearly varies according to the tasks. While women prefer church or social institutions, men tend to work in political or administrative positions which may also be beneficial for their career.

Personality: Most studies try to distinguish personality traits of volunteers from those of people who do not volunteer. By way of conclusion, findings have shown that self-confident, sociable, optimistic people with dominant tendencies are more likely to engage themselves to voluntary work.

4.4   Motivation of Volunteers

Voluntary engagement is the result of many different motives. Often the main motive cannot even be defined, since it is a combination of altruistic and egoistic motives which leads
to voluntary work (Moschner, 2002). Motivation explains the direction, the intensity and
duration of human behavior (Thomae, 1965). Motivation research therefore focuses on the
reasons and driving forces of human behavior.

4.4.1   Volunteer to Serve: The Altruism Debate

The concept of altruism goes back to the French sociologist Auguste Comte who postulated
that there had to be a binding morale within a society. This morale should help to emphasize the corporate feeling rather than egoistic behavior (Comte as cited in Fuchs-Heinritz,
1998).

4.4.1.1   Theories of Altruism

Altruism theories are based on the assumption of selflessness. Altruistic behavior can be
theoretically explained through three different approaches. These are the theory of empathy-related reactions, the empathy-altruism hypothesis and the altruistic personality
(**Figure 4.2**). The theoretic assumptions result from earlier processes which are defined
either by empathy, that is compassion, or by inner norms or values which lead to an altruistic motivation (Bierhoff, 2004).

The theory of empathy-related reactions was developed by Eisenberg. It focuses on character traits because these create empathy. Empathy is experienced, and therefore the readiness to help others increases if a situation is characterized by great sympathy, emotional
intensity and emotional regulation of the spectator. The emotional regulation has to be
emphasized in this context because it is characterized by the limitation to substantial issues,
little impulsivity and high self-control (Eisenberg, 2000).

Figure 4.2   Altruism Theories

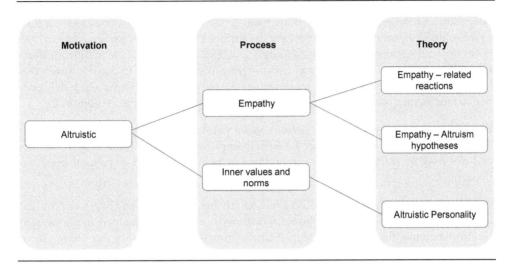

Own illustration based on Bierhoff (2004)

The empathy-altruism hypothesis is based on situation-related empathy which is triggered by another person's actual emergency situation. The basic assumption is that several factors increase or decrease the observers' empathy in a specific situation. Empathy increases if the observers know the victims personally (family or friends). It also increases if there are similarities or commonalities between victim and observer so that the observers can better put themselves in the victim's position, which will result in greater compassion (Bierhoff, 2002). In a series of experiments, Batson studied how the existence of escape possibilities influences a person's readiness to help. Emphatic persons will help the victim, no matter if they could escape from the situation or not, and thereby display a great altruistic motivation, while less emphatic persons will only help if they cannot escape (Batson, 1991).

The altruistic personality is defined by empathy and inner values. Volunteers often show a higher level of empathy and emotional stability. In addition, a greater interest in other people's needs also characterizes an altruistic personality. This applies to voluntary commitment as well as to emergency situations (Bierhoff and Schülken, 2001). Social responsibility is a norm which makes us feel a moral obligation to help others who are in an emergency. This includes that we want to meet justified expectations of others and to follow social rules (Bierhoff, 2006).

4.4.1.2   Motives of Altruism

The motives of altruism include the norm of social responsibility, a religious, charitable obligation and the aspect of reward (Moschner, 2002). Altruistic people want to contribute to the solution of social problems or at least to improve the situation. They are driven by the norm of social responsibility which includes the obligation to help people in difficult situations. They act in an altruistic manner because they like to help and to commit themselves to society, because they want to support people who have to face problems which they once had to face themselves, too, and/or because they want to take over social responsibility.

In addition to social responsibility there is also a political responsibility which focuses on societal shortcomings and generates the wish to improve these. The aim is to serve society, and this may be reached through commitment in political, societal or cultural organizations.

Another motive of altruism is the religious, charitable obligation which is based on the commandment of charity. This is the main motivation of church volunteers in the western countries because they are driven by their Christian self-concept. Most of them have grown up in Christian families or are convinced of Christian values. Their aim is to help others who are physically or psychologically in a worse situation, and they also expect others to act in a similar way (Brommer, 2000).

However, it must not be ignored that altruistic motives may also have a rewarding quality, albeit without financial aspects. One's own clear conscience and other people's gratefulness may well considered rewarding.

4.4.2   Volunteer to Meet the Own Needs: The Egoism Debate

Egoism is defined by self-centeredness, which is biologically based on instinctive and animalistic tendencies of self-preservation (Brockhaus Encyclopedia, 2005-06). Today the term "egoism" brings about strong negative connotations such as taking hard-nosed advantage of others. However it is one-sided to stick to the negative point of view because the term comprises many facets which can be evaluated in a differentiated manner from an ethical point of view.

4.4.2.1   Egoism Theories

Egoism theories are based on the individual self-interest which is caused by egoistic motives. The basic assumption is that human beings in general act selfishly. This means that for any human being it all comes down to their own well-being, their self-preservation and satisfaction of their needs. Humans strive for their own happiness, and self-interest can be regarded as a natural motive (Göbel, 2006). Two of the theories are the cost-benefit analysis and the theory of social constraint (**Figure 4.3**).

Figure 4.3   Egoism Theories

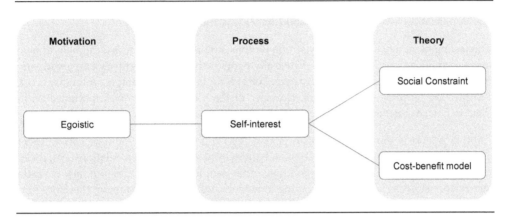

Own illustration based on Bierhoff (2004)

From the cost-benefit model the assumption can be derived that human beings decide and act in a way which best fits their cost-benefit analysis. In addition to material and immaterial costs, the consequences of one's behavior are at the center of the deliberations. These also include consequences of omission or psychological costs such as feelings of guilt or threats to one's self-perception. It is assumed that human beings anticipate such consequences and take them into account when making decisions. For example, they may deal with the following questions: What is my input in this particular action? How good will I feel when I succeed? Will I feel bad if I do not do anything? Such lines of thought occur rather unconsciously. The costs include factors such as expenditure of time, dangers, potential financial loss and degree of difficulty of the assistance. Among the positive consequences which are incorporated into the subjective cost-benefit analysis are factors such as proving one's own skills and feeling good about them, getting a positive feedback, showing compassion and solidarity and being a role model for others (Bierhoff, 2004). The higher the costs are, the lower the wish to engage oneself is, and the bigger the expected reward or benefit is, the stronger the inclination to assist others is (Bierhoff, 2006).

The theory of social constraint includes the presence of others, i.e., the role of the public. In emergency situations where help is needed the number of witnesses who could potentially provide assistance plays an enormous role (Darley und Latané, 1968). Darley und Latané proved that people's willingness to help decreases, even in threatening situations, the more „bystanders" there are, i.e., the bigger the audience is. In literature this is known as the "bystander effect". The reasons lie in the diffusion of responsibility and in the fear of disgrace (Bierhoff, 2004).

4.4.2.2   Motives of Egoism

The motives of egoism include the feeling of significance, social relationships, self-esteem and appreciation, work-life-balance and career (Moschner, 2002).

The feeling of significance is a very strong motive. Voluntary commitment can help to give one's own life a direction or a goal. Especially people who are not regularly employed (any more) can find a meaningful activity here. For elderly people for example, voluntary work can provide meaning and structure, as many of them emphasize how important it is to them to have a reason to get up every morning.

Another motive is the need for social relationships and affiliation. Voluntary commitment can reduce feelings of individualization and anonymity and create new relationships. It can provide the opportunity of getting to know other people and of building up new contacts and relationships as a means of avoiding loneliness. Voluntary commitment therefore also results from self-care because social relationships reduce the risks of illness and social isolation (Brusis, 1999). Some studies have proved the beneficial consequences of voluntary work for the volunteers' health (Badelt, 1997).

In addition, career-oriented motives can be found. Young volunteers get the opportunity to gain additional organizational and social experiences and to acquire and develop key competences such as communication skills or capacities for team-work, which may well serve to brush up their curriculum vitae. Voluntary social work can help young people to bridge the gap between the end of school and the beginning of their professional training, to gain new insights, to learn more about new topics and to make new contacts. For unemployed people, voluntary engagement may also serve as a measure of qualification. Another motive which is often mentioned is the search for new learning opportunities. Volunteers can acquire new knowledge, open up new perspectives and learn from new experiences with people of very different characters. This can help to identify one's own strengths and weaknesses very quickly (Moschner, 2002).

Richter (1980), however, also assumes that sometimes the craving for power and appreciation may prevail. When helping others one can also enjoy one's own power and greatness as opposed to the weak and needy victims. So apparent altruism may well be revealed as an especially refined strategy of egoistic self-fulfillment.

Reciprocity is also considered as the guiding motivation of mutual give-and-take. Some volunteers engage themselves in the hope of receiving help in return when they need it. However, fun and a thirst for adventure also form a very important basis of voluntary work (Moschner, 2002).

4.5 Implications for Volunteer Management

Chapter 4.4 has shown that there is a variety of altruistic and egoistic motives which may result in voluntary work. The volunteers´ primary motivation can often not be retraced since their engagement results from a variety of motives (Moschner, 2002). Measures for the promotion of voluntary work must therefore take this motivational variety into account. In order to pull the various altruistic and egoistic motives together in an organizational context, a functional approach is needed which allows us to derive implications for volunteer management. Clary and Snyder (1999) follow such a functional approach when categorizing the different needs of volunteers into compensatory and social functions, the satisfaction of a desire to learn, self-fulfillment and the fulfillment of inner moral standards (**Table 4.2**).

Table 4.2   Functions served by volunteering

Function	Conceptual definition
Values	The individual volunteers are driven by values like humanitarianism.
Understanding	The volunteer is seeking to learn more about the world or to exercise skills that are often unused.
Enhancement	One can grow and develop psychologically through volunteer activities.
Career	The volunteer wishes to gain career-related experience through volunteering.
Social	Volunteering allows an individual to strengthen his or her social relationships.
Protective	The individual uses volunteering to reduce negative feelings, such as guilt, or to address personal problems.

Own table based on Clary and Snyder (1999)

It is the human resource management's job to adjust the offers and opportunities within a social enterprise to the motives and needs of the volunteers. The better offers and needs match, the happier the workers will be and the more their commitment will grow. The interaction between person and situation is therefore decisive for the readiness to take up and to continue voluntary work.

In order to allow for an interaction between person and situation in companies which also have regular employees or in organizations which are completely based on voluntary workers, it makes sense to establish a "volunteer program" (Brudney, 2005). Such a „volunteer program" provides structures for the recruitment of new volunteers, the individual check and positioning within the organization, the assignment of duties and positions as well as for trainings that may be required. Volunteers need supervising, they need to be motivated and to gain recognition for their work, and they also should get feedback on their performance in order to develop a sense of their own productivity within the company.

Companies, however, must make certain structural adjustments in order to meet the requirements of a volunteer program. Of course, these adjustments will vary in relation to the
size of the respective social enterprise. The recruitment of volunteers and the establishment
of a volunteer program may lead to great changes within social enterprises. It is therefore
important to involve the paid employees in the processes and decisions with regard to the
volunteer program from the beginning. In a first step, the social enterprises have to define
the reasons why volunteers are to be recruited. Does the company wish to save money or to
optimize the cost-effectiveness? Another aim may be to learn more about society from the
volunteers in order to be able to raise public awareness for the company's services. On the
other hand, volunteers may have special skills which the company lacks, such as program-
ming, legal or accounting knowledge. In addition, volunteers can make very good fundraisers because they are regarded as neutral persons who do not profit directly from donations.

All social enterprises, no matter how small or large they are, will need a visible, recognized
person who is responsible for the volunteer management. If the founder cannot take over
this task, a so-called "director of volunteer services" should be appointed who functions as
a "program manager" or a "personnel manager" according to Fisher and Cole 1993, p. 18:
„In the program management approach, the volunteer administrator is a program develop-
er as well as the leader of volunteer efforts integral to the organization's program delivery.
In the personnel management approach, the volunteer administrator recruits, selects and
places volunteers and trains paid staff to work with them. In both approaches, the responsibilities of the volunteer administrator usually include job design, recruitment, interview-
ing, orientation and recognition."

In a next step, formal positions for volunteers should be created. Written task descriptions
are recommended in order to understand the range of responsibilities of different positions
within the company. These descriptions should be similar to those of regular employees in
order to provide volunteers with clear information on the company's expectations and their
respective qualification to meet these expectations. Task descriptions include (McCurely
and Lynch, 1996):

- Job title, offered position

- Purpose of the job (most important part)

- Job responsibilities and activities

- Qualifications for the position (desired skills and knowledge)

- Benefits to the occupant

- Timeframe (for example, hours per week)

- Proposed starting date

- Reporting relationships and supervision

It must, however, not be forgotten that the volunteers' leisure time is a precious good. When planning new positions, the amount of time which the individuals have at their disposal must be taken into account. It seems to make sense to create positions for a relatively short period of time at first, for example in smaller projects. In such positions, the individuals have the opportunity to get to know the company and to find out if the tasks suit them.

Most volunteers are recruited via personal contact (Pearce, 1993), so new volunteers might be won among the initial volunteers' and employees' friends. External „volunteer agencies" may also be helpful for social enterprises searching for suitable volunteers, but they should try to avoid dependencies from external sources and rather develop their own recruitment strategies.

Staffing is then done according to the applicants' motives and requirements. The activities should create added value for the company as well as for the volunteer. Social enterprises could also establish internal counseling and placement offices in order to find suitable positions for new volunteers according to their individual motives and in order to protect them against wrong expectations and disappointments.

Since the motives of volunteers may change over time, social enterprises should be prepared to react accordingly. Continued voluntary commitment is a dynamic process which is formed by feedback processes and the recognition of personal development. This process will sometimes require a modification of certain positions within the company. In addition, individual motivation incentives should be used, which, for example, may include the assignment of greater responsibility, participation in decision making processes, training opportunities, supportive feedback and performance documentation. Other tokens of esteem are of similar importance. For example, attention in the media (newsletters, newspapers), awards or social events (luncheons, banquets, ceremonies) or certificates (for tenure or special achievements) may motivate volunteers. While for some volunteers, a simple but cordial "Thank you!" will increase their motivation, others may prefer written acknowledgments (Brudney, 2005). Again, it is important that motivation incentives meet the volunteers' needs. Not everybody will appreciate an invitation to a banquet. Most motivation incentives arise from the job itself or the friendly contact with colleagues anyway (Pearce, 1993).

The development measures and incentives for voluntary commitment presented here show that the interaction of person and situation in social enterprises may be cost intensive and far from simple. The tasks of the volunteer management are very challenging and go well beyond traditional management responsibilities. It is essential to choose a leadership style that fosters trust building, cooperation, teamwork, competition, personal development, success, value creation, fun and commitment among the volunteers. "Management-by-Partnership" will lead to better results than a merely formal supervision (Walter, 1987). Although volunteer management differs from traditional personnel work in important aspects such as the lack of contractual obligations, this does not mean that volunteers must not be asked to leave the company in case of deviance or bad behavior (Drucker, 1990). Tolerating volunteer deviance might be misinterpreted by other (paid and volunteer) staff members and lead to further misconduct and loss of leadership awareness.

By way of conclusion it can be stated that volunteering is both a hobby as well as a traditional work in an organizational context (Pearce, 1993). The deliberations on the "volunteer program" are based on the assumption that volunteering is regarded as work which legitimates the application of management practices. The attention of the management has to focus on the volunteers' performance and the customers' content. However, voluntary commitment can only take place during a person's leisure time and will, like any other hobby, only be pursued if it is fun and interesting.

4.6   Case Study

GEPA – The Fair Trade Company, one of the best-known enterprises in Fair Trade, has its home office in Wuppertal, Germany. GEPA presents itself as Europe's biggest Fair Trade Organization whose mission it is to "improve the living conditions of people, especially in developing countries, who are presently disadvantaged in the regional economic and social frameworks as well as in the global economy. GEPA wants to be a reliable partner in order to enable producers to participate in the national and international markets under humane conditions and to make an adequate living for themselves" (GEPA partnership agreement). The services offered by GEPA comprise fair prices, advance financing, long-term supply-agreements, counseling and product development, avoidance of unfair intermediate trade, direct, co-operative and long-term trade relationships and creation of market access for small organizations. Main products are victuals (coffee, tea, honey, bread spreads, choco-late, wine etc.), handicrafts and textiles which are bought from associations and trade or-ganizations in Africa, Asia and Latin America. At present GEPA co-operates with 169 pro-ducers from 43 countries.

GEPA, which has more than 170 associates by now, was founded in 1975 by church institu-tions as a GmbH (limited liability company). Based on exclusively social aims and civic engagement at the beginning, GEPA now is a successful import company with a turnover of 54.4 million Euros in 2009/2010. GEPA is financed exclusively from the revenues of the products sold. Occuring profits are not distributed among the partners but re-invested in accordance with the company aims. In Germany, the products are sold at 800 fair trade stores and by more than 6,000 so-called action groups but also at food retailing companies and via an online shop.

The fair trade stores and the action groups, which make 41.39% of the turnover, are GEPA's most important distribution channel. More than 100,000 people work there, most of them voluntarily. The fair trade stores, however, are not directed by GEPA but are independent organizations which must sustain themselves without any external funding. They are either owned by private associations or – if they are bigger – non-incorporated firms or limited liability companies. The original idea of the fair trade stores was to create a room for educa-tional discussion and examination of the challenges which developing countries have to face. Thus at first, selling the products was not the primary aim, but GEPA mainly used them to sensitize customers for unfair structures in global trade, for example to show how little the actual producers earned in contrast to the intermediate traders. Nowadays, fair trade shops are popular in other European countries as well, for example there are more than 550 in Italy and 400 in the Netherlands. Outside Europe, particularly in the U.S., there are many more shops.

The action groups (the term was coined by the "Aktion Dritte Welthandel") are exclusively formed by volunteers who organize special sales events such as Christmas bazars to sell GEPA products. These groups have no business premises and no VAT deduction. They buy products to sell them with a profit for a special aim. GEPA offers the products with a dis-count to these groups in order to enable them to support their chosen social or ecological projects.

In comparison with German shops, some foreign fair trade stores make more turnover due to their better locations and more attractive appearance. Therefore, GEPA thinks that German stores also have a potential for better turnover if they are developed as more professionally managed shops which focus on selling the products and finding new target groups. However, the educational aspect must not be neglected either but should help to balance economic and social aims. By now the stores also have salaried associates in addition to the volunteers and GEPA strives to increase their percentage. In addition to the professionalization of the existing stores, GEPA is also planning to support individuals or groups in starting new stores in Germany.

Questions:

1. What about you? Could you imagine volunteering at GEPA fair trade stores and action groups? Consider pro and contra arguments.

2. What are the reasons that so far, GEPA could rely on voluntary workers in fair trade stores and action groups for selling their products?

3. Which opportunities and risks may arise when GEPA turns the fair trade stores into more professional managed shops and shifts the volunteers' work to professionally trained personnel?

4. How would you manage the professionalization process and the start-up of new fair trade stores if you worked for GEPA?

4.7 Further Reading

[1] Clary, E.G., Snyder, M. and Stukas, A.A. (1996), "Volunteers' Motivations: Findings From a National Survey", in *Nonprofit and Voluntary Sector Quaterly*, vol. 25, no. 4, pp. 485-505.

[2] Dailey, R.C. (1986), "Understanding Organizational Commitment for Volunteers: Empirical and Managerial Implications", in Nonprofit and Voluntary Sector Quaterly, vol. 15, no. 1, pp. 19-31.

[3] Hager, M.A. and Brudney, J.L. (2004), *Volunteer Management Practices and Retention of Volunteers*, The Urban Institute, Washington, DC.

[4] Omoto, A.M., Snyder, M. and Martino, S.C. (2000), "Volunteerism and the Life Course: Investigating Age-Related Agendas for Action", in *Basic and Applied Social Psychology*, vol. 22, no. 3, pp. 181-197.

[5] Van Vuuren, M., de Jong, M.D.T. and Seydel, E.R. (2008), "Commitment with or without a stick of paid work: Comparison of paid and unpaid workers in a nonprofit organization", in *European Journal of Work and Organizational Psychology*, vol. 17, no. 3, pp. 315-326.

4.8 Bibliography

[1] Badelt, C. (1997), *Handbuch der Nonprofit Organisation: Strukturen und Management*, Schäffer-Poeschel Verlag, Stuttgart.

[2] Batson, D.C. (1991), *The Altruism Question. Toward a social-pschological answer*, Lawrence Erlbaum Associates, Inc., Hillsdale, New Jersey.

[3] Bierhoff, H.W. and Schülken, T. (2001), "Ehrenamtliches Engagement", in Bierhoff, H.W. and Fetchenhauer, D. (eds.), *Solidarität. Konflikt, Umwelt und Dritte Welt*, Leske + Budrich, Opladen, pp. 183 – 204.

[4] Bierhoff, H.W. (2002), *Einführung in die Sozialpsychologie*, Beltz Verlag, Weinheim, Basel.

[5] Bierhoff, H.W. (2004), "Handlungsmodelle für die Analyse von Zivilcourage", in Meyer, G., Dovermann, U., Frech, S. and Gugel, G. (eds..), *Zivilcourage lernen. Analyse – Modelle – Arbeitshilfen*, Bundeszentrale für politische Bildung, Bonn, pp. 59-69.

[6] Bierhoff, H.W. (2006), "Entwicklung prosozialen Verhaltens und prosoziale Persönlichkeit", in Bierhoff, H.W. and Frey, D. (eds.), *Handbuch der Sozialpsychologie und Kommunikationspsychologie*, Hogrefe Verlag GmbH & Co KG, Göttingen et al., pp. 158 – 165.

[7] Brockhaus – Die Enzyklopädie (2005 – 06), in 30 Bänden. 21., neu überarbeitete Auflage, F. A. Brockhaus, Leibzig, Mannheim.

[8] Brommer, U. (2000), "Die Motivation humanitärer Helferinnen und Helfer", in *Zeitschrift für Politische Psychologie*, vol. 8, pp. 505-522.

[9] Brudney, J.L. (2005), "Designing and managing volunteer programs", in Hermann, R.D. and associates (eds.), *The Jossey-Bass handbook of nonprofit Leadership and management*, 2nd ed., John Wiley and Sons, San Francisco, pp. 310-345.

[10] Brusis, I. (1999), "Politik und Gemeinwohl:Zwischen Globalisierung und Individualisierung", in Alemann, U. Von, Heinze, R. G. and Wehrhöfer, U. (eds.), *Bürgergesellschaft und Gemeinwohl: Analyse, Diskussion, Praxis*, Leske + Buderich, Opladen.

[11] Clary, E.G. and Snyder, M. (1999), "The Motivations to Volunteer: Theoretical and Practical Considerations", in *American Psychological Society*, vol. 8, no. 5, pp. 156-159.

[12] Cnaan, R.A. and Cascio, T.A. (1998), "Performance and Commitment: Issuues in Management of Volunteers in Human Service Organizations", in *Journal of social service research*, vol. 3, no. 4, pp. 1-37.

[13] Darley, J. and Latané, B. (1968), "Bystander intervention in emergencies: Diffusion of responsibility", in *Journal of Personality and Social Psychology*, vol. 8. no. 4, pp. 377-383.

[14] Drucker, P.F. (1990), *Managing the Nonprofit Organization: Practices and Principles*, Harper Collins, New York.

[15] Eisenberg, N. (2000), "Emotion, Regulation, and Moral Development", in *Annual Review of Psychology*, vol. 51, pp. 665-697.

[16] Felfe, J. (2008), *Mitarbeiterbindung*, Hogrefe Verlag GmbH & Co. KG, Göttingen et al.

[17] Fisher, J.C. and Cole, K.M. (1993), *Leadership and Management of Volunteer Programs: A Guide for Volunteer Adminstrators*, Jossey-Bass, San Francisco.

[18] Fuchs-Heinritz, W. (1998), *Auguste Comte – Einführung in Leben und Werk*, Westdeutscher Verlag GmbH, Opladen/Wiesbaden.

[19] Göbel, E. (2006), *Unternehmensethik*, Lucius & Lucius Verlagsgesellschaft GmBH, Stuttgart.

[20] Holzer, C. (2005), "Ehrenamtliches Engagement – Motive pro und contra gemeinwohlorientierter freiwilliger Einsatz", online: http://www.claudiashome.at/pdf/ich_ueber_mich/diplomarbeit.pdf., accessed date: ???.

[21] Mayerhofer, H. (2001), "Ehrenamtliche als Personal in Nonprofit Organisationen", in Zeitschrift für Personalforschung, vol. 15, no. 3, pp. 263 – 282.

[22] McCurley, S. and Lynch, R. (1996), *Volunteer Management: Mobilizing All the Resources in the Community*, Heritage Arts, Downers Grove, Ill.

[23] Moschner, B. (2002), "Altruismus und Egoismus – Was motiviert zum Ehrenamt?", in *Bielefeld 2000plus – Forschungsprojekte zur Region*, discussion paper, vol. 20, pp. 1-20.

[24] Mroß, M.D. (2009), *Personale Arbeit in Nonprofit Organisationen*, Martin-Meidenbauer Verlagsbuchhandlung GmbH & Co. KG, München.

[25] Pearce, J.L. (1993), *The organizational behavior of unpaid workers*, Routledge, New York.

[26] Richter, H.-E. (1980), "Lernziel: Verantwortung für den Nächsten", in *Die Zeit*, march 14th, p. 16.

[27] Rosenkranz D. and Schill, J. (2009), "Aktivierung der Aktiven", in *Sozialwirtschaft*, vol. 3, pp. 6-9.

[28] Scott, J. C., Jr (1957), "Membership and Participation in Voluntary Associations", in *American Sociological Review*, vol. 22, pp. 315-26.

[29] Strecker, C. (2002), *Vergütete Solidarität und solidarische Vergütung – Zur Förderung von Ehrenamt und Engagement durch den Sozialstaat*, Leske + Budrich, Opladen.

[30] Thomae, H. (1965), "Zur allgemeinen Charkteristik des Motivationsgeschehens", in Thomae, H. (ed.), *Motivation. Handbuch der Psychologie*, Bd. 3., Hogrefe, Göttingen, pp. 45-122.

[31] Walter, V. (1987), "Volunteers and Bureaucrats: Clarifying Roles and Creating Meaning", in *Journal of Voluntary Action Research*, vol. 16, no. 3, pp. 22-23.

[32] Wöhe, G. and Döring, U. (2005), *Einführung in die Allgemeine Betriebswirtschaftslehre*, 22nd ed., Vahlen, München.

5   Collaborations and Partnerships

Heike Schirmer & Heather Cameron
Freie Universität Berlin

Learning goals
Upon completing this chapter, you should be able to accomplish the following:

- Describe different reasons for social entrepreneurs to form and participate in partnerships.

- Describe different types of partners for social entrepreneurs and their particular advantages.

- Explain different dimensions of collaborative value chain integration and specific types of collaboration.

- Recognize potential risks and challenges for social entrepreneurs when working together with other entities.

- Explain how a collaboration can be established.

5.1   Introduction

Scaling social impact requires many resources. Social entrepreneurs are constantly looking for ways to cooperate with others to achieve their social mission.

Cooperating with other organizations, companies, and institutions is an effective and efficient way to mobilize resources, gain complementary capabilities, and capture synergies. Networks, alliances and collaborations offer the potential to generate social impact "far beyond what the individual contributors could achieve independently" (Wei-Skillern et al., 2007, p. 191).

There are many ways of working together from accessing informal networks to franchising to joint ventures. The goal of this chapter is to show the spectrum and impact of working collaboratively. Therefore, the focus is first on emphasizing why partnerships and collaborations are an attractive scaling opportunity for social entrepreneurs. Next, collaborations with different types of partners and various forms of collaborations are introduced. Then, risks and challenges, which have to be considered when partnering with others, are highlighted. Finally, this chapter proposes guidelines for establishing a collaboration. The case study, *Dialogue in the Dark,* at the end of this chapter demonstrates a successful example of how partnering with local entities in the form of social franchising can spread a social innovation throughout the world.

According to Webster "collaboration" can be understood as an act of working together with others. It is an *integrated* process where the involved parties create an *integrated* solution. "Cooperation" can be understood as joint operation. In contrast to "collaboration" solutions are created parallel instead of in an integrated way. "Partnership" has a similar meaning to "collaboration" but emphasizes the *legal* relation between the parties. The focus of this chapter is on "collaboration" and "partnership" since integrated solutions are central. The term "alliance", which some authors use as a synonym for "cooperation" or "collaboration", is only been used in the specific form of "strategic alliance", which is defined on page 10.

5.2   Reasons for Crafting Collaborations

There are many reasons for social entrepreneurs to work collaboratively. A main reason is certainly the access to resources, and in particular, to complementary resources.

The resource-based view (RBV) is a useful approach to point out how social entrepreneurs can use initial resources, such as existing relationships and networks in order to acquire additional resources and create value. RBV assumes that sources for competitive advantages can be found in an organization's *internal* environment, in terms of its resources and capabilities (Barney, 1991)[3]. *Resources* are firm-specific assets and include tangible re-sources, such as equipment, real estate, financial assets, and intangible resources, such as expertise, information, and brands. *Capabilities* refer to an organization's ability to improve the efficiency and effectiveness of the firm's own resources. Resources and capabilities together provide the basis for a firm's strategy. If the strategy is value-creating and cannot easily be copied by other organizations a competitive advantage can be attained. By acquiring and managing valuable resources an organization can *achieve* competitive advantages. To *sustain* competitive advantages the core competencies must not be replicable by others. Therefore, ideally, resources and capabilities need to be valuable, rare, inimitable, non-substitutable, and imperfectly mobile between firms (Barney, 1991). The choice of resources is thus central to an organization's strategy, growth, and long term success. By reconfiguring existing resources or acquiring new resources, an organization can increase its sphere, for example, by offering additional services or new products or by growing geographically (Haugh, 2009).

Social entrepreneurs, especially when they are in an early stage, often have a low resource base. However, they can use initial resources to acquire more resources and capabilities (Haugh, 2009). A study by Haugh with three social entrepreneurs over several years showed, for example, that in particular "human resources and social networks were essential in the early stages of venture creation, as they conferred venture-specific capabilities in the form of knowledge and network relationships" (Haugh, 2009, p. 112). These resources and capabilities can then be used to support acquiring financial or other necessary resources. In other words, human and social resources enable the access to further resources.

However, access to resources is only one benefit when working with other entities. Partnerships can also increase efficiency and effectiveness and lead to achieving greater impact with the same input of resources. When, for example, a social entrepreneur collaborates with an organization offering similar services, efficiency gains can reach from a simple reduction of administrative costs and realization of economies of scale to optimized resource allocation through specialization. Additionally, more and better services can be offered to beneficiaries. Therefore, collaborative activities can lead to sustainable mission impact and to increased effectiveness (Wei-Skillern et al., 2007).

---

[3]   RBV stands in contrast to theories and models focusing on a company's *external* competitive environment, such as Porter's five forces model.

5.3   Different Collaboration Partners

Commercial entrepreneurs can collaborate with partners from the same sector, the private sector (for example, large corporations or small start-ups), or across sectors thus with institutions from the public sector or the civil sector. For *social* entrepreneurs it is very much the same. The subtle difference, however, is that the sectoral affiliation of social entrepreneurs is not always clear. Depending on their mission and approach, social entrepreneurs can be actors of the public, the private, or the civil sector and mostly their area of activity is in-between two sectors (Nicholls, 2008; Leadbeater, 1997). Nevertheless, social entrepreneurs can collaborate with different types of partners, and as illustrated in **Figure 5.1**, each sector has its own characteristics[4].

Figure 5.1   Zones for social entrepreneurship

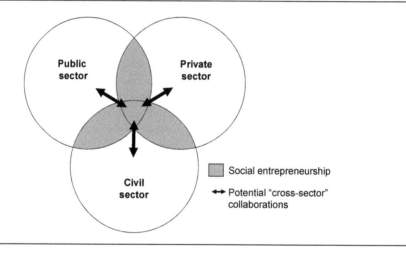

Own illustration based on Leadbeater (1997)

---

4   It has to be mentioned that the sector logic has some shortcomings. First, it is difficult to define boundaries between different sectors. Second, especially for the *civil sector*, also referred to *third* or *non-profit-sector* various different understandings exist of what is part of this sector and what is not (see, e.g., Brandsen, van de Donk and Putters 2005; Evers and Ewert 2010). Nevertheless, the sector logic is used here to illustrate some general characteristics of different collaboration partners.

5.3.1   Collaborating with the Private Sector

Collaborations between social entrepreneurs and private sector actors can reach from a pure philanthropic interaction, which is mainly a supplicant-benefactor relationship, to an integrated stage, where the collaboration has a major strategic value for both sides and resources are exchanged in both directions (see Austin, 2000 for further information).

In particular, integrated collaborations seem offer advantages for both social entrepreneurs and corporations when working together. Bill Drayton (2010, p. 57), CEO and founder of Ashoka, summarizes the benefits for both sides by saying, "Businesses offer scale, expertise in manufacturing and operations, and financing. Social entrepreneurs and organizations contribute lower costs, strong social networks, and deep insights into customers and communities." More and more collaborations between social entrepreneurs and corporations have emerged in the recent years. They can be found in developing as well as in industrialized countries. In "bottom-of-the-pyramid" markets, often located in least-developed countries, these collaborations enable corporations to access markets, which would be difficult to enter without local knowhow and a deep understanding of customers' needs. For social entrepreneurs such collaborations allow them to scale up their social impact by offering access to cheaper capital and also to non-financial resources (Drayton and Budinich, 2010).

Ashoka has created the *hybrid value chain framework* to promote interactions between social entrepreneurs and businesses (see Ashoka, 2007 for further information). Successful examples can be found in India, where Ashoka brought mortgage companies and local citizen groups together to stimulate the housing market. Another example can be found in Mexico, where Ashoka and local social entrepreneurs convinced a water-conveyance company to serve low-income farmers as customers. The local social entrepreneurs organized the farmers in loan groups, help them getting access to financial resources, promoted irrigation, and even installed systems. This contributed to an increased efficiency and a significantly higher income of the farmers due to the new water-conveyance products (see Drayton and Budinich, 2010 for further information).

In industrialized countries, collaborations between corporations and social entrepreneurs can be found in the field of fair-trade, financial services (e.g., micro financing for disadvantaged people), or job creation (e.g., for disabled people). In many cases the resources contributed by the corporations go far beyond financial aspects and can include the exchange of knowhow, the provision of materials and tools, or the access to markets. In 2005 in the UK, the department, Social Enterprise Unit of the Department for Trade and Industry, published *Match Winners – A guideline to commercial collaboration between social enterprises and private sector business* in order to promote this type of partnerships (DTI, 2005).

In both developing and industrialized countries, when collaborating with social entrepreneurs, corporations can benefit from insights into new markets and increased market-share, and go far beyond the model of corporate social responsibility (CSR). Corporations benefit from access to new business models and networks as well as offer their staff a greater sense of useful engagement such as contributing their skills to problems in their own community.

5.3.2   Collaborating with the Public Sector

Social entrepreneurs also collaborate with the public sector. The principles of such collaborations follow these of so called public-private-partnerships (PPP). PPP are long-term,
mainly contractually regulated, collaborations between public sector authorities and private
parties to deliver services, products, or projects traditionally provided by the public sector
(Akintoye, Beck and Hardcastle, 2003). The partners combine the financial and non-
financial resources (e.g., capital, knowhow, human resources) for the mutual benefit and
distribute the operational risk equally.

Specific examples of collaborations with public sector actors can be found between social
entrepreneurs and public health insurance companies. Frank Hoffmann launched the project *Discovering Hands* where blind women are trained for palpation for breast screening. So
far, two health insurance companies have agreed to bear the cost for the medical examination and the participation of further insurances is expected. The reimbursement by the
insurance companies supports the spreading of this social innovation while at the same
time the innovation enables the insurance companies to enlarge their prevention services.
Another example is the Ashoka fellow, Heidrun Meyer, who developed a program to prevent behavioral disorders and to promote social-emotional competence in preschool children. She works together with several statutory health insurance companies in Germany to
spread the innovative approach.

Some social entrepreneurs consider themselves as important innovator for the public or as
the research and development department of their government. These social entrepreneurs
work to achieve proof of principle and then lobby for a responsible government agency to
take their idea to scale and basically absorb the work of the social entrepreneur into government programs. This is similar to a start-up being bought out by a much larger company. While conventional entrepreneurs could see the government taking over their intellectual property as nationalization and theft, publicly minded social entrepreneurs are motivated by effective spread of the mission.

In the last years, Anglo-American governments have launched extensive programs to push
partnerships between social entrepreneurs and government. In 2009 in the United States,
for example, the *Social Innovation Fund (SIF)* was founded with roughly $50 million of public money. Through the SIF grant competition the best social innovations are identified and
the fund supports them to scale up and expand their reach throughout the country.

In Britain in 2010, Prime Minister David Cameron presented *Big Society*, a socio-political
program that aims "to create a climate that empowers local people and communities, building a big society that will take power away from politicians and give it to people" (Number10.gov.uk 2010). The plan includes the set up of the *Big Society Bank*, which will help
finance charities, voluntary groups, and social entrepreneurs. This program was not the
first program the UK government launched to support social innovations. Already in 1996,
the Millennium Commission launched the *Millennium Award Scheme* where national lottery
gains are given to individual people working on community projects. Since 2002, the

awards have been available through the foundation *UnLtd*. UnLtd is the trustee of the Millennium Award Trust to which the Millennium Commission granted an endowment of £100 million.

The idea behind SIF and Big Society is that governments no longer solve society's problems alone. Rather than simply contracting out the delivery of public services as it used to be done (e.g., waste-services, nursing homes, etc.), incentive systems are set up, where innovation, diversity, and responsiveness to public needs are critical. Citizens, non-profit organizations, foundations, and social entrepreneurs interact closely with governments to address social needs. Governments cannot only provide a better fiscal but also a better legislative environment, which can be especially helpful for social entrepreneurs.

5.3.3   Collaborating with the Civil Sector

When collaborating with civil sector actors (such as non-profit organizations, foundations, charities) the big advantages for social entrepreneurs are in general the similarity of the intensions and missions of the involved parties. Or in the words of the former Managing Director of the Schwab Foundation, Pamela Hartigan (2005): "These [foundations and philanthropists] are best placed to support social innovators, as they are free of the voting booth and the financial bottom line, the forces that dominate the decisions of government and business respectively."

In particular, foundations and charities can be interesting collaboration partners for social entrepreneurs. The exact definitions of these terms are different for each country. However, to put it simply, a foundation can be understood as a non-governmental, non-profit organization with its own fund managed by its own trustees or directors. It can be founded, for example, by an individual, a family, or a corporation. A charity can generally be considered a non-profit organization that – as a main difference when compared to a foundation – can derive a significant amount of its funding from the public in addition to other funding sources.

Starting with company foundations, they can play an important role initiating cross-sectoral involvement. Markus Hipp, Executive Director of *BMW Foundation Herbert Quandt*, argues that company foundations can transfer impulses from the private sector into the public or the civil sector provided they are independent and sovereign actors (Hipp, 2009). The BMW Foundation brings together international networks of leaders from different sectors to work together to address social challenges.

Additionally, some large private foundations exist that collaborate with social entrepreneurs in the way that they support them both financially and non-financially. Non-financially, they can provide access to international platforms and prestigious networks. Alongside Ashoka, the *Schwab Foundation* and *Skoll Foundation* are probably the most famous examples on a European level.

Charities are also potentially interesting collaboration partners for social entrepreneurs. Large charities such as *Caritas* often have dense networks and established structures, which could – effectively and efficiently – support the scaling and expansion of a social innovation. However, to date, collaborations between charities and social entrepreneurs are rare. Among other reasons, this could be due to the fact that they may see themselves more as competitors than as collaboration partners.

Social entrepreneurs can also team up with each other – independent from sectoral boundaries. Some of the network examples described in the following section illustrate these kinds of collaborations.

5.4   Designing a Collaboration

When examining how collaborations can be designed, social entrepreneurs can learn a lot when looking at their commercial counterparts, since collaborative growth strategies are well established in the field of general business administration. Collaborations between different organizations, so called inter-organizational collaborations, occur in various forms such as R&D partnerships, loose corporate networks or equity joint ventures. To distinguish inter-organizational collaborations, different criteria exist. Examples for such criteria are the collaboration intensity (e.g., exchange of information, mutual market presence, joint foundation), the geographical reach (e.g., local, national, international), or the dimension of a collaboration with regard to the value chain. The following section introduces first different dimensions of collaborative value chain integration followed by an introduction of specific types of collaborations.

5.4.1   Different Dimensions of Collaborative Value Chain Integration

The dimension of a collaboration refers to the involved stages of the value chain. Depending on the relationship the partners have along the value chain, three dimensions can be distinguished: vertical, horizontal, and diagonal collaborations. See **Figure 5.2**. (Volkmann and Tokarski, 2006; Volkmann, Tokarski and Grünhagen, 2010).

Linkages between organizations at successive stages of the same value chain are called **vertical collaborations**. They enable the optimization of interfaces due to better coordination between the organizations. A classical example would be the collaboration between a supplier and a producer. In the area of social entrepreneurship the collaboration between Nestlé UK and the Fairtrade Foundation demonstrates a vertical collaboration. Since the beginning of 2010 KitKat bars in the UK and Ireland have been Fairtrade certified.[5] Nestlé

---

[5]   In the value chain of chocolate bars, the cacao production, represented by the Fairtrade Foundation, is upstream of the chocolate bars manufacture, done by Nestlé.

made a long-term commitment to purchasing Fairtrade certified cocoa. The premium, which farmers' organizations receive, can be used to invest in community and business development projects of their members, such as education and healthcare. Nestlé can use Fairtrade's respected and well-known label, which contributes to its image.

Horizontal collaborations are collaborations between organizations on the same stage of the value chain (therefore often competitors) where products or services of the organizations are similar or even identical. The motivation for horizontal collaborations can be to combine resources and capabilities, to realize larger projects, or to share risks and costs. A classical example would be a research partnership between different automobile manufacturers. In the field of social entrepreneurship *SEEP* is a good example of a horizontal network focusing on connecting microcredit practitioners. Founded by a group of practitioners in 1985 and with more than 120 member organizations worldwide today, SEEP creates a global learning community, supports the exchange of knowhow, develops practical guidelines and tools, and sets standards regarding micro financing.

Diagonal collaborations are the collaborations between parties of different industries, also known as complimentary collaboration. A series of reasons exists for diagonal collaborations, one of which being to access new markets or customers. *Payback* is a classical example of a diagonal collaboration where (non-competing) corporations from various industries, such as retailers, rental car companies, hotel chain, etc. developed a joint bonus program to increase customer loyalty. The collaboration between Grameen and Veolia (detailed in the next section) can be considered as an example of a diagonal collaboration in the area of social entrepreneurship. Both organizations come from different areas and combine their forces to provide drinking water in rural Bangladesh.

Figure 5.2   Different collaboration dimensions

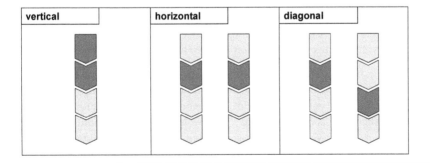

Own illustration

5.4.2   Specific Types of Collaborations

In this section the four most relevant basic types of collaborations are introduced: joint ventures, strategic alliances, networks, and social franchising. While strategic alliances usually represent horizontal collaborations and (social) franchise systems represent vertical collaborations, networks and joint ventures can exist as *horizontal, vertical,* and *diagonal* collaborations.

Joint ventures

A joint venture is a legal entity formed between two or more organizations to realize collaboration objectives. All partners are legally and financially involved into the new entity. Next to the contribution of financial resources the partners also bring material and immaterial resources, like human and social capital into the joint venture. In particular, the contribution of complementary resources makes a joint venture valuable. A joint venture can, for example, help to overcome market-entry barriers or minimize research and development risks for each organization (Volkmann and Tokarski, 2006; Volkmann, Tokarski and Grünhagen, 2010).

The Nobel Laureate Muhammad Yunus significantly shaped the term *joint venture* in the social context. Since 2006 he launched several collaborations between large corporations and Grameen, a multi-faceted group of for- and non-profit organizations, which he established. Objectives of these collaborations are to improve people's daily lives by offering essential products like water or food at affordable prices and to promote business opportunities in rural Bangladesh. One such collaboration involves Grameen Bank and Veolia Water setting up a company called Grameen-Veolia Water Ltd, which is jointly owned at parity by the two founders. Its task is to build and operate several water production and treatment plants in rural areas of Bangladesh. Veolia Water, a world leader in water and wastewater services, brings technical knowhow into the partnership while Grameen provides local knowledge and networks.

Strategic alliances

Although the relevance of strategic alliances has been rising in the recent years, no uniform definition currently exists in the collaboration literature (Glover and Wasserman, 2003).

Essentially speaking, a strategic alliance can be understood as an agreement for collaboration among two or more organizations where the organizations themselves remain independent. Unlike a joint venture, they do not create a new legal entity. Strategic alliances focus on a particular business area (e.g., joint research and development activities), and therefore only exist between current or potential competitors, making them horizontal collaborations (Hagenhoff, 2004). In the area of social entrepreneurship an example would be the collaboration of social entrepreneurs active in the same field (e.g., economic development of disadvantages regions) working together to improve the legal situation or influencing government policy.

Networks

(Corporate) networks have experienced increasing attention in the current management literature. The partners involved in a network coordinate their functions with one another

and strive for a lasting collaboration, which is not limited to a single task. A network consists of a minimum of three partners. While the collaboration is long term, partners can
leave the network and new partners can join. The types of arrangements reach from informal understandings to written agreements such as memorandums of understanding
(Hagenhoff, 2004).

The *HUB* is an example of a global network to support solutions for social and environmental change. It has locations in five continents in more than 20 cities. By offering working
space, professional tools, and an online social networking platform it supports its members
to realize and scale their ideas. The local community in each HUB, as well as the online
community, plays an important role in exchanging ideas and knowhow. Informal learning
and free peer consulting contributes to the success of this network. For a fee different levels
of membership are available and allow access to the services and tools needed.

On a European level, the network *Social Innovation Europe (SIE)* founded by the European
Commission was launched in March 2011. The goal of this emerging network is to create a
virtual and real meeting place for social innovators, social entrepreneurs, non-profit organizations, policy makers, and other relevant actors to exchange knowhow, facilitate new
relationships, and develop specific recommendations to scale social innovations all over
Europe. For example, with its call for large scale European social innovative initiatives, the
SIE increases the visibility of social entrepreneurial projects and thereby supports the
growth of social entrepreneurship in Europe.

Social franchising

Franchise systems can be understood as a specific type of network with a hierarchical structure, where a parent organization collaborates with local entities to grow. McDonalds is one
of the most famous examples of a successful worldwide franchise system. Commercial
franchising can be defined as a contract-based relationship between two independent companies. The parent company, called the franchisor, has developed a market-tested product
or service and allows another firm, called the franchisee, to produce and market the prod-
uct/service under the franchisor's trade name according to a format specified by the parent
company (Curran and Stanworth, 1983).

Social franchising uses the structure of commercial franchise systems to achieve social impact. It has been established as a promising scaling mechanism for social activities in the
last years (Tracey and Jarvis, 2007). It is valuable because it allows the franchisee to leverage local knowledge with tested models from the franchisor. The social entrepreneur with
the franchise idea can expand the effects of his/her work without having to build the entire
infrastructure him-/herself. Social franchising, like commercial franchising, creates opportunities to scale an idea quickly; however, the involvement of multiple stakeholders and the
adaption of the business model to local circumstances can potentially lead to loss in quality
or a drift from the original mission. One example of a successful social franchise is *Dialogue
in the Dark*, a social enterprise offering exhibitions and workshops in total darkness lead by
people with visual impairment. The idea and the concept are presented more in-depth in
the case study at the end of this chapter.

5.5   Potential Risks and Challenges

The different examples mentioned in this chapter emphasized that building collaborations can lead to outcomes a social entrepreneur would not be able to realize alone. However, partnering with other organizations does not work in every situation and can include risks and challenges that jeopardize the social mission.

A common challenge for collaboration partners is that expectations are not communicated clearly. Especially between for-profit and non-profit organizations the communication style can be very different. Vague arrangements or unclear assignments of tasks in the beginning can lead to unsatisfactory performance and outcomes. Being aware of cultural differences and ensuring written agreements with defined deadlines and deliverables, including clear expectation management, can help to prevent this from happening.

Additionally, the comparability of the values of the involved organizations influences the success of a collaboration. Focusing on resources and capabilities when searching for a collaboration partner is important; however, when mission-driven ventures, such as social entrepreneurs, are involved values and missions of both organizations and their comparability need to be analyzed as well (Wei-Skillern et al., 2007). The challenge is to identify beforehand if there is enough common ground to build the collaboration on. Often, such characteristics are hard to identify beforehand, especially without an intensive interaction between the involved organizations.

Another challenge when working collaboratively concerns the questions of the adequate legal form – a challenge social entrepreneurs already face when founding their organizations. In many countries, fairly strict conditions exist for non-profit organizations, or organizations with charitable status, in order to get tax benefits. In the case of social entrepreneurs, generated income (e.g., from collaborations with corporations) can lead to a loss of these tax benefits. However, a charitable status is often necessary to receive donations, e.g., from foundations or charities. Finding the right legal form that also enables collaborations with various partners often requires "creative" solutions from the social entrepreneur.

A potential risk when partnering – especially with the private sector – can be reputational damage due to misconduct of the partner, or when the collaboration fails. Furthermore, building a collaboration is always combined with providing internal knowhow to another party. There is always the risk that the other organization is using the knowhow for its own gain; for example, using information of beneficiaries to market additional services or products which are not part of a collaboration. This is especially relevant as frequently, knowhow and networks are still available to the partner after the termination of a collaboration. Only in a few cases can this be regulated in advance by contract.

One of the most important points is the balance between "cost and benefit". Often, social entrepreneurs invest substantial time, energy, and resources into establishing relationships, which at the end do not necessarily contribute to creating social impact or to scaling a social innovation. It is the social entrepreneur's task to weigh input and outcome (Social Edge,

2011). The cost of maintaining the partnership must be analyzed accurately. Often managing the relationship takes a large amount of the social entrepreneur's time while collaboration partners, e.g., large corporations have more human resources to absorb this kind of "investment". This imbalance is often not seen by the partner who may expect the social entrepreneur to have similar resources in place.

Building and maintaining collaborations requires a significant amount of initial and ongoing effort and therefore the cost and benefits of these "investments" should be analyzed wisely with a view to overall alignment with the overall social mission.

5.6   Guidelines to Establish a Collaboration

Although the creation of a collaboration often follows an opportunistic, or ad hoc approach, it is helpful to use a systematic process and to structure the necessary steps. The following section presents – from a social entrepreneur's perspective – four different phases when developing collaborations and lists recommended actions for each phase to create powerful partnerships. It is based on the *Meeting the collaboration challenge workbook* (2002) by the Drucker Foundation. See **Figure 5.3**.

Figure 5.3   Guidelines to establish a collaboration

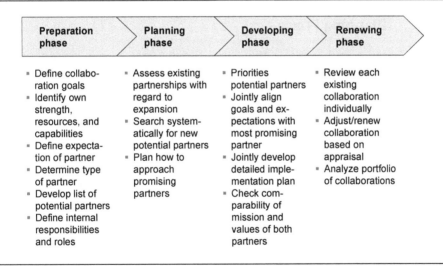

Own illustration based on Drucker Foundation (2002)

5.6.1   Preparation Phase

Before thinking about potential collaboration partners it is important to be clear about the strategic goal of the planned collaboration and to ascertain that it is in line with the social entrepreneur's overall strategy, mission, and vision. Identifying one's own strengths and being clear about the resources and capabilities he/she can contribute to a collaboration will help to specify missing assets. From there, one can begin to define the expectations of the partner and to determine the type of partner who would most likely value a collaboration (e.g., private utility companies, charities with a focus on education, etc.).

An additional action could the generation of a list of all relevant organizations with which a relationship already exists. For instance, identifying all current agreements with government authorities or existing commercial relationships with businesses, and including contacts from the personal networks can help to find potential partners.

Depending on the size of the social enterprise and the complexity of the collaboration, a helpful step is to prepare the social entrepreneur's organization for the collaboration by defining responsibilities, such as nominating a central contact person and determining his/her authority in negotiations. Additionally, it can be helpful to set parameters for ethical matters, and determine adequate guidelines in line with one's own organizational values. Including key decision makers and aligning the board of the social enterprise will influence the collaboration's success.

5.6.2   Planning Phase

To determine the most promising collaboration partner it is best to use the list of existing relationships, assess each relationship and partner in depth and consider if an expansion of the relationship could be possible and valuable when considering the intended goal. Here, the strategic fit and the ability to develop mutually beneficial projects should be taken into account. Although it is mostly easier and faster to extend or intensify existing relationships, sometimes no promising partner can be identified from existing relationships and new partners need to be found. When searching systematically, well-defined criteria can be helpful, such as geographical regions, size or maturity level of the partner organization, etc. Including middlemen or using formal and informal networks can support the search.

Once potential collaboration partners are identified, the next step is to plan how a collaboration could be approached. Relevant points to consider are: how to introduce the idea to potential partners, how to initiate a first meeting, and how to follow up. When developing this approach it helps to view potential partners as customers and to market the collaboration by addressing the other's needs and arousing interest in the joint project.

5.6.3   Developing Phase

After prioritizing these partners, which have mutual interests, closely working together is important in order to align goals and develop clear expectations of the collaboration. A useful action in this phase is to jointly develop a detailed implementation plan. This can include a time line with milestones, the resources each partner is going to contribute, and a distribution of responsibilities, tasks and eventually risks.

Even though many successful collaborations are based on oral agreements, written confirmations help to clearly align agreements and to avoid misunderstandings. In this phase particular attention should also be given to the comparability of mission and values of the partner organization since those factors are critical for the success of the collaboration (see chapter 5.4).

5.6.4   Renewing Phase

Once a collaboration is established and realized, frequent reviews and appraisals are helpful to actively manage the development and evolution of a relationship.

An appraisal of an individual collaboration can include: reviewing the strategic fit, analyzing inputs and outcomes of the collaboration, and identifying unexpected benefits or side effects. Based on the appraisal, the partners can jointly decide how to renew the collaboration, e.g., by maintaining, expanding, optimizing certain areas, or abandoning it. Changes should then be translated into a new or adjusted implementation plan. Such appraisal can lead to collaborations that develop and expand over time. A series of examples exists, where loose arrangements between non- and for-profit organizations with limited resource-sharing have evolved over time into important joint ventures with major strategic value for both partners (see, e.g., Austin, 2003).

In addition to assessing individual collaboration, it is helpful to also analyze the collaborations portfolio. Comparing different collaborations, their outcomes and contribution to the social entrepreneur's mission and overall strategy can help to decide on individual collaboration investments. Only relatively few resources should be invested in collaborations focusing on peripheral activities or showing only minor outcomes; significantly greater investments can be made in collaborations with a high importance to the social mission.

5.7   Case Study

The social enterprise *Dialogue in the Dark* is a successful example of a social franchise company. It illustrates how collaborations between the parent organization and local entities can lead to spreading a social innovation worldwide.

Dialogue in the Dark offers exhibitions and business workshops in total darkness where people with visual impairment lead sighted visitors through the dark environment. The goal is first "to raise awareness and create tolerance for Otherness in the general public, thereby overcoming barriers between 'us' and 'them'" and second to "[...] create jobs for disadvantaged people by turning deficits into potentials and thereby strengthen the self-esteem of individuals who are typically under-valued." (Dialogue in the Dark, 2009). Revenue is generated by admission fees and additional income from special events, for example, special programs, coffee shops, dinner events (Volery and Hackl, 2010).

Dialogue in the Dark was founded in 1986 by Andreas Heinecke and the opening of the first exhibition was 1988 in Frankfurt, Germany. Since then, exhibitions all over the world have taken place with more than six million visitors, over 6.000 blind and partially sighted people finding employment through them. The intensive growth could be realized by replicating the successful business model of the first exhibitions worldwide. A new company was founded in 1996, to hold the copyrights of Dialogue in the Dark and the standardized concepts of the exhibitions in the darkness. The company functions as the franchisor. Typical franchisees are organizations for blind people, museums, or other social entrepreneurs who acquire – for a license fee – the rights to use the brand and the know-how on how to set up a new exhibition. Next to the rights and licenses, the franchisor also offers advisory services to support local professionals setting up an exhibition, including support via hotline or email, a software package for booking and reservation, advice on safety requirements, etc. Furthermore, in some countries, Dialogue in the Dark offers the complete implementation of an exhibition. The franchisees are in charge of the on-site organization, in particular for the location, fundraising, marketing, sales, and the recruitment of staff. The ongoing franchise fees are charged per day throughout the time the exhibition is open plus an initial fee for the acquisition of the concept. The fees also depend on the scope of service received from the franchisor. The selection of franchisees is made by the parent organization of Dialogue in the Dark and it is "particularly important to ensure that partners' selection guarantees that the franchise's overall objective can be successfully pursued at the various locations." (Volery and Hackl, 2010). In particular, the franchisor highlights the importance of moral consensus. Identification with the objective of Dialogue in a Dark and a desire for social contribution are expected from potential franchisees. Furthermore, adequate business skills are important and required.

Since the launch of the franchising model over 140 exhibitions in more than 20 countries have been initiated in this manner (Volery and Hackl, 2010).

Questions

1. What resources and capabilities does each partner (the franchisor and the franchisees) offer in the described case study?

2. What are the advantages for the franchisor scaling the social mission through social franchising? What are potential risks?

3. Why do social entrepreneurs have to consider the shared value of partners more carefully than for-profit partners? How are social entrepreneurs particularly vulnerable?

4. What are the characteristics of a successful collaboration?

5.8   Further Reading

[1]   Austin, J.E. (2003), "Strategic alliances: managing the collaboration portfolio", in *Stanford Social Innovation Review*, vol. 1, no. 2, pp. 48-55.

[2]   Drayton, B. and Budinich, V. (2010), "A new alliance for global change", in *Harvard Business Review*, vol. 12, no. 5, pp. 56-64.

[3]   Social   Edge   (2011),   "Rethinking   partnerships",   online: http://www.socialedge.org/discussions/business-models/rethinking-partnerships, accessed date: 11/11/2011.

[4]   Volery, T. and Hackl, V. (2010), "The promise of social franchising as a model to achieve social goals", in Fayolle, A. and Matlay, H. (eds.), *Handbook of research on social entrepreneurship*, Edward Elgar, Cheltenham.

[5]   Wei-Skillern, J., Austin, J.E., Leonard, H. and Stevenson, H. (2007), *Entrepreneurship in the social sector*, Sage Publications, Los Angeles.

5.9   Bibliography

[1]   Akintoye, A., Beck, M. and Hardcastle, C. (2003), *Public-private partnerships: Managing risks and opportunities*, Blackwell Science, Oxford.

[2]   Ashoka   (2007),   "Defining   social-business   hybrid   value   chains",   online: http://www.ashoka.org/sites/ashoka/files/HVCdefinition_0.pdf, accessed date: 11/11/2011.

[3]   Austin, J.E. (2000), "Strategic collaboration between nonprofits and businesses", in *Nonprofit and Voluntary Sector Quarterly*, vol. 29, no. 1, pp. 69-97.

[4]   Austin, J.E. (2003), "Strategic alliances: managing the collaboration portfolio", in *Stanford Social Innovation Review*, vol. 1, no. 2, pp. 48-55.

[5]   Barney, J.B. (1991), "Firm resources and sustained competitive advantage", in *Journal of Management*, vol. 17, no. 1, pp. 99-120.

[6]   Brandsen, T., van de Donk, W. and Putters, K. (2005), "Griffins or chameleons? Hybridity as a permanent and inevitable characteristic of the third sector", in *International Journal of Public Administration*, vol. 28, pp. 749-765.

[7]   Curran, J. and Stanworth, J. (1983), "Franchising in the modern economy: towards a theoretical understanding", in *International Small Business Journal*, vol. 2, no. 1, pp. 8-26.

[8]   Dialogue   in   the   Dark   (2009),   "Mission",   online: http://www.dialogue-in-the-dark.com/about/mission, accessed date: 11/11/2011.

[9]   Drayton, B. and Budinich, V. (2010), "A new alliance for global change", in *Harvard Business Review*, vol. 12, no. 5, pp. 56-64.

[10] Drucker Foundation for Nonprofit Management (2002), *Meeting the collaboration challenge workbook: Developing strategic alliances between nonprofit organizations and businesses*, Jossey-Bass, San Francisco.

[11] DTI (2005), "Match winners: A guide to commercial collaborations between social enterprise and private sector business", Social Enterprise Unit of the Department for Trade and Industry, London.

[12] Evers, A. and Ewert, B. (2010), "Hybride Organisationen im Bereich sozialer Dienste. Ein Konzept, sein Hintergrund und seine Implikationen", in Klatetzki, T. (ed.), *Soziale personenbezogene Dienstleistungsorganisationen*: VS Verlag für Sozialwissenschaften, pp. 103-128.

[13] Glover, S.I. and Wasserman, C.M. (2003), *Partnerships, joint ventures & strategic alliances*, 3rd ed., Law Journal Press, New York.

[14] Hagenhoff, S. (2004), "Kooperationsformen: Grundtypen und spezielle Ausprägungen", online: http://webdoc.sub.gwdg.de/ebook/serien/lm/arbeitsberichte_wi2/2004_04.pdf,   accessed   date: 11/11/2011.

[15] Hartigan, P. and Billimoria, J. (2005), "Social entrepreneurship: an overview", online: http://www.alliancemagazine.org/node/1345, accessed date: 11/11/2011.

[16] Haugh, H. (2009), "A resource-based perspective of social entrepreneurship", in Robinson, J., Mair, J. and Hockerts, K. (eds.), *International perspectives on social entrepreneurship research:* Palgrave Macmillan, Basingstoke, pp. 99-116.

[17] Hipp, M. (2009), "Transsektorales Engagement als Chance gesellschaftlicher Entwicklung", in *Zeitschrift für Politikberatung*, vol. 2, no. 2, pp. 269-274.

[18] Leadbeater, C. (1997), *The rise of the social entrepreneur*, Demos, London.

[19] Nicholls, A. (2008), "Introduction", in Nicholls, A. (ed.), *Social entrepreneurship: New models of sustainable social change*, Oxford University Press, Oxford, pp. 1-35.

[20] Number10.gov.uk (2010), "Government launches "Big Society" programme", online: http://www.number10.gov.uk/news/topstorynews/2010/05/big-society-50248, accessed date: 11/11/2011.

[21] Social Edge (2011), "Rethinking partnerships", online: http://www.socialedge.org/discussions/business-models/rethinking-partnerships, accessed date: 11/11/2011.

[22] Tracey, P. and Jarvis, O. (2007), "Toward a theory of social venture franchising", in *Entrepreneurship Theory and Practice*, vol. 31, no. 5, pp. 667-685.

[23] Volery, T. and Hackl, V. (2010), "The promise of social franchising as a model to achieve social goals", in Fayolle, A. and Matlay, H. (eds.), *Handbook of research on social entrepreneurship*, Edward Elgar, Cheltenham.

[24] Volkmann, C.K. and Tokarski, K.O. (2006), *Entrepreneurship: Gründung und Wachstum von jungen Unternehmen*, Lucius & Lucius, Stuttgart.

[25] Volkmann, C.K., Tokarski, K.O. and Grünhagen, M. (2010), *Entrepreneurship in a european perspective: concepts for the creation and growth of new ventures*, Gabler, Wiesbaden.

[26] Wei-Skillern, J., Austin, J.E., Leonard, H. and Stevenson, H. (2007), *Entrepreneurship in the social sector*, Sage Publications, Los Angeles.

.

Part III: The Business

Business Models in Social Entrepreneurship
Susan Müller

Selling Good: The Big Picture of Marketing for Social Enterprises
Wiebke Rasmussen

Financing of Social Entrepreneurship
Wolfgang Spiess-Knafl & Ann-Kristin Achleitner

Performance Measurement and Social Entrepreneurship
Johanna Mair & Shuchi Sharma

Strategies for Scaling in Social Entrepreneurship
Andreas Heinecke & Judith Mayer

6   Business Models in Social Entrepreneurship

Susan Müller

University of St. Gallen
Swiss Research Institute of Small Business and Entrepreneurship

Learning goals

Upon completing this chapter, you should be able to accomplish the following:

- Explain what a business model is.

- Explain the differences between business models of commercial enterprises and business models of social enterprises.

- Describe typical areas in which social entrepreneurs find and create opportunities.

- Recognize opportunities of social enterprises.

- Describe examples of business models which were successfully implemented by social entrepreneurs.

- Explain the main characteristics of different scaling and replication strategies.

6.1   Introduction

Why the social entrepreneur's business model is different
Social entrepreneurs develop and implement effective solutions for societal problems. They fight unemployment, provide basic medical care, enhance the integration of disabled people, alleviate poverty, and fight climate change. Severe societal problems are reasons why social entrepreneurs start to develop solutions and create business models to solve them; where others might see insolvable problems, social entrepreneurs are able to envision solutions. For sure, social entrepreneurship is not a cure-it-all. Social entrepreneurs will not solve the most challenging problems of humanity on their own. This will require meaningful interactions of different economic actors including commercial and social entrepreneurs, NGOs, governments, and international organizations. But social entrepreneurs can play an important part in developing and implementing decentralized solutions to address societal problems.

Social entrepreneurs have one thing in common: They create value for society. Value creation, in turn, is delivered by an organization's business model. Peter Drucker once said a business model needs to answer the following basic questions: What is the customer value provided by the company? How does the company create that value? How does the company make money? The same questions need to be answered by the social entrepreneur's business model. Just like commercial entrepreneurs their business models have to explain how value is created for their customers or beneficiaries, how they deliver the product and service, and how they generate revenues. However, there are a couple of reasons why business models of social enterprises are distinct from those of commercial enterprises:

- **Social entrepreneurs pursue different objectives.** While commercial entrepreneurs focus on value *appropriation* social entrepreneurs focus on value *creation* (Santos, 2009). This means that commercial entrepreneurs want to create value for themselves and/or their stakeholders while social entrepreneurs want to create value for their beneficiaries and for society. For social entrepreneurs, profits are a facilitator but not the primary purpose of the organization.

- **Social entrepreneurs pursue different entrepreneurial opportunities:** Social entrepreneurs often discover and create opportunities related to the social, the so-called "third sector". Often markets in the social sector are informal, not regulated, not predictable, and characterized by the idiosyncrasies of personal relationships (Robinson, 2006).

- **Social entrepreneurs take different approaches to enact opportunities.** The different objectives for starting a social business result in different approaches of how opportunities are enacted. For example, social entrepreneurs are not interested in building up a sustainable competitive advantage; instead they want to provide sustainable solutions (Santos, 2009). Thus, they are not interested in protecting their ideas or their intellectual property. Quite the contrary, they want the idea to be spread to other geographic regions or target groups.

The reasons mentioned above indicate that business models implemented by social entrepreneurs are, to some extent, distinct from business models implemented by commercial
entrepreneurs. If the business model is the key vehicle for social value creation and if social
value creation is at the heart of social entrepreneurship it becomes crucial to understand the
mechanisms of the social entrepreneur`s business model.

6.2 Opportunities for Social Entrepreneurs

Educational achievements of children often depend on their social background, even in
industrialized countries. CO_2 emissions heat up the atmosphere of the planet, cause extreme weather situations and put large areas under water. Each day 29,000 children die
from preventable and treatable illnesses. Worldwide, there are 144 million undernourished
children under the age of five. 2.1 billion people live on less than 2 USD a day. Inequality of
educational opportunities, climate change, lack of basic medical care, undernourishment,
poverty—the facts are alarming and can have a paralyzing effect. However, for social entrepreneurs, all these problems are potential opportunities to start a social venture. The
following chapters describe the nature of these opportunities and show how social entrepreneurs turn challenges into opportunities.

6.2.1 The Nature of Social Entrepreneurial Opportunities

Since 1998 the Schwab Foundation for Social Entrepreneurs tries to find the most advanced
social entrepreneurs who are then provided access to a network of people which can potentially be beneficial for their work. **Figure 6.1** shows the fields of application of the 195 social
entrepreneurs distinguished by the Schwab Foundation for Social Entrepreneurs.

Figure 6.1   Fields of activity of distinguished entrepreneurs

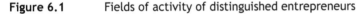
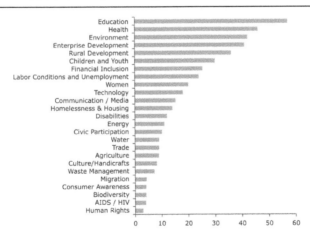

Illustration based on Schwab Foundation for Social Entrepreneurs (2011)

The figure shows that social entrepreneurs are active in a variety of fields, reaching from education to health topics such as AIDS/HIV to challenges related to migration or human rights. How is the nature of opportunities discovered or created by social entrepreneurs different from opportunities for commercial entrepreneurs? As indicated above, opportunities for social entrepreneurs are special because they are often embedded in the social sector market, which provides social services and products that benefit society. The specifics of this market are twofold. First, social sector markets are "social", which means they have an impact on society. Second, they are highly influenced by formal and informal factors, by social and institutional factors. Thus, social entrepreneurs often operate in environments characterized with little governance and oversight (Zahra et al., 2009).

In informal, hardly regulated markets, personal partnerships become important. A social entrepreneur who is not anchored in the community he wants to help (and does not manage to compensate this with partnerships) might fail, even if he could potentially help the beneficiaries (Robinson, 2009). With regard to the discovery and creation of entrepreneurial opportunities for social entrepreneurship Robinson (2009) identified the following recurring patterns:

- Successful social entrepreneurs identify opportunities in social and institutional contexts they believe they understand.

- Successful social entrepreneurs take into consideration the social and institutional factors when evaluating an opportunity.

- Social Entrepreneurs directly address social and institutional problems and their organizational goals often address social and institutional barriers to communities or markets.

6.2.2   Opportunity Recognition in Social Entrepreneurship

Opportunity recognition is the starting point for all entrepreneurial activities. But why do social entrepreneurs see problems and start to act while others don't? Zahra et al. (2009) identify three types of social entrepreneurs which vary with regard to how they discover social opportunities, how they pursue social opportunities, and how they impact the social system on a broader level. Building on the works of Hayek (1945), Kirzner (1973) and Schumpeter (1934), Zahra et al. (2009) develop a typology that identifies three types of social entrepreneurs that differ in how they address social needs, how they acquire resources and how they recognize opportunities.

- The first type of social entrepreneurs is called **Social Bricoleurs.** The name refers to the work of Hayek (1945) who proposed that opportunities can only be discovered and acted upon at a local level. Social Bricoleurs use whatever resources are available to solve the problem he or she is confronted with (Weick, 1993). Think of MacGyver using commonplace items around him to come up with ingenious solutions to escape a seemingly inescapable situation. In the same sense, Social Bricoleurs use readily available resources to address small-scale local social needs.

Their scope might be restricted and they might not aim to scale up their ventures and expand geographically. Nevertheless, they play an important role in society. Many social needs might otherwise be not fulfilled or interpreted incorrectly from afar (Zahra et al., 2009).

How do Social Bricoleurs identify and address opportunities? They have intimate knowledge about the local environment and the locally available resources. Outsiders might not recognize these opportunities because they lack the tacit knowledge needed to see and tackle the problem. Social Bricoleurs draw on local experiences and connections to the community. However, they might not see opportunities outside their realm of knowledge and might have no interest in increasing the scope of their activities.

- **Social Constructionists** typically address market failures. They address social needs that are currently not addressed adequately. They want to introduce reforms and innovations to a broader social system. Zahra et al. (2009) mention the Acumen Fund as an example, a non-profit venture fund that supports entrepreneurs of systemized and scalable solutions that work on problems with a direct influence on poverty. The Acumen Fund changes the landscape of supporting systems for social entrepreneurs. In contrast to Social Bricoleurs, Social Constructionists look at broader problems, follow a more structured path and aim for scalable solutions. They fulfill an important role in society because for-profit-businesses might not see the incentive to address the respective problem.

The concept of the Social Constructionist is based on Kirzner's work. He emphasized that an opportunity does not necessarily occur to the entrepreneur due to a specialized knowledge but rather due a general alertness towards opportunities. The Social Constructionist could even be an outsider to the specific industry who realized that existing economic actors (businesses, institutions, NGOs) inadequately address a social need.

- The **Social Engineer** is the one creating the highest level of change. He aims to mitigate systemic problems by revolutionary change. Social engineers identify complex problems that can be caused by inadequate institutions and try to change the system by establishing different social structures.

The theoretical foundation can be found in Schumpeter's work about "creative destruction". Muhammad Yunus, founder of the Grameen Bank, can be called a Social Engineer. He recognized that the underlying problem of poor people in Bangladesh was that they were trapped in owing debts to moneylenders demanding usurious interest rates. The situation was caused by the fact that the poor had no access to regular financial institutions since these would require collaterals they do not possess. Yunus changed this situation by founding a new financial institution that provided poor people access to micro-credits. Thus, he changed the institutional landscape in the financial industry.

Social Engineers can have an immense social significance on a national or even international level. They replace existing underlying structures that cause problems with new and better ones. Thus, they are an important force causing social change.

6.2.3   Examples: How Social Entrepreneurs Translate Problems into Opportunities

As stated above social challenges are opportunities for social entrepreneurs. This chapter provides examples of how social entrepreneurs translate problems into opportunities.

■ **Bringing unemployed teenagers into the job market: Job Factory** (www.jobfactory.ch)

Problem: Youth unemployment prevents young people from acquiring the necessary qualifications to find employment later on. It is also a burden to the Swiss government. Job Factory calculated that each unemployed young person costs about 47,000 USD per year.

Opportunity Recognition: Robert Roth, the founder of Job Factory, was working in a related field before. He founded a company called Weizenkorn that has grown to be the largest Swiss employer for young people with psychological problems. Over the years, he recognized that it was not only young people with psychological problems who could not find a job and had lost hope, but at-risk youth in general. This is why he started the Job Factory.

Business Model: Each year, 300 young people get the chance to work in the Job Factory during a six-month internship. During that time they can acquire marketable job skills. The Job Factory has 15 shops where the participants can work, including stores for clothing, musical instruments, and a carpenter's shop. The shops of The Job Factory are working break-even as an incorporated company (annual sales: 12 million Euros). The internship is accompanied by a targeted coaching program that addresses the capabilities and the weaknesses of the young people and is financed through donations and the public sector. By working in The Job Factory young people can get prepared for several apprenticeships.

Impact: 2000 unemployment teenagers participated in the programs since the company's foundation in 2000. Eight out of ten participants were able to find a regular apprenticeship afterwards (Schwab Foundation for Social Entrepreneurs, 2011).

■ **Eradicating poverty: Grameen Bank** (www.grameen-info.org)

Problem: In Bangladesh, 78 % of the people live underneath the poverty line of 2 USD per day. Poor people are often trapped in the vicious cycle of owing money to moneylenders who demand usurious interest rates. Since poor people have no collaterals they are lacking access to conventional financial services.

Opportunity recognition: Muhammad Yunus talked to a poor woman in Bangladesh trying to find out what it was that kept her in poverty. The woman produced bamboo stools. It turned out that the dependency of the money lender and the high interest rates prevented her from escaping poverty. Yunus gave her money to pay back the money lender. She paid off her debt, bought raw material from his private credit and was able to pay back the micro-credit after a while. Yunus tried the same model again with other people in the same village and again it worked out. In this case, opportunity recognition was not based on someone's own experiences with poverty but rather on observation and experimentation.

Business model: Muhammad Yunus has build up a financial institution that provides micro credits to poor women in Bangladesh without collaterals. Key success factors are self-selected borrower-groups of five women who are jointly responsible for the loan. If one member cannot pay back the weekly installment the peers in the group have to jump in. Thus, the group serves as a "social collateral" increasing pay back rates.

Impact: In 2009 the number of active borrowers was 6.43 million (Grameen Bank, 2011). The initiative of Muhammad Yunus has spread across the globe.

- **Fighting climate change: atmosfair gGmbH** (www.atmosfair.org)

Problem: Climate change is one of the many symptoms of our ailing environment. Travelling by plane contributes to the greenhouse effect. atmosfair, a non-profit limited liability company and registered charity located in Bonn, allows customers to offset their emissions caused by their individual flights.

Opportunity recognition: The founder of atmosfair, Dr. Dietrich Brockhagen, is a physicist and an environmental economist. He estimates that air travels are responsible for an estimated 10 % of global warming. The idea resulted from the frustration about the lack of compulsory environmental regulation that would bring the ever rising CO_2 emissions of the industry towards a pathway compatible with emission reduction targets. In order to prepare the ground for policy makers and to raise awareness among consumers for the true climate costs of air travel, atmosfair was launched as a second best voluntary approach.

atmosfair was developed from a research project financed by the *German Federal Environment Agency,* the environment and development organization *Germanwatch,* and the *forum anders reisen,* an association of German travel agencies promoting environmentally-sustainable tourism. When the results of the research project demonstrated that it was feasible to devise a voluntary offset system without compromising environmental integrity, the atmosfair company was founded by means of donations and equity provision of the founder.

Business model: atmosfair provides voluntary CO_2 compensations. Travelers can offset the greenhouse gases they create by flying. They can calculate the amount of greenhouse gas emissions created by their flight using an "emissions calculator" provided at the company's website. The calculator also shows the amount of money necessary to offset the respective emissions. Donations are made through the website or travel agencies. The donations are invested in projects in developing countries, that save a comparable amount of greenhouse gas emissions (e.g., implementation of solar or hydropower). atmosfair uses a percentage of the donations to cover administrative costs. However, administrative costs are low. According to the 2009 annual report of the company over 90 % of the revenues from donations are invested in climate protection projects. atmosfair does not receive public funding.

Impact: In 2009, customers donated about 2.2 million Euros in offset fees. The operating climate protection projects should reduce CO_2 emissions by 760,000 tons by the year 2020.

■ **Integrating mentally ill persons: Pegasus GmbH** (www.pegasusgmbh.de)

Problem: Often, mentally ill persons are not able to find a "normal" job. Instead they work in social programs, that are expensive to the government and do not allow the person to build up self-confidence.

Opportunity recognition: The founder Friedrich Kiesinger is a psychologist. Before he became a social entrepreneur he initiated an integration project aiming to prepare people suffering from depressive disorders, schizophrenia or other mental illnesses for the first labor market. The project was financed by the European Social Fund. The project failed because companies did not want to hire mentally ill people. Instead of giving up Friedrich Kiesinger founded a company himself where people with mental illnesses where integrated (brand eins, 2008).

Business model: Friedrich Kiesinger, the founder of Pegasus GmbH, provides jobs to people who are mentally ill. His company engages 100 employees of which 14 % are mentally ill. The company offers services such as facility management, catering, administrative services, services related to senior citizens. The variety of jobs allows the company to find jobs for people with different skill sets. People with mental illnesses are hired due their personal skills (Pegasus, 2011).

Impact: Mentally ill people get the chance to build up self-confidence, since they are not working in a "protected" environment but in a regular company. On the other side employees with no diseases learn how to support the others. The company generates a turnover of 3 million Euros and can sustain itself. Profits are reinvested into the company's development and growth (Pegasus, 2011).

Table 6.1 summarizes how the above mentioned social enterprises solved the respective challenges.

Table 6.1   Examples of how social entrepreneurs recognize and tackle problems

Company	Problem	Opportunity recognition	Solution
Job Factory, Switzerland	Youth unemployment	Own experiences: the social entrepreneur worked in a related field before	Engage at-risk youth in internships at the Job Factory and offer accompanying coaching
Grameen Bank, Bangladesh	Lack to regular financial institutions. People trapped in the vicious cycle of owing debt to moneylenders and paying usurious interest rates	Triggered by conversations with poor people. By experimenting with micro-credits provided by himself he saw that this was a successful intervention for escaping poverty	Provide micro-credits to self-selected borrower groups of women without collaterals
atmosfair, Germany	Climate change caused through CO_2 emissions	Developed from a research project aiming to work out an approach for implementing voluntary CO_2 compensations	Provide voluntary CO_2 compensation for flights. Donations are invested in projects saving a comparable amount of CO_2
Pegasus, Germany	Difficulty for mentally ill persons to find a regular job	An EU-sponsored project to prepare mentally ill people for the job market failed because companies did not want to hire mentally ill people. The founder eventually established a company himself where people with mental disabilities can work	Provide a variety of jobs in which mentally ill people can utilize their strengths. Work closely together with psychiatrists

Own table

6.3 Distinct Features of Business Models for Social Enterprises

The business model literature does not fully agree on the definition of a business model. Different definitions list different components of what constitutes a business model. Nevertheless, the following three elements are typically mentioned as building blocks of business models (Stähler, 2001):

- The **value proposition** describes the value that the company creates for its customers and partners. A clear value proposition needs to answer the following questions: Who are our customers? What job do we solve for our customers? What kind of value do we create for our customers and partners?

- The **value architecture** describes *how* the products and services are produced, and thus, how the value is created. This includes the value chain, the core capabilities and partners, and finally the distribution architecture used to reach and communicate to customers.

- The **revenue model** describes the sources of revenue as well as the enterprise's cost structure which depends on the value architecture.

The business model canvas in **Figure 6.2** shows the building blocks of the business model. It is important that the elements fit together. Aravind Eye Care, an organization mentioned later on in this chapter, is a good example for an organization with a coherent business model where all elements enforce each other. All three elements and the interaction between them also need to be explained in a business plan.

Figure 6.2   Business Model Canvas

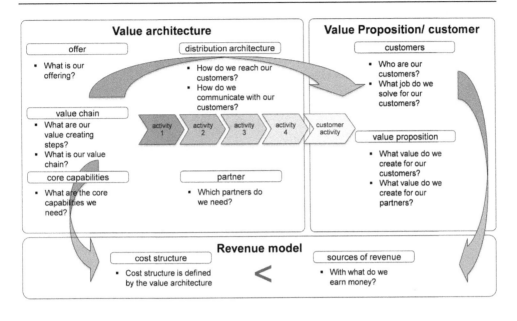

Value architecture

offer
- What is our offering?

distribution architecture
- How do we reach our customers?
- How do we communicate with our customers?

value chain
- What are our value creating steps?
- What is our value chain?

activity 1   activity 2   activity 3   activity 4   customer activity

core capabilities
- What are the core capabilities we need?

partner
- Which partners do we need?

Value Proposition/ customer

customers
- Who are our customers?
- What job do we solve for our customers?

value proposition
- What value do we create for our customers?
- What value do we create for our partners?

Revenue model

cost structure
- Cost structure is defined by the value architecture

<

sources of revenue
- With what do we earn money?

                                        Own illustration based on Stähler (2001)

Just as commercial entrepreneurs, social entrepreneurs need to define the three main elements of a business model. They need to be clear about their value proposition, define how they create and deliver the product or service and build a sustaining revenue model. However, due to the differences of social and commercial entrepreneurship mentioned in chapter 6.1 there are a couple of differences with regard to the design and implementation of the social enterprise's business model. **Table 6.2** provides an overview of some characteristics that are specific for business models of social enterprises.

Table 6.2   Specifics and principles of social enterprises' business models

Business model components	Business models of social entrepreneurs	Business models of commercial entrepreneurs	Business models of traditional non-profit organizations
Value proposition	– Create social value – Cater to basic humanitarian and environmental problems – Solving the root cause of a problem – Provide systemic solutions for complex social problems – Induce social change	– Various value propositions aiming to fulfill or create an unmet market need that promises financial gains	– Comparable value propositions than social entrepreneurs – However, the value propositions might aim to provide an instant relief instead of solving the root cause
Value architecture	– Apply innovative resource mobilization strategies (partnerships, co-creation, volunteer support) – Active participation of the beneficiaries to design or create the product	– Depends on the company's objective	– Often project-based interventions. If the project is finished employees might turn towards the next project
Revenue model	– Employing various sources of money – Revenue-generating business models that benefit social value creation – Price differentiation	– Revenue model aiming to maximize profits	– Often dependent on donations, state, or philanthropic money

Own table

In the following, the differences between the social, commercial and charity business models are being described in more detail.

■ **Value proposition:** The social entrepreneur's value proposition is typically linked to mitigating social or environmental problems. Social entrepreneurs start their company to serve basic humanitarian needs, distribute scarce resources more fairly or take care of the needs of future generations by promoting environmental behavior (Seelos and Mair, 2005). Successful social entrepreneurs are not satisfied with treating the symptoms; they want to eliminate the root cause of the problem.

Traditional entrepreneurs, in contrast, look at market opportunities with a different angle. The question is which markets promise interesting target groups and lucrative margins. Financial objectives are often an important driver. However, most entrepreneurs start their companies not solely for financial reasons. Instead, commercial entrepreneurs often start companies that allow them to follow their passion, create something by themselves, and enjoy the freedom of being their own boss.

Traditional non-profit organizations potentially work on the same problem areas as social entrepreneurs. However, there are many organizations that are providing instant relief but do not solve the core problem. For example, a non-profit organization that provides communities with used clothes, money, or food offers an instant relief but does not solve the underlying problem. In emergency situations this is surely the right thing to do! But if the support comes regularly it might cause dependencies and prevent self-initiatives. This type of aid does not help to develop internal structures allowing communities to support themselves.

■ **Value architecture:** The social entrepreneur's value architecture often engages partners and beneficiaries in the creation of the product. This can serve two purposes: First, the engagement of partners and beneficiaries can help overcome restrictions caused by resource limitations. More than commercial entrepreneurs, social entrepreneurs have to deal with severe resource limitations, a hurdle which they can overcome by building networks (Grichnik, et al., 2010) and bringing together volunteers, commercial, and non-commercial partners. Thus, innovative resource mobilization strategies are an important tool for social entrepreneurs. Second, participation of partners and beneficiaries can evoke a sense of responsibility. For example, if the social entrepreneur uses the principle of co-creation to conjointly design or create the product with the beneficiaries the chance that the product or service will fulfill the needs of the beneficiaries and will be applied is much higher. The principle of co-creation is further explained in chapter 6.4.3.

Of course, commercial entrepreneurs build complex relationships as well. However, the nature of these relationships is different. In general, partners of commercial entrepreneurs have clearly defined roles which are often regulated by legal contracts. Social entrepreneurs, on contrary, might build their relationships on a shared vision. To reach this commitment the social entrepreneur needs to be an inspirational leader with the ability to engage other parties and share leadership.

■ **Revenue model:** The social entrepreneur's revenue model might be complex and funded by different sources. The Schwab Foundation for Social Entrepreneurs distinguishes between three different types of social enterprises based on their financial model (Schwab Foundation for Social Entrepreneurs, 2011):

– **Leveraged Nonprofit:** The entrepreneur drives an innovation that addresses a market or government failure. Private and public organizations are engaged to help drive and multiply the innovation. The venture continuously depends on outside philanthropic money. However their longer term sustainability is often supported by partners with an interest in the long term existence of the business.

– **Hybrid Nonprofit:** The entrepreneur also follows a non-profit approach. However, the organization includes some degree of cost-recovery by selling goods and services. Other sources of funding can include public and philanthropic money, grants, loans, or equity.

– **Social Business:** The venture generates turnover and profits and is thus self-sustaining. Financial surpluses are reinvested in the venture and used to grow the solutions. Maximizing profits and wealth accumulation is not a priority.

Even though there are social entrepreneurs using donations, state, or philanthropy money as (part of) their income, they usually prefer earned income strategies in order to reduce dependency of outside funding. This is also a major difference to traditional non-profits that often use donations, philanthropy money, or state money as a major source of income.

Since increasing social value is at the core of a social entrepreneur's business model, they might use price differentiation to provide access to customers who could otherwise not pay for the product or service offered.

Compared to commercial businesses aiming to increase the profit for their shareholders, social entrepreneurs try to generate profit in order to develop and grow their business-es.

The business model of the Aravind Eye Clinics is a good example for a coherent business model of a social enterprise. Aravind is a social enterprise that aims to "eradicate needless blindness". The founder, Dr. Venkataswamy, had the idea of applying McDonald's princi-ples of providing the same service in a standardized manner to cataract surgery. A cataract surgery is a relative small operation in which the natural, clouded eye lens is removed and replaced by an artificial lens. Left untreated cataract causes blindness. In 2006 an estimated 20 million people were blind from cataracts worldwide, more than 80 % of them live in developing countries. Dr. Venkataswamy, a specialist in cataract surgery, thought that if McDonald's could ensure that hamburgers all over the world are delivered in the same manner and in an efficient way, why should that not be possible for performing eye sur-gery. What started as an idea and an 11-bed hospital has now evolved into a self-sustaining organization conducting more than 300,000 eye surgeries in six hospitals per year.

One key success factor of Aravind is its standardized processes. Patients from remote vil-lages are screened in eye camps and brought to the hospital in case they need an operation. Highly trained staff takes care and prepares patients for the operation while the doctor concentrates on performing the operation. Since the hospital specializes on cataract surger-ies each doctor performs about 2,000 operations a year, ten times more than an ophthalmol-ogist working in a traditional medical practice or hospital would normally encounter per year.

The streamlined procedures give Aravind the financial leeway to employ price differentia-tions according to the ability of the customers to afford the treatment. If patients cannot afford to pay they are still being treated. Roughly 40 % of Aravind's patients pay for the service. They provide enough to cover the costs for all patients being treated. Aravind even generate a surplus. However, profits are not distributed to the owners but used to develop and grow the company. The quality of treatment doesn't differ between paying and non-paying patients. The business model of Aravind is described in **Table 6.3**.

Figure 6.3   Business Model Canvas for Aravind Eye Care

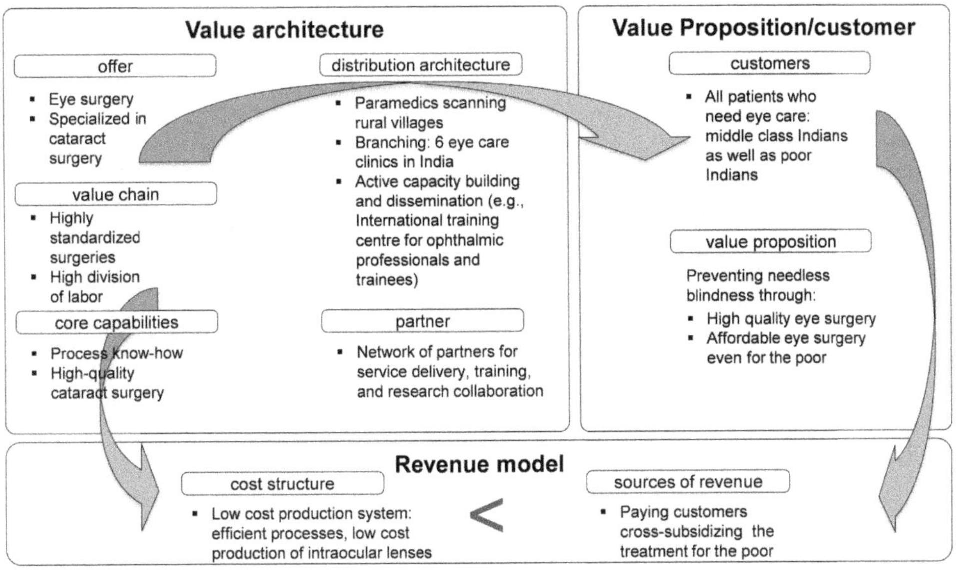

Own illustration based on Stähler (2011)

6.4   Design Principles of Social Entrepreneurship Business Models

Social entrepreneurs build very diverse and innovative business models. However, there seem to be a couple of principles that fit the idea of creating social value with entrepreneurial approaches. In the following four sub-chapters these principles are introduced and illustrated with an example.

6.4.1   Addressing the Root Cause of a Societal Problem

Social entrepreneurs are interested in addressing the root cause of a problem in order to create systemic and durable change and thus have impact. Addressing the root cause of a problem requires social entrepreneurs to understand rather complex social problems otherwise they will have difficulties reaching the core of the problem they aim to solve.

One organization that clearly targets a root cause of a problem is Agua Par La Vida, an organization providing access to safe drinking water in rural communities in Nicaragua.

The organization's value proposition is to give every home in a village access to safe drinking water. Unsafe drinking water causes serious diseases and is probably the single largest health problem in the world. By providing the villagers with access to safe drinking water, the health of the villagers improves immediately.

Marche Seibel, the founder of Health Rock, an organization based in Boston, also wants to get to the core of the problem. By increasing health literacy he aims to prevent illnesses instead of curing them. Mache Seibel, a medical doctor by profession, writes and performs health songs for children to increase health literacy. But the songs about diabetes, about brushing teeth, or H1N1 would not have any impact without changes in the children's behavior. Therefore, in order to increase the effectiveness of his music Marche Seibel tries to produce the songs in a way his target audience can relate to. Anorexia, for example, is mainly eminent in young women and therefore sung by a young woman. That makes it more credible for the target group and the likelihood that listeners act upon the song increases.

6.4.2   Empowerment of Beneficiaries

Empowering the beneficiaries is often a key element to reach the social ventures objective. Muhammad Yunus founded the Grameen Bank to eradicate poverty. To do so he does not collect donations and distribute them among the poor. Instead, he aims to empower the beneficiaries. By giving micro-credits to poor people without collaterals he gives them the opportunity to free themselves from poverty. With the success of the Grameen Bank, Muhammad Yunus showed that the poor have the ideas, motivation, and skills to secure their livelihood by themselves (Mohan and Potnis, 2010). So far, they just lacked access to the resources necessary for starting off.

6.4.3   Co-Creation

Co-creation, the integration of the target group in the design, the production or the distribution of the product or service, is often utilized as a valuable resource by social entrepreneurs. Co-creation offers two advantages. First, the social entrepreneur can leverage scarce resources. Second, the involvement of the target group can be a precondition to guarantee the sustainability of the value proposition.

For example, The Hub Zurich, a co-working space for social entrepreneurs, was built in 2010. The founders employed the principle of co-creation for financing and building the office space. Part of the money needed for building and furnishing the office space was covered by small loans provided by people who believed in the purpose and the success of the Hub. The lenders, or crowd-funders, will get their money back on an agreed upon date. Also, to crowd-build the Hub the founders organized events and invited people to build or enhance the office space.

Another social entrepreneurial venture applying the principle of co-creation is the above mentioned organization Agua Par La Vida. The value architecture works as following: Agua Par La Vida goes into villages and helps the community to build their own gravity flow pipe water systems that provides all homes in that village with access to safe drinking water. The building of the water system is only started when all families in the community agreed that they actively help in building the system. Even if it takes three or four years to reach commitment in the community, the project is not started without a prior and written commitment of the villagers.

While Agua Par La Vida provides the material, the villagers help to build the system. This approach serves multiple purposes: The organization can bootstrap scarce resources and the beneficiaries take ownership of the project and are able to maintain and repair the system. Also, the co-creation process increases acceptance of the intervention in general which is important since the water system is not only a technical intervention but requires changes in behavior to be effective. Access to fresh water has more impact if hygiene measures are taken up. Otherwise, the impact of the intervention is limited.

Bill McQueeney an American who supports Agua Par La Vida through his own US-based organization Rural Water Venture reports another important effect caused through the co-creation process. The successful completion of a project helps the villagers to gain trust in their own abilities and skills. Often the village community starts with other projects such as building streets or improving school buildings. Thus, co-creation has an impact on multiple levels.

6.4.4   Price-Differentiation and Cross-Subsidization

Social entrepreneurs want to increase social value. Often that means that they try to cater to the needs of people who are not able to afford the regular price of the product or service. Price differentiation and cross-subsidization are two principles to deal with that challenge. The Aravind Eye Clinic is one example of a social enterprise applying these principles. As described in chapter 6.3 it is Aravind's vision to eliminate needless blindness. The organization focuses on standardized eye surgeries. About 40 % of the patients can afford to pay for the service. These 40 % cover the costs for all patients being treated. If the clinic would provide the eye surgery for free to everybody, the company could not deliver its service in a sustainable manner and would depend on outside money. Also, if Aravind would not treat patients who can't afford the treatment, the social venture could not fulfill its vision which is the eradication of needless blindness—regardless of the person's ability to pay for the service. Thus, the idea that patients only have to pay if they can afford to and to use the money of paying customers to cross-subsidize the service for the poor allows the social venture to reach its mission.

6.5   Replication and Scaling-Up

In order to address social problems on a large scale, social entrepreneurs need to replicate or scale their solutions. Mostly, social entrepreneurs use the term "replication" to refer to the diffusion and adoption of their model in different settings. The term "scaling-up" is mostly utilized when the social entrepreneurs refer to a more significant organizational growth and central coordination (Dees et al, 2004). Both options, replication and scaling-up strategies, can help social entrepreneur to increase their geographic scope or reach out to a new target group.

According to Dees et al. (2004) social entrepreneurs often find it hard to scale. In many cases, the process is slow, particularly if compared to the magnitude of the addressed problem. The authors recommend that social entrepreneurs firstly define their innovation to make sure it is clear what they want to scale and whether the innovation is transferable and ask the following questions:

"What makes their approach distinctive? What is essential to their success? What internal or external factors play critical supporting roles? And what could possibly be changed without jeopardizing impact? [...] Will the core elements be as effective in different contexts? Are these elements easily communicated and understood? Are they reliant on rare skills or conditions?" (Dees et al., 2004, p.26)

If the social entrepreneurs found that they are ready to replicate they have to decide which scaling or replication strategy is good for them. Possible ways to scale include the following concepts which are explained in more detail in chapter 10:

- **Dissemination:** The dissemination of the principles is probably the most easy strategy. It means that the social entrepreneur spreads the word about his innovation and thus serves as a role model or catalyst for others (Dees et al., 2002, p.246). It can be compared to an open source strategy where an approach is made available to the public. That is in line with the thought that social entrepreneur are not interested in protecting their idea but in spreading the word so that as many people as possible will apply it.

  One social entrepreneur who successfully followed this strategy is Takao Furuno, a Japanese farmer, who started the „Duck Revolution". In the 1970s he turned his farm organic. After years of tearing out weeds by hand, he rediscovered the traditional practice of using Aigamo ducks to protect rice. Instead of using chemicals, the ducks paddling in the rice not only eat insects but also use their feet to dig up weeds. Furuno improved the method by experimentation. For example, he determined the optimal age and number of ducklings released to the field by experimentation. To disseminate knowledge about his methods he published the book „The Power of Duck: Integrated Rice and Duck Farming". Also, he holds lectures and cooperates with agricultural organizations and governments. His Impact: More than 75,000 farmers in Japan and other Asian countries already apply the method.

- **Affiliation:** The parent company works together with one or more partners on a permanent basis. The partner organization is responsible for the implementation on a local level. Three types of affiliation can be differentiated: Joint Venture, Licensing, and Social Franchising.

  - Joint Venture: In a Joint Venture two or more partners found a new company together. The different partners can bring different things to the table, including know-how or intangible resources. The joint venture allows putting together the strengths of the partners and sharing associated risks. If things go well partners can reach economies of scale and synergies. A potential disadvantage is that centralized controls might have a negative impact to the entrepreneurial behavior of the firm.
  - Licensing: Licensing means that the license holder acquires the right to use the intellectual property of the social entrepreneur. The licensing agreement could allow the licensee to use a technical innovation, a program package, or the brand name of the company.
  - Social Franchise: Social franchises use the idea and the logic of commercial franchises to achieve social goals. A contract between franchisor and franchisee is the basis for the partnership. The franchisor is responsible for the franchise package, which might include the brand, key processes, the education of the franchisee, and the further development of the concept. An example for a successful social franchise is the exhibition "Dialogue in the Dark". In the exhibition blind or partially-sighted guides lead visitors through a completely dark environment. The visitors learn to rely on other senses and develop an understanding of how blind people experience their environment. "Dialogue in the dark" was started in 1988 and has been presented to more than 30 countries and over 160 sites in Europe, Asia and America. Six million visitors have experiences the exhibitions and 6,000 employees, most of them blind or partially sighted found a job (Schwab Foundation for Social Entrepreneurs, 2011).

- **Branching:** The operative work is done on a branch level. Normally, all branches together build a legal entity. Branching allows for central coordination and local responsiveness. Generally, the strategy requires a lot of resources from the social entrepreneur. If the success is highly dependent on specific processes and quality standards branching can be the preferable strategy (Dees et al, 2004). An example is the Grameen Bank. Throughout the years the bank has lent money to more than 8 million customers. One success factor of the bank is that the money is given to the people through local branches of the bank. This ensures process quality and allows the organization's employees to get close to the customers.

It is important to notice that all efforts to scale or replicate a business model requires resources in terms of time and cost, even disseminating an idea takes up time and resources. What is the right strategy depends on the underlying idea and the business model. For example, if the success of a business model depends on some key factors that are easy to understand disseminating the idea might be the best option.

If on the other side, it is important that certain key processes are followed in detail a social franchise with strict quality control processes might be the better choice. **Table 6.3** provides an overview of the advantages and disadvantages of the different options.

Table 6.3   Advantages and disadvantages of scaling strategies

Table	Advantages	Disadvantages
Dissemination	– Low costs – The idea can spread quickly to other geographic regions – Idea might be adapted to local conditions	– Low control
Joint Venture	– Different partners with different strengths might achieve better results – Risk sharing – Reach economies of scale and synergies	– Centralized controls might decrease entrepreneurial behavior
Licensing	– No large financial requirements – Revenue generation through licensing	– Loss of control over the production and delivery of the product – Difficulty to enforce the licensing agreement
Social Franchising	– Brand consistency – No large financial resources required, franchisee invests own money – Encourages entrepreneurial spirit at the level of the franchisee	– Difficult to control whether the social mission is really followed
Branching	– Quality control – Possibility to enforce standards – Improve organizational learning – Get close to the target group	– Often requires large investments

Own table

6.6 Case Study

May 2010. Murat Vural, co-founder of ChancenWerk, and Erkan Budak (head of the Cologne branch office) are sitting in their office in Cologne discussing the future of ChancenWerk. The number of participants increased during the last months and both of them are satisfied with the impact of the program. Participation in the program allowed the school students to see how one could succeed in school and life. More than half of the program's participants already improved their grades.

The concept of ChancenWerk passed the field test. Murat and Erkan now want to implement their program in schools throughout Germany. However, they are not sure how they should organize the expansion. They do not have a lot of resources at hand and they are aware that the revenue model and the organization's structure needed to be changed, before they could scale or replicate their program.

They know that a lot of work is waiting ahead of them. On the other side, the thought that they could provide each and every child participating in their program with the chance to change his or her own life kept them going.

The Problem
The likelihood to finish school with the "Abitur", the German university-entrance diploma, is much higher for children whose parents graduated from university. Thus, in Germany, the social background largely determines whether or not a child will have a successful school career. Having experienced educational injustice himself, Murat Vural, Ph.D. candidate at the Ruhr-Universität Bochum, decided to empower immigrant children to escape the situation of underperforming in school and failing in life. Later on, he explicitly enlarged the group of beneficiaries from immigrant children to children from difficult social backgrounds.

The Idea
In June 2004 Murat and ten fellow students founded the „Intercultural Association for Education and Student Support", later renamed "IBFS ChancenWerk". To increase the educational opportunities for immigrant children Murat developed an "education chain" which draws on positive role models. The program offers an after school program that allows children to acquire the tools necessary to succeed in school and life.

The education chain called "Students helping Students" (SHS[2]) works as follows:

- A volunteer **school coordinator** is supervising the project at one school. The school coordinator is responsible for coordination, member support, and team leadership.

- One **university student** supports eight older school students with exam preparation. The student is hired and paid by ChancenWerk.

- The **older school students** do not have to pay for the supervision but have to support younger school students with their homework. Two teams, each comprised of four older school students and one university student, supervise 16 younger school students once a week. Each team conducts one session à 90 minutes per week. That means that the 16 younger school students receive two sessions per week, one provided by the first, one provided by the second team.

- The **younger school students** have to pay 10 Euros per month to participate. The fee of 10 Euros is much cheaper than commercial offers for home tutoring and can also be afforded by parents with a low-income.

- The **impact of the model:** Even though only three university students are paid, 24 school students (16 younger students and 8 older school students) benefit from the model.

Figure 6.4 provides an overview of the education chain.

Figure 6.4   Education chain of the SHS2 Model (shows one week of provided support)

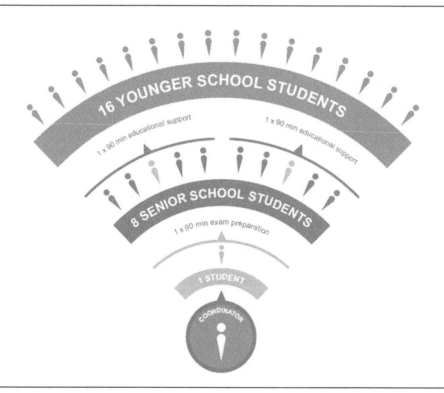

Illustration based on ChancenWerk

The idea of using role models is an important factor of the model's success. Partly, ChancenWerk hires university students who come from difficult family backgrounds themselves and who have proven that you can successfully finish school even if your starting conditions were not promising. The idea works: If you can identify yourself with somebody you are more likely to ascribe his attributes to yourself: "If he could do it, I can do it as well". Difficult family situations are then not an excuse anymore. Also, the older school students who support the younger school students not only benefit from the training they receive but also from helping the younger ones. The study groups provide the participating children with the needed appreciation, recognition, and opportunities to prove themselves.

Implementation

The first cooperation with a school was initiated in August 2004 with a comprehensive school in Castrop-Rauxel. Today, ChancenWerk is active in eight schools. In total, three salaried employees of ChancenWerk and about 50 university students reach about 400 school students.

Up to six SHS[2] models can be implemented at one school. If four SHS[2] models are offered at a school 32 older and 64 younger school students can be reached. A volunteer school coordinator is responsible for the project management and the implementation of the model at the respective school. The school coordinator is, in turn, supported by a city coordinator. One city coordinator is responsible for the introduction, implementation and further development of the model at six schools. He supports the school coordinators, hires qualified students and is in touch with local organizations and associations.

In order to be successful, ChancenWerk not only focuses on the children but bridges between schools, students, and parents. For example, Murat realized severe communication problems between schools and parents. Often parents did not come to parents' evenings. To improve the situation the employees of ChancenWerk call the parents at home and personally invite them. This might take 10 to 15 minutes per call, but the increased participation of parents shows the importance of the initiative. Since the language is often another communication barrier the employees of ChancenWerk address the parents in their respective mother tongue which could be Arab or Turkish or whatever is required. The key is to convince the parents to allow their children to participate in the program.

Before the organization's business model can be replicated and scaled the organization needs to rethink its revenue model. At the moment, the organization depends on donations. **Table 6.4** shows expenses and revenues of the model per month.

Table 6.4   Revenues and expenses of one implemented SHS² model

Supervisor	Beneficiary	Received monthly supervision	Compensation of students per 90-minutes-course	Expenses per month	Revenues per month
1 student	8 senior school students	4 x 90 min. intensive exam preparation	30 Euros	120 Euros[1]	
2 teams comprised of 1 university student and 4 older school students (each team offers 4 sessions per month)	16 younger students	8 x 90 min. homework supervision	15 Euros	120 Euros[2]	160 Euros[3]
Sum				240 Euros	160 Euros

Own table

[1] 30 Euros x 4 ninety-minutes-courses = 120 Euros

[2] 15 Euros x 8 ninety-minutes-courses = 120 Euros

[3] 16 younger students x 10 Euros membership fee = 160 Euros

However, loses occurring during schooldays are, to some degree, compensated during holidays: Membership fees are being paid throughout the year (12 months/year), while courses are only offered during school days (9 months/year). Thus, no salaries have to be paid during holiday time. Additionally, the demand at the schools is quite high. In almost all of the schools the groups reach maximum size.

The yearly revenues for each SHS² can thus be calculated with the following formula:

- Number of SHS2 models x 16 school students x 10 Euros x 12 months

ChancenWerk is a charity and is therefore tax exempted. Currently the association employs three employees and 19 volunteers. Besides the variable costs mentioned above there are a couple of other costs, that occur independent of the number of implemented SHS^2 models (e.g., overhead costs for personnel, administrative costs, coaching for the students).

Next Steps
The model is now supposed to be implemented in other schools. Murat wants more children with difficult family backgrounds to have the chance to benefit from ChancenWerk, no matter if it is children with a migration background or not. For that purpose the revenue model and the organization structure of ChancenWerk needs to be changed. The co-founder is thinking about different options to change the model so that each SHS^2 covers its cost.

- **Option 1:** Increase the fee for each participant to 15 Euros per month

- **Option 2:** Change the ratio between older and younger school students

- **Option 3:** Changes with regard to both options

Both increasing the fees and changing the ratio between supervisor and learners bring about disadvantages. Since ChancenWerk targets its services to children from socially deprived backgrounds an increase in fees might prevent children from participating in the program since their parents might not be able to afford the fees anymore. In any case, Murat and Erkan want to avoid this situation. Also, they do not want to endanger the high quality of homework supervision that might be in danger if the supervisor-learner-ratio would be changed. Murat and Erkan are also discussing alternative options for organizational structure, such as a social franchising system, build up branches, or pursuing a strategy based on partnerships.

Questions
1. Use the Business Model Canvas (see **Figure 6.2** and **Figure 6.3**) to describe the current business model of ChancenWerk.

If you were in the situation of Murat and Erkan:

2. How would you change the SHS^2 model? What are the advantages and disadvantages of your suggestions?

3. How would you change the business model in general in order to increase the organization's effectiveness?

4. What type of replication or scaling strategy would you follow? Also use the information provided in chapter 5 to answer that question.

Justify your recommendations.

6.7   Further Reading

[1]   Austin, J., Stevenson, H. and Wei-Skillern, J. (2006), "Social and commercial entrepreneurship: same, different or both?", in *Entrepreneurship Theory & Practice*, vol. 30, no. 1, pp. 1-22.
[2]   Dees, G.J., Emerson, J. and Economy, P. (2002), *Strategic tools for social entrepreneurs: enhancing the performance of your enterprising nonprofit*, John Wiley & Sons, New York.
[3]   Dees, G.J., Anderson, B.B. and Wei-Skillern, J. (2004), "Scaling social impact—strategies for spreading social innovations", *Stanford Social Innovation Review*, Spring 2004, pp. 24-32.

6.8   Bibliography

[1]   atmosfair, "Annual Report 2009", online: http://www.atmosfair.de/fileadmin/user_upload/Medien/ Jahresbericht_2009_EN_Website.pdf, accessed date: 08/06/2011.
[2]   brand eins (2008), "Sinnvolle Arbeit", online: http://www.brandeins.de/uploads/tx_brandeinsmagazine/120_b1_12_08_sozialunternehmen.pdf, accessed date: 08/06/2011.
[3]   Dees, G.J. (2007), "Taking social entrepreneurship seriously", in *Society*, vol. 44, no. 2, pp. 24-31.
[4]   Dees, G.J., Anderson, B.B. and Wei-Skillern, J. (2004), "Scaling social impact—strategies for spreading social innovations", *Stanford Social Innovation Review*, Spring 2004, pp. 24-32.
[5]   Dees, G.J., Emerson, J. and Economy, P. (2002), *Strategic tools for social entrepreneurs: enhancing the performance of your enterprising nonprofit*, John Wiley & Sons, New York.
[6]   Grameen Bank (2011), "Grameen Bank: Performance Indicators & Ratio Analysis", online: http://www.grameen-info.org/index.php?option=com_content&task=view&id=632&Itemid=664, accessed date: 08/06/2011.
[7]   Grichnik, D., Brettel, M., Koropp, C. and Mauer, R. (2010), *Entrepreneurship: Unternehmerisches Denken, Entscheiden und Handeln in innovativen und technologieorientierten Unternehmungen*, Schäffer-Poeschel Verlag, Stuttgart.
[8]   Hackl, V. (2009), *Social Franchising—Social Entrepreneurship Aktivitäten multiplizieren*, Doctoral Thesis, online: http://www1.unisg.ch/www/edis.nsf/SysLkpByIdentifier/3674/$FILE/dis3674.pdf, accessed date: 08/06/2011.
[9]   Kirzner, I. (1973), *Competition and entrepreneurship*, The University of Chicago Press, Chicago.
[10] Kistruck, G., Webb, J., Sutter, C. and Ireland, R. (2011), "Microfranchising in base-of-the-pyramid markets: institutional challenges and adaptations to the franchise Model", in *Entrepreneurship Theory & Practice*, vol. 35, no. 3, pp. 503-531.
[11] Robinson, J. (2006), "Navigating social and institutional barriers to markets: how social entrepreneurs identify and evaluate opportunities", in Mair, J., Robinson, J. and Hockerts, K. (eds.), *Social Entrepreneurship*, Palgrave Macmillan, Basingstoke.
[12] Meyskens, M., Robb-Post, C., Stamp, J., Carsrud, A. and Reynolds, P. (2010), "Social ventures from a resource-based perspective: an exploratory study assessing global Ashoka fellows", in *Entrepreneurship Theory & Practice*, vol. 34, no. 4, pp. 661-680.
[13] Mohan , L. and Potnis, D. (2010), "Catalytic innovation in microfinance for inclusive growth: insights from SKS", in *Journal of Asia-Pacific Business*, vol. 11, no. 3, pp. 218-239.
[14] Pegasus (2011), Website Pegasus GmbH, online: http://www.pegasusgmbh.de/unternehmen/das-unternehmen, accessed date: 08/06/2011.
[15] Pearce, J. and Doh, J. P. (2005), "The high impact of collaborative social initiatives", in *MIT Sloan Management Review*, 46, pp. 329–339.
[16] Santos, F. (2009). A Positive theory of social entrepreneurship. *INSEAD Working Paper.*

[17] Schwab Foundation for Social Entrepreneurship (2011), *Outstanding Social Entrepreneurs 2011.* Geneva, online: http://www.schwabfound.org/pdf/schwabfound/SchwabFoundation_ProfilesBrochure2011.pdf, accessed date: 10/23/2011.

[18] Schumpeter, J.A. (1934), *The theory of economic development*, Oxford University Press, London.

[19] Seelos, C. and Mair, J. (2005), "Social entrepreneurship: creating new business models to serve the poor", in *Business Horizons*, vol. 48, no. 3, pp. 241-246.

[20] Stähler, P. (2001), *Geschäftsmodelle in der digitalen Ökonomie. Merkmale, Strategien und Auswirkungen.* Lohmar: Josef Eul Verlag.

[21] Stähler, P. (2011), *"Open Innovation & Entrepreneurship"*, Lecture at TiasNimbas Business School, April 18th & 19th, 2011, online: www.slideshare.net/pstaehler/from-an-idea-to-a-great-and-sustainable-business-model, accessed date: 10/23/2011.

[22] Weick, K.E. (1993), "The collapse of sensemaking in organizations: the Mann Gulch disaster", in *Administrative Science Quarterly*, vol. 38, pp. 628–652.

[23] Zahra, S., Gedajlovic, E., Neubaum, D. and Shulman, J. (2009), "A typology of social entrepreneurs: motives, search processes and ethical challenges", in *Journal of Business Venturing*, vol. 24, no. 5, pp. 519-532.

7 Selling Good: The Big Picture of Marketing for Social Enterprises

Wiebke Rasmussen

Ruhr-University of Bochum
Marketing Department

Learning goals
Upon completing this chapter, you should be able to accomplish the following:

- Create awareness of the peculiarities of marketing in social enterprises, especially in relation to commercial and non for profit marketing.

- Understand a systematic approach to marketing in terms of a concerted marketing conception.

- Describe the typical process steps of a marketing conception.

- Understand exemplary tasks and challenges connected with the single process steps of a marketing conception.

- Recognize that social enterprises need individualized approaches to marketing in view of the specific service or product delivered.

7.1   Introduction

Especially for social enterprises which are usually small or medium-sized operations with scarce labor force at their disposal, people in charge need to consider which potential business functions should be focused. Hence, we start (and have to remain) on a global level by discussing the importance of marketing as a business function in terms of ensuring an organization's viability and profitability. In a next step, we will turn to social enterprises which can of course also benefit from applying an adequate marketing conception. The question is: what does adequate mean? In view of the many different forms social enterprises may take on in reality, it is hardly manageable to embrace all manifestations of social enterprise in the market and to present a single marketing approach fitting all these types of organizations equally well. At this point it is therefore more important to get a rough idea of the aspects a marketing conception contains, the potential stakeholders the social enterprise should approach with their marketing measures, and the elements of the marketing mix.

So, what is marketing about? Marketing comprises a bundle of decisions which specify the precise marketing actions (Varadarajan, 2010) which cover the design of the exchange processes and as such involve the planning and executing of a targeted strategy to ensure that products and services get to the customer. The marketing concept calls for most of the effort to be spent on discovering the needs of a target audience and then creating the goods and services to satisfy them. Hence, marketing should enable the identification of potential customers, their information about the organization's offers and offering products or services which attract these customers. Also, marketing measures follow the goal of increasing public awareness of a product or an organization to make it part of all consumers' evoked sets. In this view, marketing is a vital business function to ensure that the organization sells its products and thereby generates profits and becomes more and more accepted as an umbrella conception which ensures a customer- and market-orientated view along all organizational activities. Despite the key role marketing researchers place on their discipline in terms of ensuring sales and profit, marketing is confronted with prejudice. Some might say that marketing is about spending money on measures which mainly produce intangible, thus hardly measurable outcomes such as customer loyalty or image. Also, it is hardly verifiable if these effects are due to the distinct marketing measure or if they are a side-effect of other activities or simply a coincidence. For instance, in the past, marketing measures often focused on increasing customer satisfaction. Although this seems to be a reasonable approach, it remains unclear if a specific marketing measure taken actually affected a customer's satisfaction in the desired direction and, if so, if increased satisfaction actually implied an increase in sales. Other prejudice marketing is challenged by might say that "marketing is manipulative" or that "marketing is unethical" as the measures aim to persuade people to buy a good they have no need for. Certainly, we have all read once or twice about insurance agents disposing of life insurances to retirees. However, ethical marketers—and we assume these to be in the majority—appeal to ulterior needs consumers potentially have not been aware of before.

This aspect—appealing to ulterior motives—is especially important for marketing conceptions designed for organizations with a social mission. A phrase often used when it comes
the differences between marketing activities in commercial and in nonprofit environments
respectively is "Why can't you sell brotherhood like you sell soap?" as cited in Wiebe (1952,
see Kotler and Zaltman, 1971). The answer to this question is not easily elaborated. While
some principles of commercial marketing can be transferred to the nonprofit sector and to
social enterprises, deciders need to be aware of the fact that marketing practices in the third
sector bear peculiarities with regard to marketing research and strategy and the precise
design of the marketing mix. A differentiated approach is needed to orientate all internal
and external activities to the benefit and expectations of all stakeholders (e.g., supporters,
beneficiaries, or the general public) in order to achieve the organization's diverse goals
(Bruhn, 2005, p. 63).

Recently, the role of marketing to establish long-term and worthy relationships with different stakeholders gained acceptance in nonprofit settings. However, the big picture of how
to successfully put marketing into practice for social enterprises is still missing. This is
partly due to the fact that social enterprises hardly describe a homogenous cluster of organizations. Instead, social enterprises cover diverse social purposes and various forms of
operation. Dees (2001) for example introduced a continuum of social enterprises which he
clusters by the importance the organizations assign to social goals in the commercial exchange in relation to performance goals. Many peculiarities of specifying marketing
measures also depend on where in the value chain social entrepreneurs aim to create social
value. Accordingly, this chapter on marketing in social enterprises can only touch the surface of marketing practices for these organizations. This also means that generalizations can
only be made cautiously. Yet, the following should make readers understand marketing-
related concerns in a social enterprise environment.

The questions to be elaborated in this chapter are:

- Why is marketing important for social enterprises?

- What is special about marketing in a social enterprise?

- And what do social enterprises have to consider when elaborating a marketing concept?

7.2   Why is Marketing Important for Social Enterprises?

Diverse peculiarities of the social enterprise sector insinuate that these organizations can significantly benefit from marketing endeavors. Some researchers state that the competition taking place in the third sector can hardly be compared to the competition in business-to-consumer markets (Heister, 1994). But still: third sector initiatives often need to invoke people's willingness-to-contribute by applying marketing tools. As such, the marketing endeavors of organizations with a social mission focus on current donors (aim: creating loyalty and a higher "new share-of-wallet"), former donors (aim: regain), and potential donors (aim: convincing them to give). These objectives are typical objectives as formulated in the marketing strategy of an organization with a social mission and focus on the publicity measures to increase supporters' awareness.

Others argue that the third sector is a *particularly* competitive market because organizations with a social mission rely so heavily on financial contributions. One key argument for this reasoning is that social needs are becoming more challenging, even in industrialized countries. Accordingly, the number of nonprofits and charities is growing similarly to cater to this rising demand (Liao, Foreman and Sargeant, 2001). At the same time, governmental funds to financially sustain nonprofits' and social enterprises' missions are on a verge (Bendapudi et al., 1996; Hibbert and Horne, 1996). Although third sector initiatives target diverse social needs, they obviously face increased competition for funding (Small and Verrochi, 2009). Any organization which aims at remaining a successful player in the third sector should employ an appropriate marketing strategy to differentiate itself from the competition and to establish or retain credibility and a positive reputation. Also, the increased competition for decreasing available funds, forces nonprofits and social enterprises to actively request charitable donations, recruit volunteers, and create a trustworthy image to convince ideational supporters to spread positive word-of-mouth as a cheap and trustworthy tool of communication. As a consequence, organizations with a social mission are forced to demonstrate higher market orientation in their managerial decisions as they compete for government budgets, talents and volunteers, for supporters' scarce financial and time resources, media attention, and, ultimately, public awareness of the mission and the organization itself (Andreasen, 2002). It is equally mandatory for organizations with a social mission to initiate a customer/market orientation and to establish a brand image to differentiate themselves from their competitors. While customer orientation focuses primarily on identifying customer needs and serving these, market orientation is a broader and more reasonable concept in competitive environments as it reflects a market-related (i.e., similarly competitor-oriented) view in any intra-organizational decision and process. This market-orientation helps organizations with social missions to increase social value by becoming more effective and efficient (e.g., Zietlow, 2001).

7.3   Peculiarities Concerning Marketing for Social Enterprises

As a reaction to the ambivalent dynamics of increasing competition for support and decreasing public funding, the nonprofit sector was forced to open up to new, more commercial funding strategies. For example, some nonprofits enriched their funding strategies by offering goods at commercial conditions (i.e. by selling ribbons or offering branded giveaways) actively promoted cause-related marketing initiatives with commercial companies, and so forth. Dees (1998) formulated that the "new pro-business Zeitgeist has made for-profit initiatives more acceptable in the nonprofit world". As such, social enterprises, which apply commercial strategies for reaching a social cause, are now an accepted player in the third sector.

Social entrepreneurs, however, need to be cautious when opening up to approved for-profit approaches, as a direct transfer of methods and tools into nonprofit environments may be misleading: To either solely rely on nonprofit or commercial marketing approaches would neglect social enterprises' peculiarities. In fact, social enterprises describe organizational hybrids between purely commercial and social organizations and similarly have to challenge the commercial and nonprofit marketing techniques for their business. As such, social enterprises are advised to apply an inter-sector transfer of marketing concepts and marketing tools from the commercial (Andreasen, 2002) and the nonprofit sector. And it does not come as a surprise: the mixture of tools and methods to be applied for a single social enterprise needs to be assessed individually for any organization.

Being blind for the peculiarities of social enterprises would threaten the organization's success. For example, social enterprises are especially challenged by the fact that they are often locally embedded and thus only have a very limited market of operation. Furthermore, the value proposition social entrepreneurs offer should impact the concrete nature of their marketing activities. Also, social entrepreneurs and nonprofits equally share the fate that potential financial and resource supporters often choose not to contribute to the alleviation of a specific social need. Given this initial reluctance to contribute, it is crucial for people to feel they are satisfying an (unconscious) need when donating. This constitutes one of the main tasks of promoting organizations with a social mission. Private and public sponsors and donors are a major stakeholder group, which social organizations have to target. Therefore, to many nonprofit managers, marketing is equal to fundraising. But the social enterprise exists for more than just collecting funds. Actually, the funds collected from the supporters are (in most of the cases), simply a means to an end.

In competitive commercial markets, organizations must decide what value to create, how and under which conditions to provide the value to customers, and how to communicate the value proposition to the marketplace. Similarly, a social enterprise's main goal actually is to serve its mission, which predominantly means to serve its beneficiaries. Therewith, social enterprises have to approach beneficiaries to raise awareness for their in-kind offer and that they have access to this in-kind product or service. Hence, sales marketing to their beneficiaries is important, too. Here comes another challenge: social enterprises might even serve abstract targets such as the environment. In such a situation, the group of beneficiaries comprises society as a whole and sales marketing may resemble social marketing strategies which aim at promoting change in individual behavior to serve the overall goal.

We can therefore summarize that social enterprises have to approach both donors of time and money as well as beneficiaries. One can also say that social enterprises, despite the specific manifestation they have in the market, need to demonstrate a two-tailed marketing approach, consisting of a procurement as well as a sales marketing strategy (see **Figure 7.1**). Procurement covers activities of ensuring a constant inflow of necessary resources, such as labor or financial support, whereas sales marketing targets the positioning of the actual good being marketed with customers (in the case of social enterprises, beneficiaries and intermediaries which help to establish contact between the social enterprise and its and beneficiaries).

Figure 7.1   The Marketing Foci in Social Enterprises

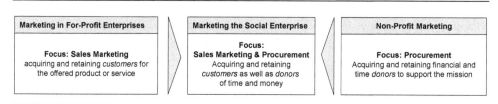

Own illustration

One can also say that social enterprises are similar to nonprofits because pursuing the social mission is what guides (or should guide) all activities related to the business, while earning sustainable income is only one of many subordinate business goals and should ensure the viability of the business. This means that social mission comes first (Dees, 1998). Supporting this argument, social enterprises often find the sourcing for funds to be the bottleneck of their activities, just as nonprofits do. At the same time, the demand for the product or service delivered by the social enterprise should usually be ubiquitous and therefore might (!) need relatively less attention.

7.4   Elaborating a Marketing Conception

7.4.1   The Elements of a Marketing Conception - Basic Framework

The process of implementing a marketing conception in a social enterprise is a complex and continuous one (see **Figure 7.2**). As an initial step, the market a social entrepreneur aims at entering needs to be screened (market analysis). It totally makes sense that any player within a market needs to know the conditions under which he or she will have to work. In view of the generated market information, the organization needs to benchmark its own capabilities, potentials, and necessities to be able to formulate challenging, yet reasonable marketing goals. These goals lay the groundwork for the competitive strategy, which, in turn, shapes the precise planning and implementation of the marketing measures taken to fulfill them. Usually, the bundle of measures planned and applied is referred to as the marketing mix. No planning process is complete without controlling the resulting figures. This means that it is necessary to control if, ex-post, the results achieved met the objectives planned or if, meanwhile, the organization is on a good way of doing so. This benchmarking task delivers status-quo information on how well the social enterprise does in achieving its mission, specifically in terms of the set marketing goals. The information generated in the controlling phase is then used as input information for a subsequent market analysis and goal formulation. In other words: along the life span of a business, the strategy and thus the marketing strategy should be regularly challenged. This is not only necessary because of changes in market conditions, i.e., new competitors or laws, but also to respond reasonably to changes in clients' demand for the product or service delivered.

Figure 7.2   The Elements of a Comprehensive Market Conception

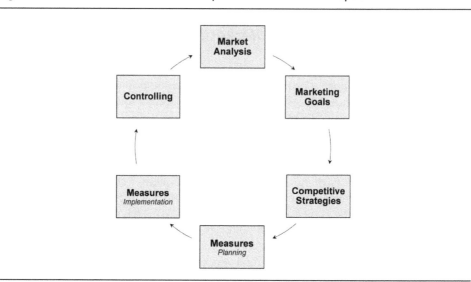

Own illustration based on Meffert, Burmann, and Kirchgeorg (2008)

7.4.2   Market Analysis

To analyze the market is especially important in the initial phase of a new venture. According to Michael Porter, it is recommendable to assess the organization's environment in terms of analyzing the forces the organization is confronted with. As described above, market orientation is a commonly accepted principle of all business functions, and hence especially of Marketing. Yet, how could an organization be market-oriented without having knowledge about the market it serves? Therefore, social enterprises need to gather information about their market environments, i.e., about its customers, their respective needs, and also about the legal and structural market environment. Any organization needs to form an idea about the market situation to formulate goals thereon.

To analyze the market, a holistic view should be taken. The actual analysis of the market situation comprises an analysis of the internal-, market-, and external conditions which the organization is confronted with. Internal conditions include such things as the present skills and structures within the organization. In fact, an organization should try to understand the external conditions of the market it serves in a similar way. Market conditions represent aspects such as the general funding climate, a comparative analysis with other organizations, and the identification of the niche or distinctive competence. External factors include, for example, the gravity of the social problem which the social enterprise aims at alleviating and economic factors like disposable tax deductions for financial donors.

Often these pieces of information are gathered within a **SWOT**-framework which let organization's assess their **S**trengths and **W**eaknesses (the internal perspective) and the **O**pportunities and **T**hreats it faces with regard to external influences.

Market research deals specifically with the gathering of information about the size of the market and expected trends. *Marketing research*, in contrast, focuses on scrutinizing the customer, or more general, the stakeholder perspective. The bottleneck for social enterprises is to win over supporting forces and to convince beneficiaries of their product or service. To do so, the social enterprises have to form an idea about what supporters need to stimulate their financial and time contributions. At the same time, social enterprises have to show that the product or service they offer actually meets the beneficiaries' demand as this might be an argument for supporters to engage themselves for the organization. Similarly, it is equally important for social enterprises to serve beneficiaries with a good they lack. What is challenging about the beneficiary analysis is that sometimes beneficiaries do not necessarily perceive the product or service as important to themselves in the first place. Dees (1998) mentions the vivid example of a social enterprise which offers counseling to abusive spouses. Like traditional social marketing, social enterprises often offer products and services which beneficiaries not deem useful in the first place.

Market analysis is about gathering competitor and stakeholder information. The primary purpose of the social entrepreneur is to create superior social value for the beneficiaries of the services delivered. However, a social entrepreneur also needs to be successful in attracting resources (capital, labor, equipment, etc.) in a competitive marketplace (Dees, 1998). Accordingly, one broad view of segmenting the stakeholders of a social enterprise differentiates beneficiaries (who Kotler and Andreasen, 2008 refer to as 'clients and publics'), supporters, stakeholders, and regulators. Because nonprofits need to target diverse stakeholders, a societal orientation in lieu of the traditional marketing orientation seems to better reflect the eclectic goal system for social enterprises (see Sargeant, Foreman and Liao, 2002). As mentioned above, marketing goals and measures should especially address two main clienteles: recipients of their services (i.e., the beneficiaries) and supporters, whom they rely on for providing essential financial and time resources (Yavas, Riecken and Babakus, 1993).

Yet, although the basic segmentation into supporters and beneficiaries entails a very important notion for nonprofits and social enterprises, these major segments are not homogenous clusters. In fact, different individuals respond differently to different charitable appeals. More detailed sub-segments should be identified which represent relatively homogenous groups in terms of socio-demographic (gender, age, profession), socio-economic (income) and psychographic (attitudes and values) criteria. This homogeneity makes it more likely that people thereon respond similarly to the certain marketing tools (promotion, positioning, pricing, and distribution).

Concerning a further segmentation of the cluster of *supporters*, one broad approach would be to distinguish public from private investors, to appeal to money donors differently as compared to time donors, and so forth. Financial donors will not receive a material compensation for their financial contributions as well as volunteers know they will not be remunerated with market salaries for their time investments. Hence, it is helpful to further segment with regard to motives. Supporters may have diverse motives to consider helping the organization. Nonprofit research has a long-standing tradition in analyzing helpers' motives and showed that beyond the warm glow of giving (the pleasant feeling because one donated) instrumental motives (prestige or career perspectives) play a role for engaging for the organization (see Clary and Snyder 1992, and their functional approach for a nice overview on volunteers motives and Bekkers and Wiepking, 2007 and numerous further articles which regard distinct motives driving charitable contributions, e.g., Harbaugh, 1998; Seoetevent, 2005; Shang and Croson, 2009). These characteristics thus make it even more important that the organization is able to satisfy donors' other, non-material motives. Compared to demographic segmentation, which insinuates for example that any woman in the age of 30 is similar, an attitude- or value-based approach allows for a more in-depth understanding of the donors motives. Although research agrees on the general usefulness of attitudes for segmenting customer markets and developing effective promotional strategies based thereon, these aspects are disproportionately harder to identify and to be served. You can imagine that it is much more challenging to gather information on attitudes and values instead of on (merely) observable aspects such as gender or age. The problem propagates in the implementation phase: even though the organization has actually designed tools to distinctly approach the sub-segments, it still remains unclear which channels to use to appeal to the right sub-segment.

Beneficiaries comprise the prime customer group of any organization with a social mission. It is important to note that the social entrepreneur's relationship with the customers and consumers of its products or services only has little in common with the commercial entrepreneurs' and their customers. The beneficiaries of a social enterprise often have little or no resources at their dispose and therefore lack alternatives. One can say that the social enterprise's beneficiaries dispose of hardly any market power. "Thus, the market mechanism through which consumers vote with their dollars is virtually absent for social entrepreneurs" (Austin, Stevenson and Wei-Skillern, 2006). Instead, supporters subsidize the products or services. It therefore comes as no surprise that many social enterprises view their donors—especially the money donors—as their primary clients. What becomes clear: supporters and beneficiaries are both targets of marketing measures, but require distinct conceptions.

7.4.3   Marketing Goals

In a subsequent step, any organization has to define specific marketing goals, which it aims to achieve by applying marketing tools. The question is: "What do we want to achieve as a result of the marketing efforts?" Merely any enterprise follows similar strategic marketing goals. Depending on the stage of maturity in which the social enterprise resides in, these strategic marketing goals differ. Recently founded social enterprises should first aim at increasing awareness of their business and the products and services they deliver. However, a lack of awareness is not only a matter of organizations in the initial phase, as a recent study by the Office of the Third Sector (OTS) reveals. Therein, only 28% of the respondents were able to name a social enterprise. 47% of the people surveyed knew nothing about them. Awareness is the precondition of getting in touch with an organization. Rightly, marketing is therefore said not only to be "the resource cited as most needed by the [social] organizations in their venturing experiences" (Self, Wymer and Henley, 2002, p. 38) or a "basic survival mechanism" to increase awareness and, ultimately, stimulate donation income (Grace and Griffin, 2006). Subsequently, the marketing goal of any social enterprise which has successfully established sufficient awareness is to create and retain a *positive* standing in the market. This is even more important for organizations with a social mission such as social enterprises because they build their business on being perceived as trustworthy and sell social benefit. Nonprofit research shows that the organization's image in the eye of a particular group affects who receives donations (Bennett and Gabriel, 2003). The success of an organization in achieving its mission can be considered an indicator of the status of that organization. The effectiveness of a nonprofit, i.e., the demonstrated reasonable usage of donations by the organizations, has been found to instill donor trust (Tonkiss and Passey, 1999). Only if supporters perceive the organization as being effective in terms of fulfilling its mission, they anticipate pride in delivering help to that organization. Pride, in turn, has been identified as one of two major drivers in triggering psychological and behavioral engagement. Also, it has been found that people need to characterize the organization they invest money and time in as trustworthy. Especially in the nonprofit sector trust plays an important role as former research confirms. This is due to the fact that the actual performance of a nonprofit is hardly observable—nonprofits provide credence goods. Hence, investors can only limitedly monitor if charitable donations are effectively used or embezzled. Therefore, marketing is responsible for providing information on the organization's activities and successes. Remember: "What consumers know about a company can influence their reactions to the company's products" (Brown and Dacin, 1997, p. 79). Trust is used as a proxy mechanism to establish lasting relationships in situations where explicit monitoring of the other party is not feasible. These lasting relationships are desirable to both parties. Consumers appreciate trusting relationships with certain providers as this helps them to reduce alternatives in the futures and thereby ease information processing, achieve higher consistency of their decisions, and perceive lower risks associated with future choices (Sheth and Parvatiyar, 1995). For example, stakeholder satisfaction is crucial to maintain existing and facilitate further relationships (Arnett, German and Hunt, 2003; Oliver and Swan, 1989). And social enterprises can save costs as it is less expensive to keep a relationship running than to establish a new one.

The other major driver for supporters' engagement and thus an aspect to be targeted in marketing is respect, which reflects that people feel they are valuable members of the organization (Bozeman and Ellemers, 2008). Triggering respect is part of an internal marketing strategy, which addresses the needs of the organization's internal stakeholders, i.e., employees and volunteers. Kotler (1991) stated that especially service marketers are supposed to implement internal marketing measures so as to ensure that those employees and volunteers have a positive attitude toward their tasks. Internal marketing measures which aim at fostering the relationships an organization holds with its employees and volunteers is especially important as the majority of social enterprises lack financial resources to pay standard market salaries. In fact, in most cases, social enterprises can only attract employees by offering a wide spectrum of benefits despite financial ones. Yet, social enterprises follow the mission of improving the standing of their beneficiaries, which is why "organizational support for individual volunteers is not self-evident" (Boezeman and Ellemers, 2008, p. 1015). Hence, social enterprises may use effective internal marketing as a tool to become an attractive employer and target time donations of volunteers.

The goals defined have diverse degrees of abstraction. A very broad and strategic goal could be to increase donor satisfaction. This very global and abstract goal needs to be refined into concrete action programs. More precisely, the social enterprise should at best be able to formulate goals which contain a deadline, a precise target value of the key figure, and the measure applied to reach the goal. For example: By the end of the year, customer satisfaction should be increased by two percent point in the major donor segment with the coupon program "We like to thank you".

7.4.4   Competitive Strategy

In view of the information gathered in the market analysis (including market and marketing research), the overall business goals (business mission) have to be defined, which in turn serve as a guideline for the strategic, tactical and operational marketing goals. One must keep in mind: Only if the activities of all other business functions are guided by the organization's business mission, the organization ensures that these are reached. Any business function should contribute to the achievement of these goals if the organization seriously follows a market- or socially-oriented approach. The accordant marketing goals serve as the basis for the precise competitive strategy the organization applies. Porter differentiates between the strategy of differentiation (i.e., providing added value to the customer), cost leadership (i.e., being able to gain a greater margin than the competitor when selling similar products), and focus (i.e., applying one of these strategies in a reasonably limited market).

In view of the chosen competitive strategy, which results from matching the defined marketing goals and the organization's internal capabilities and market conditions, marketing strategy transfers the resulting demands into a practice program. Varadarajan (2010) defines a marketing strategy as: "... an organization's integrated pattern of decisions that specify its crucial choices concerning products, markets, marketing activities and marketing resources in the creation, communication, and/or delivery of products that offer value to customers in exchanges with the organization and thereby enables the organization to achieve specific objectives" (p. 128). It is also "the total sum of the integration of segmentation, targeting, differentiation, and positioning strategies designed to create, communicate, and deliver an offer to a target market" (El-Ansary, 2006, p. 268). To define a marketing strategy might be even more difficult for a social enterprise as compared to a traditional nonprofit or a commercial business, because the latter organizations are mainly concerned with a single bottom line. Social enterprises, however, need to focus on both social mission and financial viability. Hence, marketing goals should not only ensure financial viability (by increasing sales or increasing funds collected) but should also inform the potential donors, the general public about its successes and contribution to the social mission.

7.4.5   Measures - Planning & Implementation

Subsequently, social entrepreneurs face the challenge of designing (and later implementing) a marketing mix, which helps best to fulfill the set strategy. The marketing mix is the umbrella term for product, price, promotion, and placement decisions with regard to a specific good or target group which, of course, need to be implemented practically. As reasoned above and depicted in **Figure 7.3**, social enterprises are confronted with a two-tailed marketing conception: one targeting the actual consumers of the product or service (sales marketing to beneficiaries), the other targeting the organization's money and time supporters (procurement, i.e., fundraising). Both marketing concepts will be elaborated in more detail with regard to the precise definition of the marketing mix in the following.

Figure 7.3   Marketing Mix for Beneficiaries (Sales Marketing) and Supporters (Fundraising)

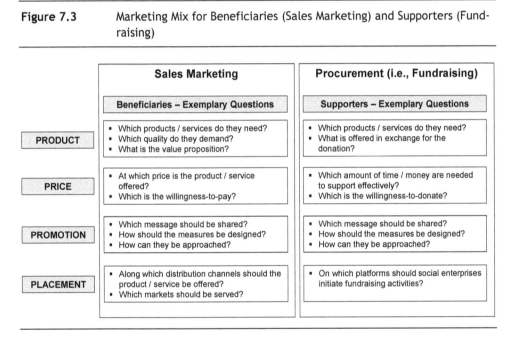

Own illustration

7.4.5.1   Procurement - Fundraising

Fundraising is a key activity for social enterprises as they aim at approaching (potential) supporters and at convincing them to cooperate with the organization. While usually connoted with financial donations, broader perspectives of the term fundraising include all resource retrieving activities, and thus comprise establishing sponsorship relations and so on, but also non-financial contributions such as time investments.

In accordance with the general marketing concept presented above, fundraising goals serve as the basis for any measures taken. These goals, on the one hand, should reflect the organization's actual financial and time necessities and thus follow an external (what do the beneficiaries' need) and internal (which resources does the organization already have at its dispose) analysis. On the other hand, it is important for social enterprises and any organization following a social mission that these resource goals are linked to precise investment targets. In a subsequent step, the organization is forced to restrict the marketing budget for its fundraising activities. In the end, the amount of money collected should be considerably higher than the money invested in these activities and should suffice to fulfill the defined goals. The same holds true for volunteers, i.e., donors of time. The effort to attract volunteers should be compensated by the value they can bring to the organization or its beneficiaries respectively. To meet the basic notions of a planned process, the fundraising activities should be scheduled for a defined period of time and people should be informed about their responsibilities in achieving the goals. As any qualified planning process, a fundraising strategy is finalized—at least temporarily—by controlling if the measures taken led to collecting the targeted funds or to positively influence public awareness of the organization.

The particular approach to raise funds is chosen from a portfolio of diverse strategies. It is actually a matter of the goal defined, which strategy fits best. It is intuitively comprehensible that the goal of winning over additional donors requires a different fundraising approach than the goal of improving the nonprofits reputation or increasing visibility. Hence, the fundraising strategy chosen should be challenged and reconciled with the current development phase the organization is in. Hence, the marketing mix also needs to reflect the specific fundraising goals. At this point, only initial thoughts on how to design the marketing mix elements in fundraising contexts can be offered. Yet, as stated above, all fundraising activities should establish lasting and trusting relationships with the supporters, i.e., measures should reflect a focus on relationships rather than transactions. With additional attention paid to a donor, the likelihood that this donor increases the financial (or time) contribution rises. Relationship marketing ensures that activities target specific segments of financial and time donors. The aim of relationship marketing is

■ to ensure that donors, who reached a certain donor segment, do not get lost as a sponsor to the organization or decrease their time or money contributions and

■ to enable donors to ascend to the next higher donor level ("upgrading", which means that donors increase their time or financial involvement).

Product
In fact, supporters of social enterprises actually do not receive material gain in return for their investment of time and / or money. Still, social enterprises need to make considerations which can be classified as thoughts on product policy. A social enterprise needs to ensure that the financial and time donors experience the satisfaction of their ulterior motives by giving to the organization. This is sometimes compared to a psychological contract which reflects that donors of time and money do not only give but also receive (Farmer and Fedor, 2001).

For financial donors, one motive to support the social enterprise could be the public an-
nouncement of the cooperation. With such conspicuous consumption, people aim at dis-
playing their contribution to the public (Grace and Griffin, 2006). Hence, in return for disposing funds, the donor receives the service to be mentioned on diverse communication
channels as a generous donor. A "product equivalent" for volunteers could be the concrete
task the volunteer is designated to as different types of volunteer tasks satisfy different
motives to volunteer (Houle et al., 2005). Rational incentives an organization might offer its
volunteers are material rewards in the form of skills acquired or certificates issued (Puffer
and Meindl, 1995). Congruence between motives and perceived rewards delivered by the
organization also positively affect volunteers' role identities with their activity in the very
organization and thereby impact satisfaction and the longevity of service.

Price

Certainly, pricing does not play a direct role for volunteering. Yet, prices reflect the value of
an exchange relationship. Hence, organizations cooperating with volunteers should ensure
that these volunteers experience high motive fulfillment via their activity which may increase the likelihood of increased time investments. Like in commercial environments, the
question is which concessions in price an organization may actually allow.

With regard to collecting funds, it may also come as a surprise to talk about pricing. There
is no market prices for donations as in most cases, donors can decide themselves about the
amount they give. This differentiates donations from sponsorship agreements which are
more contractual in nature because a specified good (e.g., money) is traded against a specified other (i.e., logo of the sponsor is printed on flyers). Could social enterprises and nonprofits not be lucky if they received any funds at all? Generating low funds is certainly
better than collecting none. However, as described above, the raised funds must ensure that
the fundraising goals in the form of specific project results are achieved. Hence, social enterprises should ensure that the amounts fundraisers ask for are justifiable (and, therefore,
well-researched) and high enough to suffice the organization's financial and time necessities. Nonprofit research showed that diverse "price" strategies help increase the funds collected. Some nonprofits frame the donation as a commercial exchange, i.e., they offer a
small material present in exchange, such as donation ribbons or postcards (Briers, Pandelaere and Warlop, 2006). In such a situation, the social norm of reciprocity applies and
people want to return the gift by making a fair donation. It becomes clear: this "pricing"
strategy is appropriate especially in situations where the organization is merely interested
in the increase of its donor base and is satisfied with small contributions. Equally, nonprofit
research discusses paltry donations, which are often traded under the motto "Even a penny
would help". The motto also signals: any contribution is legitimate. Instead, another approach for pricing donations comes into play, where the organization suggests what a reasonable donation to the social enterprise would look like. Thereby the potential supporter
can form an idea of an adequate donation in the eyes of the social enterprise (Fraser, Hite
and Sauer, 1988). Yet, the question remains where to set the anchor point to stimulate significant contributions. The organization should be careful to not set donation recommendations too high as supporters may perceive the costs of complying with the request as too
high, which may inhibit donations at all. In contrast, if the anchor point is set too low, there

will hardly be a significant difference to unspecified request and the supporters' willing-ness-to-donate (as their maximum amount available for supporting the organization) is not exploited. Yet, social enterprises are also recommended to focus on establishing funding relationships with capable funders because social enterprises often lack the infrastructure and resources to approach numerous potential donors on a wing and prayer.

Promotion and Placement

Promotion comprises the collectivity of communication measures and the adequate selec-tion of concrete measures given a defined target group and the marketing goals. Communi-cation is particularly important for cultivating an organization's relationship with support-ers. Communication policy is about ensuring that relationships with employees, support-ers, the public and potential donors and other stakeholders which are connected to the organization are built and maintained. The issues tackled here are

- how to design the message communicated to supporters and

- which communication tools and channels to use.

With institutional and major donors, which are the basic funding source for social enter-prises, the approach is comparable to a business-to-business approach—proposals need to be specified to the particular situation of the potential funder and it should become clear what the funds will be needed for in detail. Hence, conventional communication tools like TV commercials or consumer magazines—which would in any case exceed a social enter-prises promotion budget—are not of interest. Despite the lack of resources, social enterpris-es and nonprofits also know that too much advertising targeting volunteers and donors may also be perceived as non-efficient resource-spending and, thus, adversely affect organ-izational attractiveness. Promotion should rather be focused on relatively cost-efficient measures such as establishing direct contact on fairs, conventions, social gatherings, and fundraising events as well as issuing simple informational materials. Research finds (and practice often confirms this view) that most people do not donate time or money until they have been asked by an organization or a friend to do so. This said, it becomes clear that promotion and placement are as inseparable for most social enterprises as they are fre-quently in business-to-business relationships.

With regard to designing the precise message or advertisement, the motive structures as identified in marketing research should be picked up. Also, the insights generated by prior nonprofit research should be considered, e.g., insights on how to present the information. People responsible for designing advertisements often make use of emotional contagion effects. Research finds that sad people on posters arouse sadness in its viewers, given that they are at least a bit sympathetic (Small and Verrochi, 2009). Messages which aim at evok-ing sympathy have been shown to positively affect people's volunteering choices, donation targets and the size of their donations. Despite this finding, most charities refrain from portraying victims' sadness. Another finding has been that only referring to comparably abstract statistics in terms of the number of victims arouses less sympathy in potential do-nors compared to a situation, wherein the nonprofit tells the personal story of a victim (Small and Loewenstein, 2003) to personalize the impact of trading with a potential supporter. In fact, referring to the congruence model, individuals with high normative motives should be provided high normative incentives as a valued reward. Accordingly, administrators should tailor persuasive messages to different motivational perspectives of potential volunteers and match volunteers to activities that satisfy their motives (Clary, Snyder and Ridge, 1992). Persons who aim at fulfilling normative motives by volunteering, i.e., helping somebody without personal gain, are more likely to respond to incentives which symbol that the task they perform supports a good cause.

As elaborated above, donations are trust goods. With trust goods, people are unable to correctly assess the quality of the product or service. Promotion should therefore also provide information on the effectiveness and efficiency of the organization. Yet, storytelling and creating a personal relation with the beneficiary has been found to be especially helpful in cases where the supporter partakes in the personal development of the beneficiary. One very popular example from nonprofit environments is child sponsorship (see practical example 1). Prior research on donations in the nonprofit sector shows that the strategy of appealing for donations for specific needs is more successful if the organization identifies the need as short-term, and focuses on a single case, e.g., by showing how the contribution helps a specific person (Warren and Walker, 1991). The sponsorship idea can be easily transferred to those social enterprises which aim at relieving the specific situation for human beings or animals. It is practicable for organizations, which struggle with precise overall impact measurement as it is coupled with the personal well-being of a particular person or subject.

Another way to cope with the lack of public information to create trust would be to make use of objective seals of approval, which are for example used for charities. For social enterprises, explicit seals of approval informing potential donors about the organization's effectiveness and efficiency do not yet exist. An implicit seal of approval is provided by organizations such as phineo (based in Germany) and NPC (based in the United Kingdom). phineo was officially founded in May 2010 as a spin-off from the renown Bertelsmann foundation. The organization promotes organizations with a social mission by delivering recommendations for particularly efficient and effective organization. A preceding check-up of the organizations' effectiveness (fulfillment of the social mission) and efficiency (relation of administrative expenses and mission-related expenditures) serves as a basis for this assessment. Thereby, phineo addresses the perceptions which Herzlinger (1996) has found to negatively affect people's image of a nonprofit organization:

- ineffective organizations "that do not accomplish their social mission"

- inefficient organizations "that get too little mileage out of the money they spend"

- managers, employees, or board members who abuse their fund control by inappropriately allocating excessive benefits to themselves; and

- organizations that take on excessive risks (p. 98).

But again, social enterprises need to be equally cautious as nonprofits: If a potential supporter gets the impression that the organization is too successful they may interpret this
incorrectly and infer that no further support is needed. This chain reaction has been vali-
dated for volunteer help where people perceived the need for successful nonprofits as
smaller (Fisher and Ackerman, 1998). Also, social enterprises are recommended to spend
more on the social cause than on promotions which feature the good work they are doing in
order for consumers to positively judge their intentions (Yoon, 2006).

Practical Example 1: Child Sponsorship with SOS children's villages
The nonprofit SOS children's villages is one of many organizations which procure child
pence a day, "you can help provide love and care for children who have nothing and no-
one, and if you are thinking of making a regular donation to charity, child sponsorship is
one of the best ways to do it." The way of promoting the message is very clear. By making
the fate of one child dependent from the personal contribution to the charity, the sponsorship idea relates to donors' striving for learning about

- how their contribution is invested and

- which impact this investment actually made.

By accompanying and supporting a particular child along its way to adolescence and receiving documentation on its progress and gratefulness, sponsorships are a frequent target
of donations to nonprofits. **(www.soschildrensvillages.org.uk/sponsor-a-child)**

7.4.5.2   Sales Marketing to Beneficiaries

With social enterprises the problem is different from commercial organizations in that the
bottleneck seldom is in attracting beneficiaries to the product or service. Beneficiaries are
often in need, simply waiting for its provision. Still, they sometimes need to be made aware
of even convinced of the product or service.

Product
In most markets, the product will be placed in a competitive environment. Therefore, organizations need to ensure that their product or service is both visible and attractive to the
targeted public. Only by attending to concerns about product policy, an organization may
develop products and services whose features fit the clients' needs. These features should
contribute to value. This means that beneficiaries, like any other consumers, are interested
in benefits products may have, rather than their features.

Products and services a social entrepreneur may provide comprise housing to the homeless,
family planning for the rural poor, food to the needy, and jobs or loans to the disadvantaged (Dees and Anderson, 2003). These goods only have value to people who aim at ame-
liorating their hunger, homelessness, and so on. Typical issues related to product management are developing new offers in case of further market requirements or decisions on
differentiation (extension of the product portfolio with similar products), variation (re-
design of the given product portfolio), and diversification (extension of the product portfolio with products from another category). For an exemplary social enterprise which serves

the homeless by providing free lunches, product differentiation may comprise the offering of free dinner or breakfast. Product variation, instead, could mean to improve the quantity or quality of the food offered. The said social enterprise would realize a diversification strategy, if it additionally offered the homeless an opportunity to spend the night.

Price

In commercial sales marketing, pricing is a key element of the marketing mix. Prices need to be competitive (i.e., consciously set in relation to competitors' pricing) and need to include considerations about what customers' are ready to forgo for receiving the product or service.

It is also necessary for nonprofits—and social enterprises as well—to form an understanding of how demand reacts to shifts in prices, i.e., how the beneficiaries' price elasticity is shaped (Young, 1999). We can generalize: beneficiaries of social enterprises' products or services are supposed to be even more price sensitive than conventional commercial customers, simply because they have a severe bottleneck on funds. In fact, social enterprises are well-advised to price below the regular market price because its product and services should be made available to a target group which probably does not dispose of sufficient funds to consume under common circumstances. Others may not fully appreciate the value of the service being offered and thus would not "consume" if they had to pay for the service rendered. And in some cases, it would simply not be appropriate to let the intended beneficiaries pay for the received services. It is against its social mission that the International Red Cross charges a fee to earthquake victims who received emergency relief, as Dees (2001) describes so vividly. Hence, social enterprises have to ask themselves how price schedules should be designed to allow beneficiaries' to consume the product or service or if to charge prices at all.

One pricing strategy social enterprise often adopt is price discrimination. Price discrimination is characterized by the notion that one segment subsidizes the consumption of another. This strategy acknowledges that some customers (here: supporters) are willing and able to pay more for an organization's services or products than others (here: beneficiaries). Sometimes, however, beneficiaries may perceive it as demeaning to be treated as a charity case. In such situations, it might be appropriate to ask beneficiaries for at least a small contribution in order to not harm their self-image. Also, partial contributions may be adequate for social enterprise programs which depend on the beneficiaries' active participation. In these situations, charging small pricing helps to screen out those who are not sufficiently serious about the program (see Dees, 1998 for a very readable discussion thereon; the case GuateSalud by Dees, Boatwright and Elias, 1995 also gives, among other aspects, vivid insight into a exemplary price decision in the social enterprise context).

Promotion
Promotion takes care of

- informing existing and prospective customers (here: beneficiaries) about the existence of the organization's products or services and

- creating knowledge about the products' and services' features, benefits, and the potential innovative edge.

- Also, communication aims at creating a preference for a given brand.

To get through to the identified customer segments with their message, organizations need use communication channels which the targeted segments use, but which do not exceed a given communication budget. Innovative and cost-efficient communication tools over the internet, beginning with the organization's homepage and further covering social media channels, which allow beneficiaries access to information about the organization's offers. Thereby, it is easier for external stakeholders to monitor an organization and sanction its underachievement, its falling short of the aroused expectations, and its unethical behavior. This transparency is also improved by specific online-communication platforms which allow consumers to share their organization- and product-related opinion not only in their narrower circle of acquaintances but also with numerous anonymous others. Many experiments have shown that consumers do not read company's messages about the social responsibility of an organization if it is sent out by the company itself or its staff (Yoon, 2006). Of course, the downside of consumer communication is that organizations can hardly control it. It is therefore especially important for a social enterprise to behave as a responsible, caring, and trustworthy supplier to their beneficiaries (and supporters as well).

Public relations, advertising, and customer retention are the core activities placed in a social enterprise's communication mix. Also, communication for a trust good often resorts back to third-party endorsement, mostly by presenting celebrities who represent the organization. In fact, such endorsement may represent a trust surrogate as they stand behind the organization and trust (Bhattacharya, Rao and Glynn, 1995). Given the bottleneck in funds, some principally attractive communication channels are yet not accessible to social enterprises as these bear direct costs. Hence, Public Relations and internet platforms as relatively cost-efficient measures are used. If the social enterprise aims at approaching intermediaries like state agencies to convince them about promoting their products or services to potential beneficiaries, they are recommended to again chose a direct approach and contact these institutions / persons directly and individualized.

With practical example 2, we provide a recent Guerilla Marketing initiative. Guerilla Marketing can be an especially worthwhile measure to effectuate for nonprofits and social enterprises. This is due to the maxim of the Guerilla Marketing approach: Achieve as much attention with as few resources as possible. Hence, measures taken are rather unconventional and, thus, highly visible. The exemplary Guerilla Marketing initiative targeted potential beneficiaries: right-wing extremists which have toyed with the idea of dropping-out of the extremist community. The product (the t-shirt) was issued for free (price) at a festival (placement). Special promotion for this measure was not possible. However, the positive promotion effects showed *after* the festival as popular newspapers reported on the campaign.

Placement
Last, placement is about the physical distribution of a product or service to the customer. Channels in commercial marketing can be branches or online stores, for example. If you may imagine that most social enterprises are small, local-wide active organizations, complex distribution decisions are often not necessary and reasonable as the market is rather limited.

Practical Example 2: Guerilla Marketing – The Trojan T-Shirt
A donation of clothes to a festival of right-wing extremists called "Rock für Deutschland" (RFD) turned out to be the fashion surprise of the year: About 250 free t-shirts were handed out for free at the festival. At first sight, these t-shirts with a skull and the label "Hardcore Rebell – National und Frei" printed on them were a popular promotion gimmick to the festival visitors. The only "problem": after having washed the t-shirts, the skull and the label vanished. Instead, the logo of the drop-out initiative „EXIT-Deutschland" revealed along with the hint: "You can do what your t-shirt can. We help you, to escape right-wing extremism".

These t-shirts not only helped EXIT place their message on the festival, but also caused high response rates in the media. The German newspapers TAZ, SPIEGEL and Sueddeutsche Zeitung reported on this successful promotion measure. This is exemplary Guerilla Marketing for a good cause.

7.4.6   Controlling

Like any other process, the marketing concept is not a self-contained plan of procedures but it is a continuing process. Hence, the effectiveness and the efficiency of the implemented marketing measures need to be monitored and compared with defined target values. For example, an organization needs to analyze if the marketing measures taken break even or if the expected market share, the desired increase in customer satisfaction, of the target value of a specific measure's Return on Investment (ROI) have been realized. In case of out- or underperformance, the set goals need to be redefined. In fact, the goals can also be adjusted as a reaction to market dynamics.

7.5   Conclusion

The issues social enterprises have to confront when elaborating a comprehensive marketing conception are manifold. This chapter only touches key topics relevant for implementing marketing conception in social enterprises. It should help managers of social enterprises form an idea what process stages a marketing conception follows and which elements the marketing mix contains. Moreover, we have provided exemplary problems concerning each of the marketing mix elements without being too exhaustive in presenting possible issues, which should enable managers to derive reasonable conclusions with regard to a marketing conception for their own enterprise.

7.6   Case Study

Street Magazines in View of the Marketing Conception

Street Magazines can be found in nearly any bigger city in Germany. Hinz&Kuntz in Hamburg, fifty-fifty in Dusseldorf, bodo in Bochum and throughout Germany, and the Straßenfeger is sold on the streets of Berlin. Hinz&Kunzt is sold by about 400 vendors in the Hamburg city area and the suburbs. With an average print run of the newspaper of 66.500 issues, Hinz&Kuntz has higher sales than any of the other 40 German street magazines. The nonprofit association aims at supporting the reintegration of people in difficult life situations, i.e., homeless people. The business model stipulates that homeless people sell the magazine in their district instead of begging for money The homeless sell the magazine for €1.90 per piece and keep €1.00 of every sold issue. The organization itself finances itself, while 50% of funds are raised selling the magazine and advertisements and another 50% via donations. For example, E.ON Hanse, an energy company, informs on their website that the organization financially support Hinz&Kunzt.

The magazine especially provides reports on art made by the homeless, publishes social documentaries, and presents its sellers. In June 2009, the newspaper Hamburger Abendblatt reported that celebrities like news anchors or fashion designers endorse for the street magazine in a poster campaign. Six months later, in December 2009, Hinz&Kunzt acknowledged dynamics in society and changed their business model: Despite a roof over their heads, many people may suffer from poverty. Therefore, the organization now also allows people who qualify as poor to sell the magazine, and not only homeless.

Usually, street magazines cannot be bought regularly via a standing order. These are only warranted by exception, as the organizations do not want to threaten direct selling approaches by their vendors. Hinz&Kunzt defines readers living outside of Hamburg and people who are impeded from leaving their flats as eligible to a standing order.

Questions:

1. Define the mission of a street magazine like Hinz&Kunzt and elaborate which challenges the organization can be faced with in terms of marketing endeavors.

2. Which are the target groups (beneficiaries and supporters) of Hinz&Kunzt?

3. Describe in short the (presumed) decisions the street magazines made with regard to the elements of the marketing mix for supporters and beneficiaries.

7.7   Further Reading

[1]   Andreasen, A.R. and Kotler, P. (2008), *Social Marketing for Non Profit Organisations*, 7th ed., Pearson
      Prentice Hall, Harlow.
[2]   Liao, M., Foreman, S. and Sargeant, A. (2001), "Market versus Societal Orientation in the Nonprof-
      it Context", in *International Journal of Nonprofit and Voluntary Sector Marketing*, vol. 6, pp. 254-269.
[3]   Self, D.R., Wymer, W.W. and Henley, T.K. (2002), *Marketing communications for local nonprofit
      organizations: targets and tools*, Routledge, Binghamton.
[4]   Varadarajan, R. (2010), "Marketing strategy: discerning the relative influence of product and firm
      characteristics" in *Academy of Marketing Science Review*, no. 1, pp. 32-43.

7.8   Bibliography

[1]   Andreasen, A.R. (2002), "Marketing Social Marketing in the Social Change Marketplace", in *Jour-
      nal of Public Policy & Marketing*, vol. 21, pp. 3-13.
[2]   Andreasen, A.R. and Kotler, P. (2008), *Social Marketing for Non Profit Organisations*. 7th ed., Pearson
      Prentice Hall: Harlow.
[3]   Austin, J., Stevenson, H. and Wei-Skillern, J. (2006), "Social and Commercial Entrepreneurship:
      Same, Different, or Both?", in *Entrepreneurship Theory and Practice*, vol. 30, pp. 1-22.
[4]   Bendapudi N., Singh, S.N., Bendapudi, V. (1996), "Enhancing helping behavior: an integrative
      framework for promotion planning", in *Journal of Marketing*, vol. 60, pp. 33-49.
[5]   Bennett, R. and Gabriel, H. (2003), "Image and reputational characteristics of UK charitable organ-
      izations: An empirical study", in *Corporate Reputation Review*, vol. 6, pp. 276-289.
[6]   Boezeman, E.J. and Ellemers, N. (2008), "Volunteer recruitment: The role of organizational sup-
      port and anticipated respect in non-volunteers' attraction to charitable volunteer organizations",
      in *Journal of Applied Psychology*, vol. 93, pp. 1013-1026.
[7]   Briers, B., Pandelaere, M. and Warlop, L. (2006), "Adding exchange to charity: A reference price
      explanation", in *Journal of Economic Psychology*, vol. 28, 15-30.
[8]   Brown, T.J. and Dacin, P.A. (1997), "The Company and the Product: Corporate Associations and
      Consumer Product Responses", in *Journal of Marketing*, vol. 61, pp. 68-84.
[9]   Bruhn, M. (2005), *Marketing fuer Nonprofit-Organisationen. Grundlagen, Konzepte, Instrumente*. Kohl-
      hammer Verlag: Stuttgart.
[10] Clary, E.G., Snyder, M. and Ridge, R. (1992), "Volunteers' motivations: A functional strategy for
      the recruitment, placement, and retention of volunteers", in *Nonprofit Management & Leadership*,
      vol. 2, pp. 333-350.
[11] Dees, J.G. (1998), "Enterprising Nonprofits: What do you do when traditional sources of funding
      fall short", in *Harvard Business Review*, Jan/Feb, pp. 55-67.
[12] Dees, J.G. and Anderson, B. A. (2003), "For-Profit Social Ventures," in Kourilsky, M.L. and Wal-
      stad, W.B. (eds), *Social Entrepreneurship*, Senate Hall Academic Publishing.
[13] El-Ansary, A.I. (2006), "Marketing strategy: taxonomy and frameworks", in *European Business
      Review*, vol. 18, pp. 266-293.
[14] Farmer S. and Fedor, D. (2001), "Changing the Focus on Volunteering: An Investigation of Volun-
      teers' Multiple Contributions to a Charitable Organization", in *Journal of Management*, vol. 27, pp.
      191-212.
[15] Fisher, R.J. and Ackerman, D. (1998), "The Effects of Recognition and Group Need on Volunteer-
      ism: A Social Norm Perspective", in *Journal of Consumer Research*, vol. 25, pp. 262-275.
[16] Fraser, C., Hite, R.E. and Sauer, P.L. (1988), "Increasing Contributions in Solicitation Campaigns:
      The Use of Large and Small Anchorpoints", in *Journal of Consumer Research*, vol. 15, pp. 284-287.
[17] Grace, D. and Griffin, D. (2006), "Exploring conspicuousness in the contest of donation behavior",
      in *International Journal of Nonprofit and Voluntary Sector Marketing*, vol. 9, pp. 9-27.

[18] Heister, W. (1994), *Das Marketing spendensammelnder Organisationen*. Botermann & Botermann: Cologne.

[19] Hibbert, S. and Horne, S. (1996), "Giving to charity: questioning the donor decision process", in *Journal of Consumer Marketing*, vol. 13, pp. 4-13.

[20] Houle, B.J., Sagarin, B.J. and Kaplan, M.F. (2005), "A functional approach to volunteerism: Do volunteer motives predict task performance?", in *Basic and Applied Social Psychology*, vol. 27, pp. 337-344.

[21] Liao, M, Foreman, S. and Sargeant, A. (2001), "Market versus Societal Orientation in the Nonprofit Context", in *International Journal of Nonprofit and Voluntary Sector Marketing*, vol. 6, pp. 254-269.

[22] Meffert, H., Burmann, C. and Kirchgeorg, M. (2007), *Marketing: Grundlagen marktorientierter Unternehmensführung. Konzepte - Instrumente – Praxisbeispiele*. Gabler Verlag: Munich.

[23] Polo, Y. and Sesé, F. J. (2009), "How to make switching costly: The role of marketing and relationship characteristics", in *Journal of Service Research*, vol. 12, pp. 119-137.

[24] Puffer, S.M. and Meindl, J.R. (1992), "The congruence of motives and incentives in a voluntary organization", in *Journal of Organizational Behavior*, vol. 13, pp. 425-434.

[25] Self, D.R., Wymer, W.W. and Henley, T.K. (2002), *Marketing communications for local nonprofit organizations: targets and tools*. Routledge: Binghamton.

[26] Small, D.A. and Verrochi, N.M. (2009), "The face of need: Facial emotion expression on charity advertisements", in *Journal of Marketing Research*, vol. 46, pp. 777-787.

[27] Tonkiss, F. and Passey, A. (1999), "Trust, Confidence and Voluntary Organisations: Between Values and Institutions", in *Sociology*, vol. 33, pp. 257-274.

[28] Varadarajan, R. (2010), "Marketing strategy: discerning the relative influence of product and firm characteristics", in *Academy of Marketing Science Review*, no. 1, pp. 32-43.

[29] Yavas, U., Riecken, G. and Babakus, E. (1993), "Efficacy of perceived risk as a correlate of reported donation behavior: An empirical analysis", in *Journal of the Academy of Marketing Science*, vol. 21, pp. 65-70.

[30] Zietlow, J.T. (2002), "Releasing a New Wave of Social Entrepreneurship", in *Nonprofit Management and Leadership*, vol. 13, pp. 85-90.

8 Financing of Social Entrepreneurship

Wolfgang Spiess-Knafl & Ann-Kristin Achleitner

Technische Universität München
KfW Endowed Chair in Entrepreneurial Finance
Center for Entrepreneurial and Financial Studies (CEFS)

Learning goals
Upon completing this chapter, you should be able to accomplish the following:

- Describe the characteristics of the financing structure of social enterprises.

- Explain the financing instruments available for social enterprises.

- Describe the financing institutions in the social capital market.

- Explain the trade-off between social and financial return.

8.1   Introduction

As discussed in the chapter *What Social Entrepreneurship is and what it isn't* social entrepreneurs are often described as individuals approaching a social problem with entrepreneurial spirit. Success stories such as "Dialogue Social Enterprise" (described in the case study) demonstrate the potential of an entrepreneurial approach in solving a social problem. One of the most important elements in fulfilling the social mission is access to capital which can either be generated internally or provided externally. The following **Figure 8.1** shows the different financing sources and instruments which are available for social enterprises.

Figure 8.1   Internal and External Financing

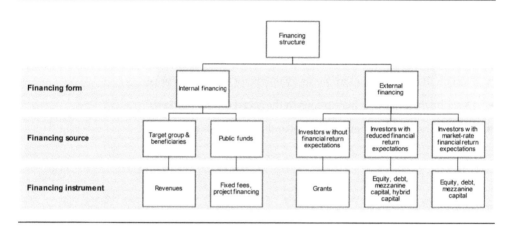

Own illustration based on Achleitner, Spiess-Knafl and Volk (2011)

Internal financing is provided by cash flows generated through the provision of services or products. The services can be paid by the target group or third-party beneficiaries (e.g. employers, visitors or parents) if they have the financial means to cover the costs for the products or services provided. This income stream is oftentimes accessible, but there are also exceptions. Areas such as human rights or violence prevention usually do not offer potential for this strategy. An alternative financing source which can be classified as internal financing is the public sector. Public authorities are often legally obliged to fund the services and products provided by social organizations or can use their discretionary power to fund projects on a cost base. This financing source is usually not accessible for for-profit enterprises and therefore constitutes one of the differences within the financing structure.

External financing is either used to cover temporary negative operating cash flows or to finance long-term investments such as buildings, equipment or infrastructure. Social enterprises have access to external financing sources which are not available to for-profit companies. Traditionally, donations play an important role in the social sector and are important to secure operations if there are no other available financing streams. More recently, social enterprises began to use equity, debt or mezzanine capital within their financing structure. However, capital providers have to consider that the social mission limits the financial capabilities of social enterprises and have to adapt the financing instruments accordingly. There are basically two mechanisms to modify the financing instruments. Capital providers can reduce the rate of financial return they expect (e.g. capital preservation with interest costs set at inflation rate). Moreover, capital providers can structure the financing instruments to better suit the needs of social enterprises. Those modifications can include a deferred repayment schedule, a conversion of loans into grants in the case of unexpected low performance or risk sharing.

In line with the financing instruments, capital providers can thus be classified according to their financial and social return expectations. Capital providers aiming for social and financial return are often referred to as *double bottom line investors*. That means that low financial return requirements are compensated by higher social returns. Social returns are those returns which are generated for society and are not appropriated by the social enterprise. Social return thus represents the value created for society and especially the target group, and is measured in monetary terms.[6]

Heister (2010) has developed a framework for this trade-off. The return curve represents the trade-off between the financial and the social return which can be observed in a range of industries and will have a different form in each industry. This trade-off can be observed for hospitals, elderly care centers or education providers with market participants as diverse as non-profits and listed public companies. However, companies in more business-oriented areas such as online encyclopedias, hearing aid devices, microfinance or the solar energy also have to face these decisions.[7]

Thus, a social enterprise has to decide how to position itself on the return curve shown in the following **Figure 8.2**. A kindergarten operated by a social organization might be on the left side whereas a kindergarten operated by a for-profit company might choose to increase the financial return and position itself on the right side of the curve. There are no studies on the quality of the services provided but the kindergarten with the lower financial return requirements might include otherwise excluded segments and offer additional services.

---

[6] Non-monetary components can include higher self-esteem or easier access to cultural activities which are hard to measure in monetary terms.

[7] See Carrick-Cagna and Santos (2009) for the discussion on the positioning of microfinance institutions and Schwartz (2006) for online giving portals.

Figure 8.2   Trade-Off between Social and Financial Return

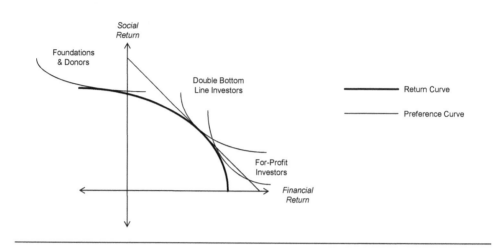

Own illustration based on Heister (2010)

The return curve shows the trade-off between social and financial return from the perspective of a social enterprise. However, capital providers also have preferences which are illustrated as preference curves in **Figure 8.2**. Donors and foundations would be willing to fund the income gap of the social enterprise. The double bottom line investor will prefer a model with a modest financial return while traditional capital providers prefer a model maximizing the financial return. Traditional capital providers have a steep trade-off curve which means that a small reduction of the financial return has to offer a high gain in terms of the social return. On the other side, individual donors are willing to accept a small increase of the social return with a disproportionate reduction of the financial return.

The existence of capital providers which have different objectives is also unique in the financing structure of social enterprises.[8] This divergence of the preferences of the investors is one of the key challenges for social enterprises which they need to address in their strategy, communication and further corporate development.

---

[8]   Family firms are another exception as they also have multiple goals (e.g. family succession).

8.2   Financing Instruments

As social is not equivalent to non-profit, social enterprises can chose from a number of legal forms ranging from non-profit to for-profit status. Moreover, there are satellite models which combine non-profit and for-profit entities. In some countries, even special legal forms for social enterprises have been set up.[9]

That explains why social enterprises have access to the same financing instruments as traditional companies. These financing instruments are equity, debt and mezzanine capital which can be modified according to the needs of social enterprises. One of the key modifications is the amount of interest or dividends a social enterprise has to pay. Equity capital can be provided as "patient capital" without dividends being paid. Debt capital can be provided as an interest-free loan with no interest payment requirements.

Additionally, social enterprises have access to donations and hybrid capital. Both forms are described below in more detail. The range of financing instruments depending on the repayment ability of the social enterprise is shown in **Figure 8.3**.

Figure 8.3   Financing instruments

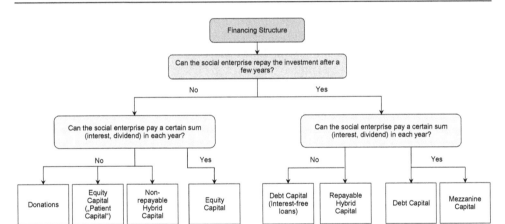

Own illustration based on Achleitner, Spiess-Knafl and Volk (2011)

---

9   Those legal forms include the L3C (low-profit limited liability company) in the US, the CIC (community interest company) in the UK or the gGmbH (public-benefit limited liability company) in Germany.

8.2.1   Donations

The traditional form of financing in the social sector is based on donations. Donations are usually provided by foundations or individuals in monetary or non-monetary form[10]. Donations are attractive as they are not repayable and do not give any enforceable control or voting rights to the donors. Moreover, the social enterprise secures the opportunity to pursue activities without income-generating potential. Victims of domestic violence, illegal immigrants or culturally interested teenagers within low-income families can hardly pay for the services and public authorities usually do not fund very innovative or experimental concepts. For those reasons donations continue to be an important part of the social sector.

Despite their importance, donations have a range of shortcomings. They are usually provided only for project-related costs as the donors are unwilling to cover more than a minimum share of the administrative costs or any expenditure for corporate development. Moreover, they are short-term oriented and have significant fundraising costs.[11] Some capital providers address these issues by providing stipends or using a venture philanthropy approach.

Individual donors or foundations sometimes contribute a significant part of the social enterprise's income and a loss of these contributions can have serious implications for a social enterprise. Therefore, individual donors or foundations need to consider exit strategies to secure the sustainability of the social enterprise. There can either be a follow-up financing or the social enterprise becomes self-sustainable and is no longer dependent upon donations. If both options are not achievable and the social enterprise cannot continue its operations, liquidation remains the last option (as shown in **Figure 8.4**). The remaining assets are then usually given to a charitable social organization.

---

[10]   Non-monetary donations include volunteering or in-kind contributions such as pro bono services or products free costs for a social enterprise.
[11]   Sargeant et al. (2009) have shown that the median fundraising costs for generating £1.00 amount to £0.21.

Figure 8.4   Exit options

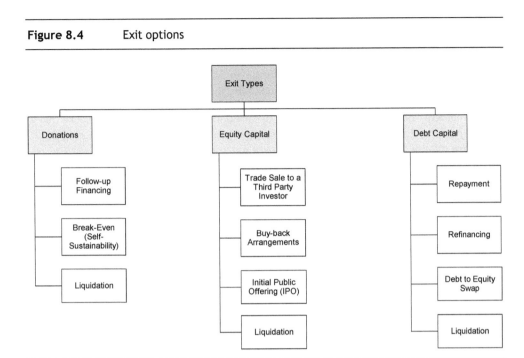

Own illustration

8.2.2   Equity Capital

The shortcomings of donations have led to the use of other financing instruments within the financing structure of social enterprises. Equity capital is used to finance working capital, long-term investments or to cover temporary negative operating cash flows.

Equity capital can be provided by informal sources such as the founder himself or friends and family (often referred to as 4F meaning "founders, friends, family and fools") as well as more formal sources such as social business angels and venture philanthropy funds. In exchange for providing capital, a certain percentage of the shares is transferred to the investor. A share of the enterprise gives the social investor control and voting rights. Those ownership rights can be executed through a supervisory board or an advisory board. The final governance structure depends upon the legal requirements and the articles of association.

Equity capital is the financing form with the highest risk as the investor participates from profits as well as possible losses.[12] The distribution of profits depends upon the philosophy

---

[12]   There are no statistics on the profitability of social enterprises. Most social enterprises appear to be low-profit or dependent upon donations. However, some segments do provide profit opportunities such as "bottom of the pyramid" business models, microfinance or intermediary services in the social sector.

and the legal form of the social enterprise. Certain social enterprises have committed to reinvest all their earnings while others distribute part of the earnings. The non-distributing form of equity capital is shown in **Figure 8.3** as "patient capital". In the UK, community interest companies (CIC) can pay dividends up to 35% of the distributable profits with further restrictions based on the paid-up value of the shares (CIC Regulator, 2010).

At the moment, there is a limited number of opportunities to exit the investment. The investor can pass the shares to another investor via a trade sale or an initial public offering (IPO). There are various efforts to set up a fully functioning social stock exchange described below. Depending upon the financing ability of the social entrepreneur, there can also be buyback arrangements in which the social entrepreneur takes over the shares of the investor at the end of the investment period. The last option is the liquidation of the company and the sale of the remaining assets (also see **Figure 8.4**).

8.2.3   Debt Capital

Debt capital can be used to finance working capital as well as long-term investments which promise stable and predictable cash flows. Those long-term investment include equipment or buildings. Debt capital receives regular interest payment but no share of the profits. As illustrated in **Figure 8.1** and **Figure 8.3**, debt capital can be provided from traditional debt capital providers such as banks as well as social investors. Therefore, the interest rate can be variable ranging from 0% (interest-free loan) to normal market return rates.

Debt capital has to be repaid at the end of the payment period. As shown in **Figure 8.4**, there are various exit options. The social enterprise can either repay the debt or refinance the loan with another capital provider. In case of financial distress the debt capital can be converted into equity capital giving the investor a share of the company. If the continuation of the operations is not promising the investor can institute bankruptcy proceedings and recover part of the invested capital through the liquidation of the enterprise.

8.2.4   Mezzanine Capital

Mezzanine capital combines elements of debt capital and equity capital and can be structured flexibly according to the needs and requirements of the social enterprise. Usually, there is a fixed interest rate and a repayment obligation (debt capital character) as well as an additional variable performance-related interest rate or an equity kicker (equity capital character). An equity kicker gives the investor the opportunity to receive a share of the increase in the equity value of the enterprise.

This financing form is especially attractive for social investors as the investment is repaid like a loan with the option of a performance-related compensation in case of financial success. Thus, mezzanine capital is a suitable financing instrument for social investors aiming at a market-rate return.

8.2.5   Hybrid Capital

As illustrated in **Figure 8.5**, hybrid capital combines elements of debt capital, equity capital and donations. Hybrid capital can be an attractive financing instrument as it addresses the specific business models of social enterprises. The grant character can be explained through the fact that there are no interest costs and the financing is converted into a donation in certain pre-agreed scenarios.

Figure 8.5   Financing instruments

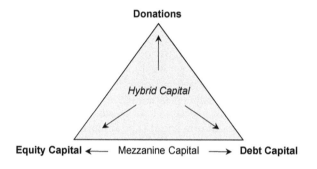

Own illustration based on Achleitner, Spiess-Knafl and Volk (2011)

Financing instruments which can be classified as hybrid capital are:

■   Recoverable grants

■   Convertible grants

■   Forgivable loans

■   Revenue share agreements

A recoverable grant is attractive when the project is likely to be income-generating. It is a loan which has only to be repaid in case of success (e.g. sustainable income generation and positive earnings). If the project is not able to repay the loan, the recoverable grant is converted into a grant. However, the investor has to consider the structure as the social enterprise can have an incentive to be unsuccessful as there is then no need to repay the loan. A convertible grant uses the same mechanism with the difference that the investment is converted into equity if the project proves to be successful.

A forgivable loan uses the opposite mechanism as the loan is forgiven if certain pre-agreed milestones are reached. This structure can be attractive for public authorities which want to finance a project and secure the long-term pursuit of the social goal. It can also be used as a conditional stipend which forgives a portion of the loan each year.

Revenue share agreements are financing instruments where the investor funds a project and receives a share of the future revenues. This approach looks promising as the social investor and the social enterprise share the risk of a project and there are no exit issues as the investor receives a share of the revenues on a regular basis. Projects in countries with high political risks (e.g. risk of civil war or endemic corruption) can be financed through such an arrangement as the social enterprise is not facing bankruptcy in case of a write-off caused by political changes.

8.3   Financing Institutions

In the last decades, the external financing of the social sector was mainly based on dona-tions with social enterprises having limited access to other financing instruments. In the 1990s, wealthy entrepreneurs with a background in IT, venture capital, private equity or banking began applying new and innovative funding strategies for their philanthropic activities. Social entrepreneurs also aimed at using debt and equity capital to increase the entrepreneurial flexibility and the planning certainty.

Both trends led to the development of a social capital market with a range of institutions each focusing on a given segment of the social sector. In the following **Figure 8.6** the institu-tions in the social capital markets are shown with the equivalent traditional capital market institutions shown on the left side.

Figure 8.6   Social Capital Market

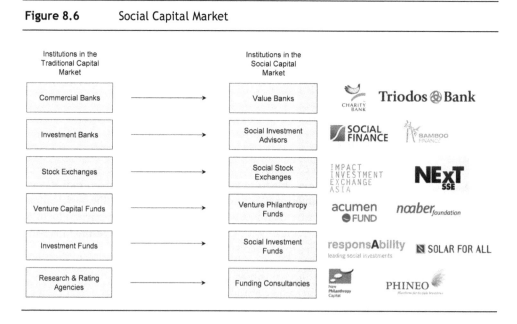

Own illustration

8.3.1   Value Banks

Value banks perform the same role as commercial banks in the traditional capital market. Those banks accept deposits from savers and give loans to enterprises or individuals. As value banks are focused on the social sector, they have a better understanding of the different business models and the specific needs and requirements.[13]

However, they also have to minimize the default rate and therefore focus on the lower risk capital expenditures in the social sector. Some social enterprises have stable and predictable cash flows as their services are paid by insurances or public funds (e.g. hospitals or elderly care centres) giving them a low-risk profile. Alternatively, they have assets which can be pledged as security which can be sold by the bank in case of default. Those assets can be buildings, equipment or farmland.

8.3.2   Social Investment Advisors

The social sector can be characterized by a high fragmentation and high transaction costs. Social investment advisors reduce these transaction costs by bundling investments and structuring appropriate financing mechanisms. One of those mechanisms is described below.

A social impact bond is a mechanism in which the public sector commits to pay a sum dependent upon the outcome of the social measures. This mechanism shifts the social risk of a lower than expected outcome to the social investors who receive a financial return to compensate for this risk. The financial return depends upon the savings for the public sector. This mechanism is shown in the following **Figure 8.7**.

Figure 8.7   Mechanism of a Social Impact Bond

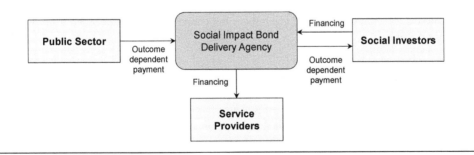

Own illustration based on Bolton and Savelle (2010)

---

13   Globally, some banks formed the "Global Alliance for Banking on Values" (www.gabv.org).

Social Finance, an UK-based financial intermediary, set up the first social impact bond in 2010. The underlying social problem is that 60% of short sentence prisoners are re-offending within one year. A reduction of this re-offending rate would reduce the costs for the prison system and the crime rate.

Over a period of six years, social investors will fund a range of social organisations to provide support to 3,000 short sentence prisoners. After this period, social investors will receive a share of the long term savings if the re-offending rate drops by a certain percentage (for more information see www.socialfinance.org.uk).

One of the key challenges for social impact bonds is the measurement of the savings for the public sector. Crime prevention, healthcare or employment programs are certainly areas where social impact bonds can be used whereas projects in education or integration are not feasible due to the problems of calculating the savings for the public sector.

8.3.3   Social Stock Exchanges

As described in chapter 8.2, there is only a limited number of exit options for equity capital investors. A fully functioning social stock exchange could be an attractive exit option for social investors as well as an additional funding source for mature social enterprises with a proven business model. There are currently various initiatives to set up a fully functioning social stock exchange.

The key issues are the valuation of the social enterprise, the protection of the social mission and the social reporting. There is not yet a valuation method for social enterprises and it remains to be seen if social investors are paying a premium or a discount on a relative valuation. The protection of the social mission can be achieved through various measures also common on traditional capital markets. Examples are the control of a minority stake (e.g. above 25%) by a foundation to lock the social mission, the set-up of articles of associations with reference to the social mission or poison pills to avoid unsolicited take-over bids.[14] Social enterprises also need to report their social activities. Examples are the Social Reporting Standard (SRS) in Germany or the Impact Reporting & Investment Standards (IRIS) in the United States.

8.3.4   Venture Philanthropy Funds

Venture Philanthropy funds are the equivalent of venture capital funds in the traditional capital markets. The starting point for the development was an article published by Letts, Ryan and Grossman (1997). The concept has become popular and there are 31 funds organised within the European Venture Philanthropy Association (EVPA, 2010). Those funds

---

[14] Social enterprises have sometimes built up significant assets through unpaid labour (volunteering), in-kind contributions or donations. Those assets should be protected for the fulfillment of the social mission.

generally have a regional and a sector focus to gain experience and transfer knowledge within their portfolio.

John (2006) defines Venture Philanthropy as having the following characteristics:

- High engagement
- Non-financial support
- Tailored financing
- Multi-year support
- Organisational capacity-building
- Performance measurement

Venture Philanthropy funds support the social enterprise in their day-to-day business through access to their networks or management consulting (*high engagement* and *non-financial support*). Venture philanthropy funds not only use equity and debt capital but also provide donations (*tailored financing*). Contrary to foundations or individual donors they support the organisations over a long time period between 3-7 years (*multi-year support*). Moreover, they provide funding for the management and overhead costs and secure a proper governance structure (*organisational capacity-building*). One of the key differences to foundations is their approach to measure and monitor the performance of the social ventures (*performance measurement*). Venture philanthropy funds also use a multi-stage selection process with an initial screening of the applications and various interviews including a site visit (Achleitner, Heister and Spiess-Knafl, 2010).

8.3.5   Social Investment Funds

Social investment funds perform the same role as investment funds in the traditional capital markets. Social investment funds bundle capital from various investors and invest those funds in certain asset classes. Attractive investment segments are microfinance institutions or enterprises with a sustainable and income-generating business model. Those enterprises can be active in the solar industry or health care.

The social investment funds need to consider social and financial return requirements and there is normally a side condition or constraint. If the fund is maximizing the social return there is a financial constraint or financial side condition which formulates that the fund has to deliver at least a capital-preserving return. If the fund is maximizing the financial return there is a social constraint or social side condition which formulates that the fund has to be active within a certain social segment or deprived area. These side conditions are also known as "Impact First" (financial constraint) and "Financial First" (social constraint) (Palandjian, 2010).

8.3.6   Funding Consultancies

Social investors or foundations pursuing a rational instead of an emotional investment approach typically face difficulties in their capital allocation decisions. Those difficulties can be explained through the high fragmentation and a lack of transparency of the social sector as well as a lack of quantitative measures such as social impact or social value creation.

Funding consultancies advise social investors on their capital allocation decisions. Phineo in Germany and New Philanthropy Capital (NPC) in the UK operate as funding consultancy and publish research reports on social issues or advise social investors and foundations in their funding strategies. Their equivalent in the traditional capital market would be rating or research agencies.

8.4   Case Study

Andreas Heinecke has started the concept "Dialogue in the Dark" in 1988 and is a serial social entrepreneur since 1995. Andreas was honored as the first Ashoka Fellow in Western Europe and named Outstanding Social Entrepreneur by the Schwab Foundation for Social Entrepreneurship.[15]

Dialogue Social Enterprise and its subsidiaries (hereinafter DSE) seek to overcome barriers between "us" and "them" and to redefine "disability" as "ability," and "otherness" as "likeness" (Dialogue Social Enterprise, 2011). To reach this goal, DSE runs exhibitions in which blind guides lead visitors through a complete dark environment to experience the daily routine of blind persons. The visitors are led through a real-life environment which includes supermarkets, a city theme or a café. Based on this concept, the social enterprise has also developed "Dialogue in Silence" and workshops for corporate clients. Since the foundation, 7 million visitors have experienced the exhibition and 7,000 blind persons have gained access to the employment market through their work with DSE.

The social enterprise has two revenue streams. The concept is scaled globally using a franchise system which provides DSE with income to provide for planning and development support. Additionally, DSE operates permanent exhibitions in Frankfurt and Hamburg and conducts workshops with corporate clients on all continents. The annual revenues amount to around €5 million without dependence on federal funding or donations and the stable business model makes DSE suitable for financing through Venture Philanthropy funds.

In 2005, a subsidiary of DSE was provided a loan by the Munich-based Venture Philanthropy fund BonVenture to open a permanent exhibition in Frankfurt. The loan was repayable within 5 years. In 2010, DSE decided to offer more workshops to corporate clients and took on equity and debt capital from French Venture Philanthropy fund PhiTrust to cover the capital requirements. The equity capital was provided at nominal value with a buy-back arrangement at the end of the loan period. Both funds provided management consulting, strategic advice and access to their networks to the social enterprise. Those elements proved to be crucial for the further development of the social enterprise.

Questions
1. What are the key differences between a bank loan and a loan from a social venture capital fund?

2. What can be the problems around the exit of an investment?

3. Why did DSE not focus on donations for the international expansion of its business?

4. What could have been other financing sources for DSE?

---

[15]   Also see www.dialogue-se.com for a complete overview of the social enterprise and
       www.ashoka.org/fellow/3661 or
       www.schwabfound.org/sf/SocialEntrepreneurs/Profiles/index.htm?
       sname=179427 for more details regarding the social entrepreneur Andreas Heinecke.

8.5   Further Reading

[1] Achleitner, A.-K., Heinecke, A., Noble, A., Schöning, M. and Spiess-Knafl, W. (2011) "Social Investment Manual", online: http://ssrn.com/abstract=1884338.

[2] Fama, E.F. and Jensen, M.C. (1983), "Agency problems and residual claims", in *Journal of Law and Economics*, vol. 26, no. 2, pp. 327-349.

[3] Fedele, A. and Miniaci, R. (2010), "Do Social Enterprises Finance Their Investment Differently from For-profit Firms? The Case of Social Residential Services in Italy", in *Journal of Social Entrepreneurship*, vol. 1, no. 2, pp. 174-189.

[4] Fischer, R.B., Wilsker, A.L. and Young, D.R. (in press), "Exploring the Revenue Mix of Nonprofit Organizations: Does it Relate to Publicness" in Nonprofit and Voluntary Sector Quarterly, online: http://nvs.sagepub.com/content/early/2010/04/08/0899764010363921.abstract,   accessed   date: 06/05/2011.

[5] Foster, W. and Fine, G. (2007), "How Nonprofits Get Really Big", in *Stanford Social Innovation Review*, Spring 2007. pp. 46-55.

[6] Jäger, U. (2010), *Managing Social Businesses - Mission, Governance, Strategy and Accountability*, Palgrave Macmillan, Houndmills, New York.

8.6   Bibliography

[1] Achleitner, A.-K., Heister, P. and Spiess-Knafl, W. (2010), "Venture Philanthropy und Sozialunternehmertum", in Hoelscher, P., Ebermann, T. and Schlüter, A. (eds.), *Venture Philanthropy in Theorie und Praxis*, Lucius & Lucius, Stuttgart, pp. 81-89.

[2] Achleitner, A.-K., Spiess-Knafl, W. and Volk, S. (2011), "Finanzierung von Social Enterprises - Neue Herausforderungen für die Finanzmärkte", in Hackenberg, H. and Empter, S. (eds.), *Social Entrepreneurship - Social Business: Für die Gesellschaft unternehmen*, VS Verlag, Wiesbaden, pp. 269-286.

[3] Bolton, E. and Savelle, L. (2010), "Towards a new social economy - Blended value creation through social   impact   bonds",   online: http://www.socialfinance.org.uk/sites/default/files/Towards%20A%20New%20Social%20Economy%20web.pdf, accessed date: 06/05/2011..

[4] Carrick-Cagna, A.-M. and Santos, F. (2009), "Social vs. Commercial Enterprise: The Compartamos Debate   and   the   Battle   for   the   Soul   of   Microfinance",   online: http://www.insead.edu/facultyresearch/centres/social_entrepreneurship/research_resources/documents/compartamosfinal-w.pdf, accessed date: 06/05/2011.

[5] CIC Regulator (2010), "Information Pack", online: http://www.cicregulator.gov.uk/guidance.shtml, accessed date: 06/05/2011.

[6] Dialogue Social Enterprise (2011), "What do we do?", online: http://www.dialogue-se.com/what/what-do-we-do, accessed date: 06/05/2011.

[7] European Venture Philanthropy Association (EVPA) (2010), "European Venture Philanthropy Directory 2010/2011", online: http://evpa.eu.com/wp-content/uploads/2010/11/EVPA-Directory-2010-113.pdf, accessed date: 06/05/2011.

[8] Heister, P. (2010), *Finanzierung von Social Entrepreneurship durch Venture Philanthropy und Social Venture Capital*, Wiesbaden.

[9] John, R. (2006), "Venture Philanthropy - The Evolution of High Engagement Philanthropy in Europe",   online: http://www.sbs.ox.ac.uk/centres/skoll/research/Documents/Venture%20Philanthropy%20in%20Europe.pdf, accessed date.

[10] Letts, C., Ryan, W. and Grossman, A. (1997), "Virtuous Capital: What Foundations Can Learn from Venture Capitalists" in *Harvard Business Review*, vol. 75, no. 2, pp. 36-44.

[11] Palandjian, T. (2010), "Investing for impact: Case studies across asset classes", online: http://www.parthenon.com/ThoughtLeadership/InvestingforImpactCaseStudiesAcrossAssetClass es, accessed date: 06/05/2011.

[12] Sargeant, A., Lee, S. and Jay, E. (2009), "Communicating the "Realities" of Charity Costs: An Institute of Fundraising Initiative", in *Nonprofit and Voluntary Sector Quarterly*, vol. 38, no. 2, pp. 333-342.

[13] Schwartz, R. (2006), "Profit taboo in social enterprise country?", in *Alliance*, vol. 11, no. 3, pp. 31-32.

9 Performance Measurement and Social Entrepreneurship

Johanna Mair
Hertie School of Governance &
Stanford University
Stanford Center on Philanthropy and Civil Society

Shuchi Sharma
Bennett Day School Chicago

Learning goals
Upon completing this chapter, you should be able to accomplish the following:

- Understand the origins of the current momentum in measuring social impact

- Be familiar with key approaches

- Critically evaluate efforts to measure social impact

9.1   Introduction

While *entrepreneurs* are the innovative leaders and enterprisers of the business sector, *social entrepreneurs* are the visionary change makers of the not for profit and for-profit social sectors[16]. Social entrepreneurs and their venture-capital-like investors aim to achieve positive long-term, large-scale, sustainable social goals and non-financial impact using business principles and practices. An entrepreneurial approach and performance based investment allows social enterprises[17] to maximize the value of their limited resources and creatively leverage additional resources beyond their direct control to create greater impact, while staying relentlessly focused on their missions (**Figure 9.1**).

Figure 9.1   Social Venture in Social Entrepreneurship

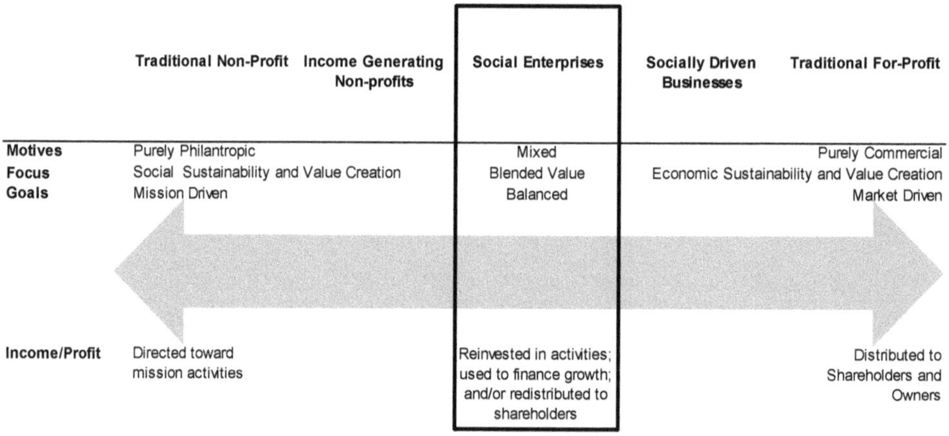

	Traditional Non-Profit	Income Generating Non-profits	Social Enterprises	Socially Driven Businesses	Traditional For-Profit
Motives **Focus** **Goals**	Purely Philantropic Social Sustainability and Value Creation Mission Driven		Mixed Blended Value Balanced		Purely Commercial Economic Sustainability and Value Creation Market Driven
Income/Profit	Directed toward mission activities		Reinvested in activities; used to finance growth; and/or redistributed to shareholders		Distributed to Shareholders and Owners

Own illustration based on Dees (1998) and Alter (2006)

Unlike businesses and corporations where profit is the primary goal, social enterprises prioritize *social and/or environmental impact* over personal or shareholder wealth. In contrast to traditional not for profits, they stress good business planning, measurable outcomes, achievable milestones, and high levels of financial accountability.

---

[16] The 'social sector' is also known as the global citizen sector, voluntary sector, third sector, independent sector, and mission-based sector.

[17] A type of social venture that prioritizes double or triple bottom line impacts over financial gains. Unlike a not for profit, it tries to achieve some level of financial sustainability; and in contract to a social business, it prioritizes non-financial returns on an investment.

They differ in terms of their investor base, and their strategies and approaches toward achieving a specified level of social change and financial self-sufficiency (**Figure 9.2**).

Figure 9.2   Spectrum of Financial Strategies

| | Traditional Non-Profit | Income Generating Non-Profits | **SOCIAL ENTERPRISE** | | | Socially Driven (or Responsible) Businesses | Traditional For-Profit |
			Social Enterprise Approaching Self Sufficiency	Social Enterprise Approaching Self Sufficiency	Self Sufficient Social Enterprise		
Financial Strategy	Require full financial support	Partial self sufficiency	Cash flow self sufficiency	Operating self efficiency	Complete financial self sufficiency	Complete financial self sufficiency	Complete financial self sufficiency
Subsidies	100%	Mostly subsidized	Subsidies needed to bridge deficit b/w earned income and expenses, capital investment, and growth subsidy	Partial subsidies needed to cover cost of capital	No subsidies	No subsidies	No subsidies
Viability through Earned Income	Not viable • Dependent on grants and donations for survival	Not viable • Dependent on grants and donations for survival	Approaching viability • Cost structure and growth are subsidized	Viability expected • Subsidies diminish	Viable • No subsidies *Non-profit social enterprises may change its legal status to a for-profit entity at this stage*	Viable • No subsidies	Viable • No subsidies

Own illustration based on Dees (1998) and Alter (2006)

Social entrepreneurs pursue *double or triple bottom line goals, or blended financial and non-financial value,* where performance is measured in terms of both social impact (positive/negative) and financial performance (profit/loss). In this emerging industry, *social performance* relates to the effective translation of an organization's mission into practice via interventions and can be measured at its different stages using a variety of different approaches.

Performance measurement helps organizations monitor what interventions and approaches work, and what results they achieve. Assessment promotes a culture of (1) discipline by helping organizations develop internal controls and relevant measures to strategize, monitor progress, and use social, operational, and financial performance information to make decisions; (2) accountability by holding social ventures to their mandates; and (3) organizational transparency and legitimacy through reflection and communication of their progress towards meeting their objectives. It allows ventures to plan and implement more effectively, and facilitate social change and financial sustainability. However, social enterprises are expected to produce results and report their progress to multiple authorities from different sectors that pursue different interests, define success differently, and often have different expectations for measuring and reporting performance and return on investment.

The individuals that fund and invest in social entrepreneurs and their ventures represent a spectrum of capital, and range broadly across sectors, geographies, and in their role, purpose, and expectations (**Figure 9.3**).

Figure 9.3   Sources of Capital, Spectrum of Capital and Investment Sectors

SOURCES OF CAPITAL		SPECTRUM OF CAPITAL					SECTORS
		High Risk			*Low Risk*		
Foundations							Agriculture
Individuals	Investment Type	Grants	Patient Capital	Pure Equity	Equity Like	Loans	Water
Local government	Expected Loss	100%	20-50%	10-20%	10-20%	1-8%	Housing
Community Development Financial Institutions	Financial ROI	0%	10%	No Limit	0-30%, Variable	5-18%, Fixed	Education
Program related investments (PRIs)	Terms of Investment	Often Short	Long-term	Success-based	5-7 years	Fixed	Health
Bilateral and multilateral lenders	Involvement in Business	Often Low	Some (Through Partners)	High, Success-based	High, Success-based	Low	Energy
Nonprofit social investors							Financial Services

Adapted from Emerson, Jed and Sheila Bonni, The Blended Value Map: Tracking the Intersects and Opportunities of Economic, Social and   *Adapted from IRIS*
Environmental Value Creation, September, 2003, www.hewlett.org.

Own illustration based on Dees (1998), Alter (2006) and
JP Morgan, Rockefeller Foundation, GIIN (2010)

Common to all social- or impact-investors is the double or triple bottom line approach that they take towards their capital and decision making processes. They attribute real value to the social and environmental return, and will often tradeoff financial returns for nonfinancial impact. These impact investors are passively or actively involved in their portfolio companies, and typically use tools that are similar to venture capital to make grants and investments in innovative, high-growth and high-impact social ventures. Impact investors typically have a clear strategy and investment goals, and are looking to achieve measureable and meaningful impact. They aim to use performance data to efficiently direct their investment towards building strong and financially sustainable organizations that can deliver social (and/or environmental) benefits rapidly and on a large scale.

This group of social impact investors and funders includes a variety of individual philanthropic investors and intermediary impact investors, such as:

■ progressive **Foundations**, such as the *Bill & Melinda Gate's Foundation*, that try to leverage its resources for program related investments,

■ **Development finance institutions**, like the *International Finance Corporation (IFC)* that uses impact evaluations to evaluate interventions, maximize its efforts, and measure its results,

■ **Pension funds**, such as *Calvert Investment's Sustainable & Responsible Mutual Funds*, seeking to diversify their risk, while delivering competitive double bottom line returns to their stakeholders,

■ **Venture philanthropy firms**, like the *New Profit* or *New Schools Venture Fund* which provide capital and expertise to transform ideas into mission-driven, high-performing, sustainable organizations,

- **Social funds that have been founded and capitalized by one or more high-net indi-vidual(s)**, similar to both *Ashoka* and the *Acumen Fund*

- **Individual donors** like those looking to invest with *Kiva* and *Ashoka*, and help catalyze social change, and

- **Government** organizations at the local, state, or federal level that takes on the role of an investor or funder.

Over the past decade, this new, emerging industry of impact investors has experimented with various approaches and instruments to ensure an effective and efficient use of financial and non-financial resources invested in social ventures. More recently, eading social impact investors also proactively engage social entrepreneurs in discussions and the development of instruments. The development of performance measurement instruments is seen as an important tool to ensure interests of internal and external stakeholders of social ventures and at the same time an important mechanism to gain legitimacy and support for the newly created impact investment industry.[18]

9.2   Why Accountability in Social Entrepreneurship is Crucial

One of the promises that many associate with the field of social entrepreneurship is greater transparency and new regulatory frameworks for market based activity that prioritizes social value creation. An additional positive spillover of this would be to rejuvenate the not for profit sector. Since their inception, not for profit organizations (NPO) and traditional grant making foundations have claimed to be less bureaucratic, and more flexible, innovative, resourceful, cost-effective, and responsive to the needs of their beneficiaries than the government. However, these organizations regarded as constituting the not for profit sector have to a large extent fallen short of this promise. Nonprofits and their grant making organizations have been criticized for their failure to: to (1) manage resources efficiently, (2) build internal capacity to scale operations, and (3) become financially sustainable. The systematic inefficiencies of charitable giving and grant making have driven the recent shift from transactional funding models to venture-type performance-based, results-oriented, investment models that stress transparency, accountability, and returns to all stakeholders in the social sector.

Impact investing offers a new alternative for channeling large scale private capital for social benefit and change. Investors identifying themselves with this newly created community – or industry as some would argue – want to know if and how their investments are achieving the desired results. As a result they "encourage" organizations they invest in to use analytical tools and strategies to measure, manage, and report their performance, build internal capacity, and scale their operations and impact creation in a sustainable manner.

---

[18]   In this chapter, we use the terms impact investing and venture philanthropy interchangeably.

Social entrepreneurs that take on such investments to finance their ventures are therefore often seen at the forefront of using and co-creating such tools.

The success of social ventures depends on how well they deliver their product or service to their **beneficiaries**. Success however also depends on how well they communicate their returns and performance improvement to their **internal and external stakeholders** (**Figure 9.4**), as such social ventures are held accountable by **all stakeholders.**

While accountability in social enterprises is generated internally, it is driven externally by multiple stakeholders that typically have conflicting views on responsibility, accountability, and performance. All investors expect a social enterprise to use the funds to grow their organization to enhance their future earnings or their social impact by (1) increasing their volume of business; (2) reducing internal costs at existing level of business; or (3) increasing the impact created per dollar invested at existing level of business.

Figure 9.4   Internal and External Accountability to Stakeholders

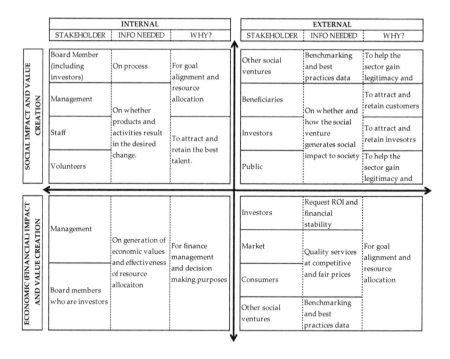

Own illustration

However, managing and delivering a social mission and at the same time achieving financial sustainability and operating at scale not an easy task. At times, to improve profitability and scale their operations, social ventures compromise their mission and their focus on social outcomes. Their efforts to raise funds to scale may result in an exit from a community that needs their products or services the most. Social impact assessment is regarded as a tool to support social ventures to achieve financial results without compromising their mission, i.e., to avoid mission drift.

When done right, so the argument goes, measurement allows organizations to become better planners and more effective implementers. It helps them to efficiently allocate scarce resources, anticipate and reassess key performance hurdles, and identify opportunities to improve, grow, and effectively serve their beneficiaries. Assessment also seen as facilitating accountability, supports communication with stakeholders, and can help communicate proven success, which would thereby facilitate and stimulate capital flows for future growth and more successfully bring initiatives to scale.

For investors, social and financial performance data is increasingly used to inform the decision making and investment allocation processes, and ensures that they are making the desired (sound) investments by estimating potential impact and assessing the quantifiable social return on the investment.[19] It provides them with critical information about their investment on how, in comparison to other investment options, their investment has made the best possible impact. However, while financial performance is arguably simpler to measure, the often intangible social benefits of a venture's activities and inputs have proven to be difficult to measure in an efficient, timely, and reliable way.

9.3   Impact Measurement

Impact can be defined as the change or effect created by a social venture, which in effect can either directly or indirectly change or transform a social system. The resulting change is driven by the combination of inputs, activities, processes of a mission driven organization, and may be positive and/or negative effects on a social system.

Impact measurement serves as a means to monitor, manage, and report the **performance and double bottom line value** ('the bang...') created by a social venture **in terms of both financial and non-financial inputs or investments** ('...for the buck') to both of these parties. Managers measure their impact to efficiently manage their resources and determine the degree of progress that they have made toward achieving their mission-based goals. Similarly, impact investors use measurement to determine how best to allocate and assess the performance of capital invested in social impact creation, as well as to help shape the execution and evolution of an entity.

---

[19]   They want to ensure that the impacts of a project are measureable, sustainable, cost-effective, and scalable.

9.3.1   Measuring Outputs and Outcomes

The proclaimed ultimate goal of all social entrepreneurs and impact investors is to create impact. Yet, prior to creating and assessing impact, an organization must first identify its objectives and validate its complex interventions and social development goals, towards which its progress can be mapped, measured, and tracked in the future.

The *Impact Value Chain* is a simplified model that was developed as a research initiative in 2005 to categorize the varying stages, methods, and degrees of social impact and value creation of a social enterprise (**Figure 9.5**). It provides a window into a social venture's objectives and strategic design implications in relation to its activities, capabilities, and resources. In addition, this framework also helps distinguish the key differences between measuring (1) social performance (monitoring processes via inputs, activities, and outputs; (2) social outcomes (short-term results and affects on beneficiaries); and (3) social impacts (long-term results and systemic changes that are attributable to a social venture's activities and interventions).

Figure 9.5   Impact Value Chain

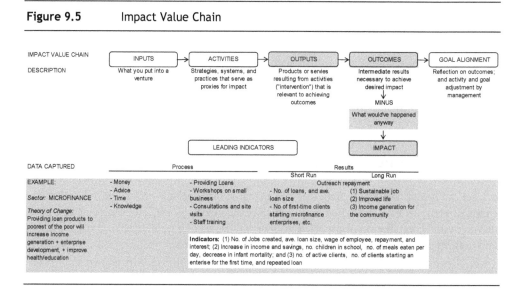

Own illustration based on the Impact Value Chain in *The Double Bottom Line Catalogue*, Clark, Rosenzweig, Long, and Olsen and the Rockefeller Foundation (2003)

Leading indicators are metrics that serve as proxies for impact. They shed light on what and how an organization would need to do to create a desired change; and are used to monitor a ventures progress and performance towards achieving its outcomes and impact.' These specific operational metrics are similar to financial indicators, and can be directly and independently measured and assessed by a venture via its activities and outputs. In the microfinance sector, for example, leading indicators for poverty alleviation would include number of jobs created, loan repayment, and number of repeat clients taking out loans.

Outcomes denote the ultimate desired changes, *or impact,* to be made into society and represent both the intended and unintended side effects of a ventures activities and operations. Measurement using lead indicators helps discern the net portion of an outcome which has been directly influenced by the activities of an organization, versus other external factors that may have caused the change. While it is often very difficult to measure changes in outcomes (especially in the short-term), most ventures have some idea about the outcomes or ultimate social change that they desire. Despite these challenges, outcomes are generally expected to be concretely measureable and should be managed towards achieving the desired results. For example, a microfinance institution's ultimate desired incomes would relate to their ultimate goals of improving life standards, such as, three meals a day and higher savings accounts and income levels.

9.3.2   Approaches to Measuring Social Impact

A variety of approaches have been developed for social impact assessment. These approaches include *tools* that assess performance based on fixed indicators; and *methods* like the *Impact Value Chain* that suggest methodological guidelines and process steps for evaluation. They vary in terms of the **data captured; the use of the data; their application; and the techniques involved.**

9.3.2.1   Data Captured

Social impact assessment is used to capture data on organizational effectiveness, social impact, or both (Figure 8). Data on organizational effectiveness (financial and non-financial) relates to the health, functionality, and efficiency of a social enterprise. This data is used to help track and monitor ongoing operational processes in terms of outputs; and their focus lies in the financial, human capital, and technology, rather than on results and social impact.

Figure 9.6   Data Captured by Measurement Approaches

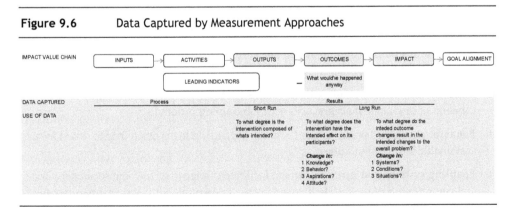

Own illustration based on the Impact Value Chain and Logic Model

On the other hand, social impact data relates to outputs and outcomes (results). Such data used to assess changes in social, cultural, environmental, economic, and/or political conditions in terms of specific interventions, and by the ultimate desired changes to individuals and families, communities and organizations, and/or society and systems.

9.3.2.2   Use of Data

Impact measurement and performance data is used by nonprofits, governments, foundations, social enterprises, and/or social investors, and can be measured in terms of an Intervention and/or the Stage of the Solution. The data is used by enterprises and investors for screening for investment; partnership formation; operations management; scaling; external reporting; exit; and or retrospective evaluation.

Interventions and the Varying Stages of a Solution

Interventions are the planned efforts taken by social enterprises to influence or alter a situation to invoke social change processes. They can be classified into four stages of planning or implementation:

- Stage 1: Defining and understanding the social problem that an enterprise hopes to solve

- Stage 2: Brainstorming ideas and developing an approach to solving the problem

- Stage 3: Demonstrating an approach at a limited scale to test and refine a solution

- Stage 4: Scaling a program and embedding social impact in the status quo

The impact an organization has depends on the degree to which it plans, budgets, and implements its interventions via its *inputs, activities, and outputs* to achieve and manage the desired outcomes and impacts. McKinsey & Company has identified and defined social sector interventions to fall under the following six categories:

- **Knowledge development** for the purpose of solving existing or expected problems (e.g., education in child survival, reproductive health, and HIV/AIDS prevention for the poorest entrepreneurs or education in strategies to manage money and save);

- **Service or product development and delivery** to fulfill the unmet needs of constituents (e.g., loans for the poorest of the poor);

- **Capacity enhancement and skills development** to help organizations improve their capabilities or change their practices (e.g., job training programs);

- **Behavior change** for positive social benefits (e.g., using loans or savings to invest in sustainable farming initiatives);

- **Enabling systems and infrastructure** to facilitate change (e.g., forming social networks and communities of practice to increase borrower accountability and ensure repayment of loan); and

- **Policy development and implementation** to promote or resist change (e.g., **lobbying,** behavior change campaigns, or public will campaigns).

9.3.2.3   Application

Evaluation is used by nonprofits, governments, program clusters, foundations, social enterprises, and/or social investors for *assessment*, *management*, and/or *certification* purposes. Approaches are either generally used to assess interventions in any sector, or are *sector specific*; they are also geographically-specific for use in developing countries, developed countries, or both.

Assessment approaches evaluate the characteristics, practices, results, and/or valuation of an intervention both pre- and post-funding (e.g., Progress Out of Poverty). Results are measured and summarized in terms of a fixed or customized set of indicators, at a specific point in time. Unfortunately, these tools and methods cannot be used to track and manage operational data over the long run.

Management approaches provide information that can be used to monitor progress and manage detailed operational information about the drivers of impact and their results (e.g., Balanced Scorecard that includes Impact). They are used post-investment, and assist social entrepreneurs and their investors to track, learn, and make midcourse corrections to their interventions on an ongoing basis.

Certification is determined by independent, external review, with an objective systematic approach to publicizing the organizations rating, and is based on certain fixed and desirable characteristics (e.g., Fair Trade). This approach serves as a risk reduction mechanism for attracting and retaining consumers and investors. I.e., it assists consumers, investors, and institutions in making purpose driven consumption, investment, and purchasing decisions; and entrepreneurs in managing their double bottom line performance.

9.3.2.4   Techniques Involved

There are three types of techniques that are used to define, gather, and/or assess social impact: (1) Planning; (2) Data Gathering; and Data Evaluation (**Figure 9.7**).

Figure 9.7	3 Types of Techniques Used to Measure Impact

Planning Techniques	Data Gathering Methods	Data Evaluation Methods
Stakeholder Consultation	Interviews	Benchmarking
Logic Model	Focus Groups	Cost Analysis
Issue Mapping	Direct Observations	Descriptive Statistics
Evaluability Model	Participant Surveys	Expert Review
Formative Evaluation	Program Data Collection	Mapping Methods
	External Data Collection	Multidimensional Indices
		Regression Methods
		Strategic Assessments

Own illustration based on TRASI Foundation's Tool's and Resources Catalogue

Planning Techniques relate to the strategies prescribed by a methodology or best practices (e.g., formative evaluation for ongoing decision making or action). On the other hand, *Data Gathering Approaches* refer to methods involved in obtaining data (such as, interviews, direct observations, etc.). Finally, *Data Evaluation Methods* describe approaches that are used to inform judgment and conclusion (e.g., benchmarking and cost analysis).

9.3.3   Issues in Measuring the Performance of Social Enterprises

While donor and lenders of social enterprises desire to know where their money is going, and social entrepreneurs wish to evaluate the effect of their organization's work in both the short- and long-run, there are difficulties and challenges in measuring, interpreting, and communicating social impact and performance measures.

Currently, there is a discrepancy between the commitment made by stakeholders to creating a positive social or environmental impact and their actual impact. This is because almost all of the measurement approaches for social impact (1) in terms of cost and/or time, may not feasible for the average social entrepreneur or grant giving organization; (2) may be subject to credibility and validity issues, especially since most outcomes are self reported, do not follow an established industry standard; and/or (3) may need to be used in combination with several other approaches to provide a 'big picture' of the performance of an organization – which may only be observable in the long-run.

The challenge has been in the creation of an evaluation system that is affordable, and that combines and balances the assessment of impact (for investors or investment managers) with the assessment for impact (for the social enterprise and its beneficiaries). So far, since most models have typically been developed by investors for investors, the latter, which is far more critical in the creation of impact, has not been a viable option for the cash-strapped social entrepreneurs and their stakeholders. The fragmented development of methodologies and social impact metrics has also limited the use and comparability of the effectiveness and efficiency of the results produced by social ventures.

Since most approaches are proprietary, a commonly accepted standard does not exist with social impact metrics. A system of indicators is absolutely critical for the field as it is useful for academic and practitioners alike. There must be an agreed upon model which defines: (1) a minimal set of common metrics for measurement; (2) common tools for collecting metrics; and (3) common reporting tools with common formats. Best practices will set the stage for increased comparability and increased credibility in the field.

9.4 Case Study

Kiva is a not for profit organization with a mission to connect people through lending to alleviate poverty that was founded by two social entrepreneurs – Matt Flannery and Jessica Jackley – in October 2005. Kiva is a person-to-person micro-lending site that connects over 600,000 individual lenders to 136 microfinance institutions (MFI's/Field Partners) in over 60 countries. These individuals make loans via MFI's of as little as $25 to social entrepreneurs, primarily women, who lack access to traditional banking systems. In addition to individual lenders, who often make optional donations, Kiva is funded by individual and institutional investors, grant makers, corporate sponsors, and foundations.

Kiva's investments account for over $240,000 in loans made to poor social entrepreneurs. While Kiva does not pay a financial return, they return your capital in full and promise an implied social impact via the loan.

Kiva Fellows are a group of over 450 volunteers that work with the MFI's to administer and channel the loans in the field. They also visit and interview the borrowers; and edit and translate their stories for reporting and communication via online journals and blogs.

Kiva has been using Kiva Fellows to help MFI's complete the CERISE Social Performance Indicators (SPI) Assessment. This excel based tool focuses on process management to compare an MFI's intentions with its actions to determine whether or not an institution has the means to attain its social objectives. It analyzes social performance using indicators that have been grouped under four dimensions. This tool has been designed to compare institutions, promote peer group analysis, and analyze the relationship between social and financial performance.

In recent years, social performance has become an increasingly important topic for investors, lenders, and grant makers. So far, Kiva reports their performance with indicators that they claim are proxies for impact; that indirectly helps determine how many people they have connected to achieve their mission of alleviating poverty.[20] Aside from fellow reports, they do not employ any other measures for assessing the social impact created by their loans. As a result, the Rockefellar Foundation provided Kiva with a $300,000 grant to help them develop and deploy social performance measurement (agreed upon metrics) across its platform to promote transparency and accountability, and attract more stakeholders to the industry. Similarly, Fishman-Hillard has provided Kiva with pro-bono communications support to help them generate awareness of one-to-one lending and ultimately attract new lenders, borrowers, MFIs and partners to the industry. Nonetheless, MFI social impact measurement and performance reporting is still uncommon, and not required by Kiva.

---

[20] Kiva indicator include: (1) Kiva Lenders; (2) Loans; (3) Repayment Rate; (4) Field Partners; (5) Number of Volunteers around the world; (6) Number of countries they help lend to.

Questions

1. How can measurement benefit and/or hurt its investors, lenders, Kiva, its MFIs, an end users?

2. What are Kiva's challenge to measuring and managing it social impact?

3. How can Kiva help compare the impacts of a loan made via local MFIs in a developed country versus an underdeveloped country?

4. How can Kiva measure, communicate, and differentiate the impact made by the investments made by Rockefeller Foundation and Fishman-Hillard?

9.5   Further Reading

[1]   Clark, C, et all. Double Bottom Line Project Report: Assessing Social Impact in Double Bottom
      Line   Ventures: Methods   Catalogue.   January   2004.   www.riseproject.org/
      DBL_Methods_Catalog.pdf.
[2]   Emerson, J. and Sprizter, J. (2007), *From Fragmentation to Function: Critical Concepts and Writings on
      Social Capital Markets, Structure, Operation, and Innovation.* October 2007.
[3]   Olsen, S. et al. (2008), *Catalog of Approaches to Impact Measurement: Assessing Social Impact in Private
      Sector,* Version 1.1. May 2008.
[4]   O'Donohoe, N, et al. (2010), *Impact Investments: An Emerging Asset Class.* November 2010.

9.6   Bibliography

[1]   Acumen Fund et al. (2007), *Impact Reporting & Investment Standards (IRIS).* April 2007. www.iris-
      standards.org.
[2]   Bonbright, D. (2007), *The Keystone Method, Keystone Accountability,* London.
[3]   Bonini S. and Emerson J. (2005), *Maximizing Blended Value – Building Beyond the Blended Value Map
      to Sustainable Investing, Philanthropy and Organizations.* January 2005.
[4]   Clark, C, et al. (2004), *Double Bottom Line Project Report: Assessing Social Impact in Double Bottom Line
      Ventures: Methods Catalogue.* January 2004. www.riseproject.org/DBL_Methods_Catalog.pdf.
[5]   Clark C. (2009), *Social Impact Assessment and Building Your SROI.* January 2009, GSVC Mentor
      Workshop.
[6]   Dees, J.G. (2003), *Scaling for Social Impact: Designing Effective Strategies for Spreading Social Innova-
      tions.* Center for the Advancement of Social Entrepreneurship, Duke University, The Fuqua School
      of Business, November 2003.
[7]   Emerson, J. *The 21st Century Foundation: Building Upon the Past, Creating for the Future.* Undated.
[8]   Emerson, J. (2003), *The Blended Value Map: Tracking the Intersects and Opportunities of Economic,
      Social and Environmental Value Creation.* October, 2003.
[9]   Emerson, J. and Sprizter, J. (2007), *From Fragmentation to Function: Critical Concepts and Writings on
      Social Capital Markets, Structure, Operation, and Innovation.* October 2007.
[10] Kramer, M., Parkhurst, M. and Vaidananathan, L. (2009), *Breakthroughs in Shared Measurement &
      Social Impact.* July 2009.
[11] Kramer, M. and Cooch, S. (2006), *Investing for Impact: Managing and Measuring Proactive Social
      Investments.* Foundation. Strategy Group for the Shell Foundation, January 2006.
[12] Nicholls, A. (2009), *'We Do Good Things, Don't We?': 'Blended Value Accounting' in social entrepre-
      neurship,* in Accounting, Organizations and Society, 34, 2009, pp. 755–769.
[13] Olsen, S. et al. (2008), *Catalog of Approaches to Impact Measurement: Assessing Social Impact in Private
      Sectors.* Verson 1.1. May 2008.
[14] Tuan, M. (2008), *Measuring And/Or Estimating Social Value Creation: Insights Into Eight Integrated
      Cost Approaches.* December 2008.
[15] Zeller, M. (2003), *Measuring Social Performance of Micro-Finance Institutions: A Proposal.* October
      2003.

10 Strategies for Scaling in Social Entrepreneurship

Andreas Heinecke

European Business School
Department of Strategy, Organization & Leadership
Danone Chair for Social Business

Judith Mayer

Technische Universität München
Chair in Entrepreneurial Finance, supported by KfW Bankengruppe
Center for Entrepreneurial and Financial Studies (CEFS)

Learning goals
Upon completing this chapter, you should be able to accomplish the following:

- Explain the difference between organizational growth and replication by others.

- Explain major scaling strategies and their distinctive features.

- Understand advantages and disadvantages of the scaling strategies.

- Recognize the perspective of social investors towards scaling.

- Explain implications of scaling and how hurdles could be overcome.

10.1   Introduction

The concept of social entrepreneurship is getting a lot of attention from the business-, the educational-, and research field (Hoogendoorn, Pennings and Thurik, 2010). Several business schools have set up centers for education and research in the area of social entrepreneurship and many articles dealing with social entrepreneurship have been published within the last 10 years. However, there is not yet a common definition (Mair and Marti, 2006). According to chapter two of Huybrechts and Nicholls in this book, we define social entrepreneurs as individuals who try to solve a social problem with an entrepreneurial approach. The pursuit of a double bottom line with social and financial goals typically distinguishes social enterprises from for-profit enterprises and nonprofit organizations (Martin and Osberg, 2007).

Former US President Bill Clinton once said: "Nearly every problem has been solved by someone, somewhere. The challenge of the 21st century is to find out what works and scale it up." (quoted in Olson, 1994). Practitioners as well as researchers put high emphasis on the importance of scaling successful approaches of social enterprises (Bloom and Smith, 2010; Tracey and Jarvis, 2007). Funding organizations emphasize the entrepreneur's ability to scale his approach as a crucial selection criterion for investment decisions. Investors who provide equity or debt to social enterprises often demand scaling in order to guarantee refund of their resources. Sometimes, scaling successful approaches is even seen as an "obligation" of social enterprises in order to increase the number of beneficiaries and improve the social impact (Ahlert et al., 2008).

Scaling is defined according to Dees (2008) as "increasing the impact [...] [of an approach] to better match the magnitude of the social need or problem it seeks to address". The definition of scaling already indicates that scaling of social enterprises does not correspond to growth of business enterprises. Whereas the former focus on expanding the impact for society, which is hardly measurable, the latter mainly focus on parameters like economic success or shareholder value (Uvin, 2000). Thus, scaling of social enterprises does not necessarily imply organizational growth, but includes replication of the approach by others as well. Furthermore, business enterprises benefit from increased revenues as well as decreasing costs per unit due to economies of scale when they are growing. In contrast, social enterprises often have limited possibilities to generate own income and mostly offer services that require big adaptations to local peculiarities and thus provide only minor possibilities for economies of scale. Another important distinction is that social enterprises rarely offer mainstream products or services like many business enterprises, but rather address niches. Thus, it is not possible to simply transfer growth strategies of business companies to scaling of social enterprises.

In the following, strategies for scaling of social enterprises will be outlined and promoting as well as inhibiting factors to scaling will be named. While addressing barriers to scaling, solutions are identified as well.

10.2   Theory on Scaling

In general, it is distinguished, whether a social organization is scaling deep, i.e., addressing more aspects of a single problem in order to provide a more holistic solution, or scaling wide, i.e., increasing the number of beneficiaries (Bloom and Chatterji, 2009). This chapter mainly focuses on scaling wide. However, most aspects can be transferred to scaling deep as well.

10.2.1   Prerequisites

Before scaling their approaches, social entrepreneurs have to consider several prerequisites. First of all, social enterprises should have identified a precise definition of their mission and their core values as well as developed an established business model (Dees, Anderson, and Wei-Skillern, 2004). Furthermore, there must be an objective evidence of success often referred to as "proof of concept" i.a. to emphasize the relevance of scaling in front of stakeholders and to obtain acceptance when targeting a new area (Roob and Bradach, 2009). If scaling takes place too early or too quickly and takes up too many resources of a social enterprise, there is a danger that advancing the enterprise's approach is sacrificed to maximize scale. Thus, it might be better to scale the approach to a limited extent in the first place. After a reevaluation, it might be scaled further. An illustrative lifecycle of a social enterprise that takes into account the considerations mentioned above, is presented in **Figure 10.1**.

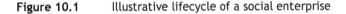

Figure 10.1   Illustrative lifecycle of a social enterprise

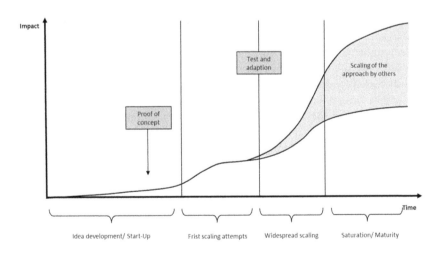

Own illustration

The x-axis displays time and the y-axis the impact achieved. In order to measure the impact key performance indicators are defined. A common measure to express impact is number of beneficiaries. Certainly, the impact will not always increase as smoothly as illustrated in the figure, but may decrease at times due to reasons like economic condition or bad management. However, decreasing impact is neglected in the figure due to reasons of simplification. As will be shown in the following, scaling does not take place just within a single organization. Instead, organizations could collaborate with others and imitators may appear that further scale the approach. Replication of the approach by others is depicted in the grey area.

Besides strategy, organizational resources for scaling should be in place (Dees, Anderson, and Wei-Skillern, 2004). Resources include, for example, capital, managerial talent and local knowledge. Furthermore, the circumstances under which an approach should be applied have to be considered and it has to be determined whether the approach can be adapted to changing conditions and whether there is a clear social need as well as sufficient market potential. When an organization has proofed that its approach is ready to scale, the question of how to reach scale arises.

10.2.2   Scaling Strategies

Referring to Dees Anderson and Wei-Skillern (2004), we focus on dissemination, affiliation, and branching. Furthermore, franchising as a form of tight affiliation is mentioned.

10.2.2.1   Dissemination

Dissemination is comparable to the open source approach in IT. The founding organization makes its social innovation available by providing information and sometimes technical assistance to others interested in replicating the approach (Dees, Anderson, and Wei-Skillern, 2004). The main advantages are the speed of reaching scale and low costs and efforts. Furthermore, people adopting an approach of an existing organization to their region know local peculiarities and take them into account. A disadvantage lies in the lack of control mechanisms for the original organization regarding who replicates the approach and whether they preserve its quality (Ahlert et al., 2008). Open source approaches seem to be more appropriate for social enterprises than for business enterprises because social enterprises have the primary goal of increasing their social impact and thus focus mainly on value creation for society. In contrast, business enterprises seek to capture the value created using their approach and thus primarily strive for value appropriation of their owners (Santos, 2009). Common strategies for dissemination are publications (e.g., brochures, manuals, and public speeches), training, consulting and definition of standards sometimes in conjunction with accreditations.

Example of dissemination – Montessori Schools
The training methods of Montessori schools are an example for a dissemination strategy. Maria Montessori developed a concept for kindergartens and basic education that focuses on self-determined learning in the early 20th century. The approach quickly attracted interest from others. In order to give them the possibility to implement the approach, a book explaining the concept was published, trainings for teachers were offered and educational material was made accessible. Nowadays, the concept is applied in schools all over the world. **(www.montessori-ami.org)**

10.2.2.2   Affiliation

Affiliation is another type of scaling. It is defined as the collaboration of a parent organization with one or more partners who are responsible for the implementation of the approach in a specific area. The relationship is defined by an agreement between the parent organization and its partners. Agreements may have general or specific guidelines concerning areas such as the use of a common brand name, program content, funding responsibilities, and reporting requirements (Dees, Anderson, and Wei-Skillern, 2004). The relationship between both parties can range from loose cooperation between organizations sharing the same mission to strongly linked affiliate systems. In case of tighter systems, it is referred to social franchising. Affiliates normally benefit from network synergies. In comparison to dissemination, affiliation allows the parent to gain more control over its adopters. However, compared to dissemination, affiliation takes longer to establish, and needs more resources as well as more support from the originating organization. Since local partners are involved, affiliation also takes geographic peculiarities into account. Two common forms of affiliation of business enterprises are joint ventures and licensing. In a joint venture, two or more partners found a new company and share know-how, resources, and risks. Licensing refers to transferring rights like the right to use intellectual property to license holders.

Example of affiliation – Parliamentwatch (German: abgeordnetenwatch)
Parliamentwatch offers a webpage where citizens can inform themselves about parliament members and ask them their questions. The aim of Parliamentwatch is to increase political transparency and participation of citizens in the democratic process. They have implemented their approach for most German parliaments as well as for German representatives in the EU parliament. In order to scale its approach across German borders, Parliamentwatch offers to partner with interested entrepreneurs or organizations. Parliamentwatch sets up the website for the partners, offers maintenance and gives partners access to their system. On exchange, partners pay a monthly license fee. Partners are free to operate under their own names and each partner adapts the approach to the political framework of its own country. In addition to technical services, Parliamentwatch offers a lot of information material. So far, partner organizations have been set up in Austria and Luxembourg. **(www.abgeordnetenwatch.de/international-248-0.html)**

10.2.2.3   Social Franchising

Social franchising is a very tight form of affiliation. Recently, it gained significant promi-
nence in the social sector (Tracey and Jarvis, 2007). Franchising offers the possibility to
adopt an already proven approach and to benefit from network synergies as well as systematic know-how transfers among franchisor and its franchisees. Similar to business franchises, social franchises allow a large number of units to operate under the same business
model and brand name in different locations (Hackl, 2009). Within franchising systems,
brand consistency is regarded as critical to mobilizing resources because consistent appearance of the individual units seems to facilitate the creation of reputation, trust as well as
visibility of the brand (Ahlert et al., 2008). However, social entrepreneurs have to be aware
of the threat of mission drift and reputational loss: If a franchisee presents himself in a way
which contradicts the mission of the founding organization, the reputation of the organization as a whole can get damaged. Therefore, the franchisor has to select his franchisees
carefully considering characteristics such as trustworthiness or allegiance. Furthermore, he
should set up appropriate control mechanisms. However, this is a difficult balancing act
because independence of franchisees is considered as an important aspect of social franchising (Ahlert et al., 2008). Compared to franchising of business enterprises, reporting and
justification of the franchisees are often neglected in the early stages of social franchising.
Furthermore, franchising of social enterprises is often not conducted as systematically as
franchising of business enterprises and regulated approaches are often developed too late
(Schöning, 2007). As social enterprises mostly offer services, it is often hard to define the
value proposition for the franchisees besides brand name and initial know-how transfer.

Example of social franchising – Dialogue in the Dark
Dialogue in the Dark offers exhibitions where blind guides lead visitors in total darkness.
After opening exhibitions and offering workshops in Germany, the founder, Andreas Heinecke, has scaled his approach via social franchising to over 30 countries. Within his model
only basic standards are defined to ensure a quality level. The model is depicted in the
following **Figure 10.2. (www.dialogue-in-the-dark.com)**

Figure 10.2   Franchising model of Dialogue in the Dark

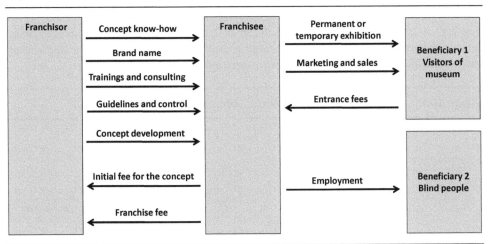

Own illustration based on Hackl (2009)

10.2.2.4   Branching

Branching refers to the creation of local sites through one organization, similar to company owned stores, offices, or plants in the business world (Dees, Anderson, and Wei-Skillern, 2004). It represents the strategy in which scaling can be controlled best by the founding organization. Thus, branch structures are particularly convenient when successful implementation of the approach depends on tight quality control, specific practices and tacit knowledge (Dees, Anderson, and Wei-Skillern, 2004). A central coordination of all branches may help to build a recognized brand, exploit economies of scale, and transfer intangible assets such as culture (Dees, Anderson, and Wei-Skillern, 2004). However, there is the risk that the central organization focuses too much on coordination of its subsidiaries and thereby disregards the day-to-day running of its business leading to decreasing quality in service provision. High costs resulting from the need of more resources and slow progress in reaching scale denote further drawbacks. Additionally, it is difficult for a central organization to take local peculiarities into account as it mostly lacks local knowledge (Ahlert et al., 2008).

Example of branching – Ashoka

In 1980 Bill Drayton founded "Ashoka – Innovators for the Public" in the US. Ashoka supports leading social entrepreneurs by providing living stipends as well as non-financial support and helps to build an infrastructure for social enterprises. Nowadays, Ashoka is represented in over 60 countries worldwide. All subsidiaries of Ashoka pursue the same mission of promoting positive social change. Ashoka has managed to provide high quality services and build up strong networks in all countries where it is represented. The ultimate decision-making power over the selection of leading social entrepreneurs resides by an international board in order to guarantee that the standards of Ashoka are maintained by every subsidiary. **(www.ashoka.org)**

10.2.3   Choosing the Appropriate Scaling Strategy

Social entrepreneurs have to consider several aspects, before deciding which strategy to apply. Generally, there are strategies with rather tight or loose control of scaling. Furthermore, the resources required for a specific strategy have to be considered. The approaches can be classified according to the framework depicted in **Figure 10.3**.

Figure 10.3   Scaling Strategies of Social Enterprises

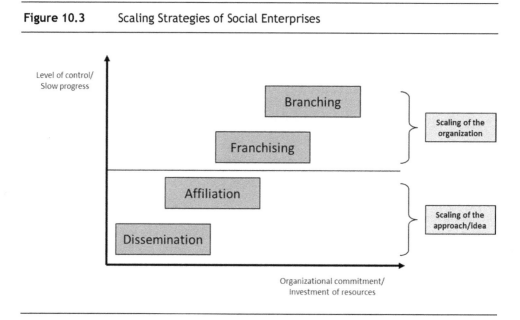

Own illustration based on Ahlert et al. (2008)

While dissemination and loose affiliation require lower commitment and may scale an approach more quickly, these benefits are only of value if the approach is spread in a form that guarantees the required quality standard. In some cases, greater coordination and slower scaling via branching might be desirable to assure high quality despite the high costs that branching brings along (Dees, Anderson, and Wei-Skillern, 2004).

Branching has been applied frequently by business enterprises and is therefore well-known and researched. In contrast, there is not much knowledge on dissemination strategies (Waitzer and Paul, 2011). Previous studies have shown that social enterprises tend to use dissemination or affiliation strategies instead of branching due to the increasing organizational complexity and the high funding requirements that branching induces (Waitzer and Paul, 2011). Often, different scaling strategies are combined to reach the full scaling potential of an approach.

10.2.4   Scalability from the Perspective of Investors

Achleitner and Heister (2009) investigated the assessment of scalability of social enterprises by social investors. According to their framework, scalability is positively influenced by the utility perceived by stakeholders. The utility gain of stakeholders has an even greater influence on scalability, when stakeholders have possibilities to influence the success of a social enterprise. In fact, it has been shown that ideas spread more quickly when recognition for their success is shared (Waitzer and Paul, 2011). Another factor positively related to scalability is the percentage of service provided by the target group and other persons not working for the social enterprise. By empowering stakeholders to take part in the service provision process of a social enterprise, dependence on the founding organization is decreased and thereby transferability is increased. Thus, beneficiaries and other stakeholders should be integrated into the service provision process of a social enterprise and thereby be transformed into co-creators (Waitzer and Paul, 2011). Others have fewer possibilities to participate in the service provision process if a great amount of know-how is required. Thus, the factor "service provision of target group and others" is negatively moderated by the knowledge necessary for service provision (Achleitner and Heister, 2009). Figure 4 depicts the relations.

Figure 10.4   Factors influencing scalability

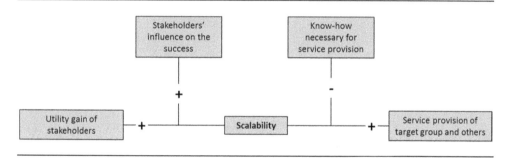

Own illustration based on Achleitner and Heister (2009)

10.3   Implications of Scaling: Barriers and Solutions

In the past, scaling of social enterprises took place quite slowly and seemed cumbersome due to barriers like financial and human resource mobilization (Hoogendoorn, Zwan, and Thurik, 2011). Hoogendorn, Zwan and Thurik (2011) even talk about social enterprises as start-up phenomena that rarely overcome the start-up stage. In the following, barriers to scaling are named and categorized into managerial factors relating to quality control and factors relating to human resources and financing. Potential solutions are also identified. Figure 5 shows the barriers integrated into the lifecycle of a social enterprise. While financing seems to be scarce all the time, it especially constitutes a problem after the initial start-up phase till maturity. Funders either provide low amounts, only sufficient for surviving during early start-up, or make deals that are not suited the financing needs of scaling activities because the deals are, e.g., too large or contractual agreements do not fit scaling (Milligan and Schöning, 2011). Other barriers relate to human resources of a social enterprise because new staff with relevant management skills is often hard to find. Quality control becomes important when others replicate an approach of a social enterprise. See **Figure 10.5**.

Figure 10.5   Hurdles within the lifecycle

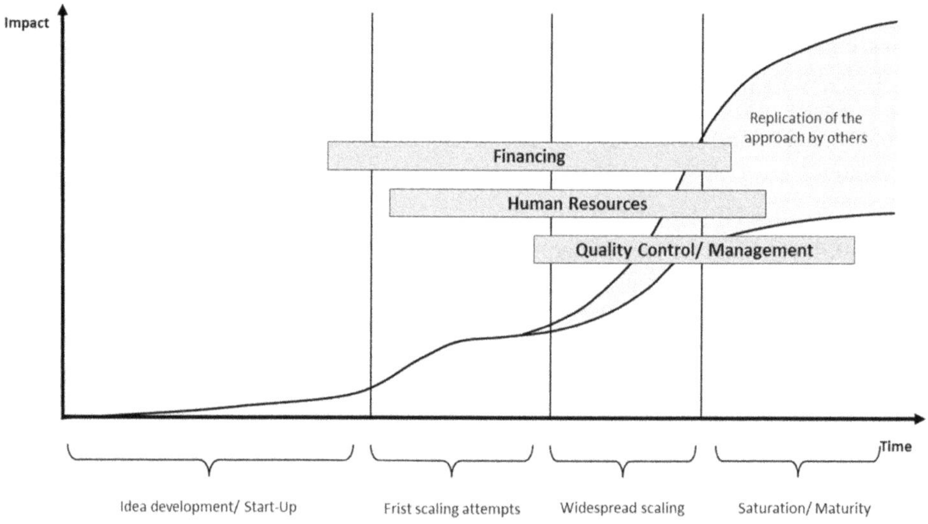

Own illustration

10.3.1   Financing

Social enterprises have a wide range of funding possibilities that even go beyond traditional sources and instruments of business enterprises or conventional nonprofit organizations (see *Financing of Social Entrepreneurship* in this book). Venture philanthropy funds e.g., apply principles of venture capital to the funding of social enterprises. Despite the various possibilities, access to finance is still perceived as a strong barrier to scaling (Hoogendoorn, Zwan, and Thurik, 2011).

10.3.1.1   Internal Financing

Concerning internal financing, social enterprises have the possibility to charge fees for their services. Fees are either paid by beneficiaries, by third parties, or by public authorities. Beneficiaries are often not able to pay for the service they receive (Glaeser and Shleifer, 2001). Furthermore, public funding imposes high liabilities on social enterprises and governments are often not prepared to cater the specific funding needs of social enterprises.

In order to solve the problems concerning internal financing, social enterprises could try to generate additional revenue streams, e.g., by selling merchandising products. Furthermore, governments should develop funding programs taking into account the specific characteristics of social enterprises. Governments could strengthen market mechanisms, especially competition, in the social sector by regularly inviting tenders to apply for funding and linking funding to the impact achieved. The government of Australia already allocates funds to social enterprises by giving out licenses for addressing problems that were formerly handled by governmental organizations. Those licenses are reallocated regularly (Obermüller, 2009).

10.3.1.2   External Financing

External financing possibilities of social enterprises include grants, equity, debt, mezzanine capital and hybrid capital (see *Financing of Social Entrepreneurship* in this book). It is difficult to obtain external financing for scaling activities because foundations and other investors like to see themselves as "social change agents" and therefore primarily fund new and innovative projects instead of scaling processes (Ahlert et al., 2008; Sharir and Lerner, 2006). Classical for-profit investors mostly retain from funding social enterprises as the legal form of social enterprises often restricts profit distribution and they mostly do not have the necessary know-how to fund social enterprises. Furthermore, social enterprises often lack knowledge about financing options for their venture and therefore do not address social investors properly.

In order to attract more investors to finance scaling of social enterprises, governments could set up programs that take on the risks related to financing social enterprises. Such programs include co-investments, guarantees or underwriting of loans. Experiences of Venturesome, a social investment fund, suggest that giving out guarantees for social enterprises actually requires only small amounts of money as the funds go undrawn in 90% of the cases (Venturesome, 2009). More information on external financing is also given in the chapter *"Financing of Social Entrepreneurship"* within this book. Furthermore, financial education of social entrepreneurs needs to be enhanced. A very good first step constitutes the Social Investment Manual (Achleitner et al., 2011).

10.3.2   Human Resources

Concerning human resources of a social enterprise, the founder and his team have to be considered. The founder is treated separately because practitioners as well as researchers put high emphasis on the founding entrepreneur. The social innovation school of thought observes the individual when researching social entrepreneurship (Hoogendoorn, Pennings, and Thurik, 2010) and awards are mostly granted to innovators instead of innovations (see Ashoka, Schwab Foundation for Social Entrepreneurship and Skoll Foundation). Sharir and Lerner (2006) even state that a founder's resignation is likely to induce a collapse of a social enterprise.

10.3.2.1   Founder Level

The founder often seems to be the bottleneck in times of scaling due to several reasons. First, a single person cannot be at every location at every time and thus needs to delegate a great amount of his work. However, social entrepreneurs are quite reluctant to give up control (Waitzer and Paul, 2011). Second, social entrepreneurs rarely possess all skills necessary for scaling. Often a lack of management capabilities poses a challenge. Limited creativity in adapting business models, e.g., often results in small income from revenue streams, another inhibiting factor. Third, the personality of the social entrepreneur might not fit scaling and social entrepreneurs often get frustrated during scaling (Dees, 2008) because their tasks change. During start-up, social entrepreneurs fulfill operational tasks that include working directly with the target group as well as strategic tasks, their work during scaling is mainly concerned with strategic purposes and includes governance of their organizations in large part. Additionally, social entrepreneurs have no incentive to become managers of large organizations when they only get paid a fraction of the salary of traditional managers. The problem of overreliance on a single person is especially relevant when thinking about succession.

Instead of transforming social entrepreneurs into managers of large organizations, it might be a good idea to replace the founder by a more appropriate manager when an organization gets too big to handle for the founder. Replacing the founder would free him up for new developments. The public, especially funding organizations and the research field, need to stop focusing on a single person and instead emphasize the importance of a team that possesses all relevant skills. If skills are missing, investors could demand a completion of the team as a prerequisite for their investment. Additionally, social entrepreneurs need professional coaching to disseminate their approaches. A central question is, how social entrepreneurs can learn to let others take over their approach (Waitzer and Paul, 2011). Social entrepreneurs need to be aware that they are inhibiting creative initiatives of replicators if they are acting in a way that is too self-absorbed (Bloom and Chatterji, 2009). In order to survive over the long term, succession plans have to be developed early on. Succession plans are of high relevance because social entrepreneurs are more often found in higher age categories than business entrepreneurs (Hoogendoorn, Zwan, and Thurik, 2011).

10.3.2.2   Staff Level

Concerning the team, social enterprises work with employed staff and volunteers. It is often assumed that staff and volunteers in the social sector have a high intrinsic motivation that compensates for low salaries (Mirvis and Hackett, 1983). In the beginning, social entrepreneurs are sometimes supported by their friends and family. In order to scale an approach, it is not a good strategy to rely strongly on intrinsic motivation and the help of family and friends. It is questionable, whether the team that enabled a social enterprise to reach its current level is appropriate for scaling because the former staff is often not prepared and motivated to fulfill management tasks that scaling brings along (Waitzer and Paul, 2011). Furthermore, the team is often unsatisfied with scaling because the working climate changes and more emphasis is put on efficiency instead of soft factors like visible outcome of their own work. However, when those people are alienated, a part of the spirit of the organization gets lost. New talented and capable staff members are difficult to attract because they often have no motivation to work in the social sector as salaries and prestige are low. Furthermore, it is hard to find persons with a mindset appropriate to the value proposition of social enterprises: focusing on the social value but also keeping in mind financial sustainability. The goal structure should be aligned in order to minimize agency conflicts.

Incentives to work for a social enterprise should be created in order to attract skilled personnel. Solutions might include forms of extrinsic motivation like recognition. Once people experience the endowment with meaning when working for a social enterprise, they might develop intrinsic motivation of their own. In order to motivate young people, governments could incorporate working at a social enterprise within programs like voluntary year of social services. Furthermore, topics related to social entrepreneurship should be included in management education like MBA programs to increase the awareness of such topics among students (Pirson and Bloom, 2011). For experienced management consultants, the possibility of a social leave could be set up, similar to a PhD- or MBA-leave. After the leave, the employees have the possibility to get back into their prior career. Thereby, experienced consultants could overcome the fear of stepping backwards in their career when working for a social enterprise. Similar programs could be structured by non-consulting companies in order to lend experienced managers to social enterprises for a limited amount of time. A good example is the I-Cats program of LGT Venture Philanthropy which offers scholarships for managers supporting selected social enterprises (http://www.icatsprogram.com/). The same could be done for outplacement of elder employees. Furthermore, pro bono services like free consulting or legal advice will always be important and should be promoted in corporate volunteering programs in order to assign volunteers based on their expertise.

10.3.3   Quality Control and Management

Social entrepreneurs need to have a clear strategy in order to scale successfully. However, social entrepreneurs often do not advance their scaling systematically but rather act arbitrary, seizing opportunities when they seem convenient. In order to avoid misuse of their approach, quality checks need to be in place. However, social enterprises face several challenges concerning a controlled scaling of their approaches.

10.3.3.1   Difficulties Concerning Quality Management

Controlling the replication of an approach is difficult because transparency is low and measures for social performance are limited (Achleitner et al., 2009; Austin, Stevenson, and Wei-Skillern, 2006). Furthermore, it is often not possible for social enterprises to apply for a patent in order to protect their approach from misuse because social entrepreneurs mostly offer services not suited for patents. Additionally, it is hard to judge whether adopters are serious about implementing an approach. In contrast to adopters of business models, adopters in the social sector often do not have to provide start-up-capital, because the initial costs are covered by someone else like a franchisor or a donor (Ahlert et al., 2008). Thus, adopters might behave opportunistically and their motivation to stick to the rules might be lower because there is no danger of capital loss (Ahlert et al., 2008). In case of the misuse of an approach, social entrepreneurs often have no possibility to sanction such behavior as there are mostly no contractual agreements that would enable them to enforce such an action.

10.3.3.2   Approaches to Ensure Quality

To overcome the problem of lack of transparency, performance indicators used by social enterprises should be gathered and consolidated to set up a pool of consistent measures. Programs like Social Reporting Standard (http://social-reporting-standard.de/) or Impact Reporting Investment Standards (http://iris.thegiin.org/) are already addressing this short-coming. However, those programs need to be spread more in order to accomplish higher consistency and transparency. Instead of applying for patents, social enterprises could at least protect their trademark to avoid misuse or dilution of their brand name. Further pos-sibilities to protect approaches of social enterprises include auditing, certifications, licens-ing fees, or setting up umbrella organizations that charge fees for membership. Fees induce that only persons that are serious about implementation join because misconduct would lead to exclusion (Gugerty, 2009). Furthermore, social entrepreneurs need coaching on how to evaluate concepts like empathy, trust, credibility, solidarity or endurance in order to assess adopters. Organizations like Ashoka might advise social entrepreneurs on the evalu-ation of adopters because their selection process takes into account such criteria.

10.4   Outlook

Considering barriers related to resource mobilization, it might be a good strategy for social entrepreneurs to partner with organizations that can provide the necessary infrastructure: After a social entrepreneur developed an idea, got it ready for the market and scaled it to a limited extent, he could partner with existing nonprofit organizations that possess the in-frastructure and overhead needed to further scale his approach. By delegating a great amount of his responsibilities, a social entrepreneur would have time to develop new ideas. Thereby, social entrepreneurs would be turned into research and development facilities of larger organizations. Alliances of social entrepreneurs with larger organizations have previously been described as alliances of bees and tress (Mulgan et al., 2006). By partnering with well-known organizations, the viability of a social enterprise is increased. Furthermore, it is unlikely that well-known organizations misuse an approach as they would risk damaging their entire reputation. However, large organizations are often perceived as rigid and detrimental to innovations. So far, social entrepreneurs seem to be quite reluctant to cooperating with others in the sector.

Example for cooperation with nonprofit organization: Childline and Unicef
Childline, founded in 1986, offers a free and confidential hotline for children and young people in the UK. In order to scale its approach, Childline began to cooperate with Unicef in 2007. Childline gave Unicef the right to promote its service internationally using the concept as well as the name of Childline. In case of misuse of their concept, Childline pertains the possibility to withdraw these rights from Unicef. With the help and funding of Unicef, Childline has reached further countries such as Malaysia, India and Trinidad and Tobago. **(www.childline.org.uk)**

It is also conceivable that social entrepreneurs partner with business enterprises. However, the risk of a mission drift has to be kept in mind when partnering with for-profit organizations.

Example for cooperation with business enterprise: Grameen and Danone
Grameen and Danone entered a joint venture in 2006 to produce and distribute yogurts for children to fight malnutrition and provide employment possibilities in Bangladesh. Via this cooperation, Danone's expertise in health foods as well as financing was brought together with Grameen's market knowledge.
(www.danone.com/en/what-s-new/focus-4.html)

Sometimes, a social enterprise's approach is not suited for wide scaling. A reason might be that the approach does not work under changing conditions. In that case, social entrepreneurs should rather stick to their region and scale deep by reducing the problem's negative impact more dramatically and increasing the quality of their services.

Example for scaling deep: Iq consult
Iq consult, founded in 1994, initially just provided job training for unemployed and disadvantaged people in Berlin, Germany. Until today, iq consult has not spread widely or been replicated elsewhere. Instead, iq consult has expanded its impact by extending its program. Nowadays, iq consult provides training, mentoring as well as funding to long-term unemployed people who aim to become self-employed. Furthermore, Norbert Kunz, the founder, seeks to sensitize private and public decision makers for the topic of supporting long-term unemployed people and thereby indirectly widens its impact by targeting a system change. **(www.iq-consult.com)**

10.5   Case Study

Andreas Heinecke has founded "Dialogue in the Dark" in 1988. He is a senior Ashoka Fellow and has been honored by the Schwab Foundation as an outstanding social entrepreneur. For a description of Dialogue Social Enterprise (DSE) please see the case study in the chapter *Financing of Social Entrepreneurship* and *Collaboration and Partnerships* in this book. As described beforehand, DSE applies franchising to scale its concept of Dialogue in the Dark. Together with Ashoka, the founder, Andreas Heinecke, identified hurdles to scaling that DSE was facing. The hurdles are presented in the following **Figure 10.6**.

Figure 10.6   Lifecycle of Dialogue Social Enterprise

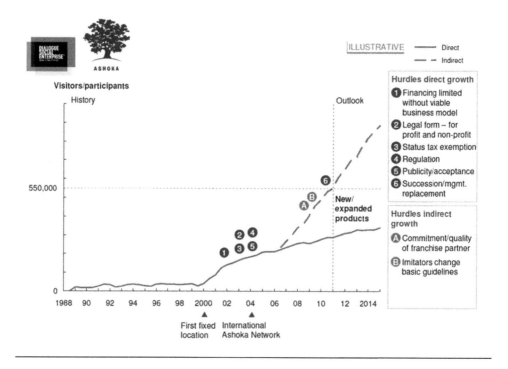

Own illustration based on Ashoka

In addition to scaling the exhibitions via franchising, DSE also scaled deep. Business workshops for teams and leaders were developed and are now conducted in Germany together with Allianz Global Investors[21]. Furthermore, DSE expanded by offering exhibitions and workshops on non-verbal communication (called Dialogue in Silence).

---

[21]   For more information please see: http://dialogue.allianzgi.com/en/Pages/default.aspx

Questions:

1. What are the advantages and disadvantages of the chosen scaling strategy?

2. What is the value proposition for the franchisees of Dialogue Social Enterprise?

3. What can be solutions to tackle the hurdles shown in Figure 10.6?

4. What would be your advice for further scaling the approach of DSE?

10.6   Further Reading

[1] Ahlert, D., Ahlert, M., Duon Dinh, H.V., Fleisch, H., Heußler, T., Kilee, L. and Meuter, J. (2008), *Social Franchising: A Way of Systematic Replication to Increase Social Impact*, Bundesverband Deutscher Stiftungen, Berlin.

[2] Dees, J.G., Anderson, B.B. and Wei-Skillern, J. (2004), "Scaling social impact", in *Stanford Social Innovation Review*, vol. 1, pp. 24–32.

[3] Bradach, J. (2003). "Going to Scale The Challenge of Replicating Social Programs", in *Stanford Social Innovation Review*, vol. 1, pp. 19-25.

[4] Waitzer, J.M.P. and Paul, R. (2011), "Scaling Social Impact: When Everybody Contributes, Everybody Wins", in *Innovations: Technology, Governance, Globalization*, vol. 6, no. 2, pp. 143-155.

10.7   Bibliography

[1] Achleitner, A.-K., Bassen, A., Roder, B. and Spiess-Knafl, W. (2009), "Reporting in Social Entrepreneurship". Paper presented at the *6th Annual NYU-Stern Conference on Social Entrepreneurship*, New York.

[2] Achleitner, A.-K., Heinecke, A., Noble, A., Schöning, M. and Spiess-Knafl, W. (2011), "Unlocking the mystery - An introduction to social investment", in *Innovations*, vol. SOCAP11: Impact Investing Special Edition, pp. 41-50.

[3] Achleitner, A.-K. and Heister, P. (2009), "Deal flow, decision-making process and selection criteria of venture philanthropy funds". Paper presented at the *6th Annual NYU-Stern Conference on Social Entrepreneurship*, New York.

[4] Ahlert, D., Ahlert, M., Duon Dinh, H.V., Fleisch, H., Heußler, T., Kilee, L. and Meuter, J. (2008), *Social Franchising: A Way of Systematic Replication to Increase Social Impact*, Bundesverband Deutscher Stiftungen, Berlin.

[5] Austin, J.E., Stevenson, H. and Wei-Skillern, J. (2006), "Social and commercial entrepreneurship: Same, different, or both", in *Entrepreneurship Theory and Practice*, vol. 30, no. 1, pp. 1-22.

[6] Bloom, P. and Smith, B.R. (2010), "Identifying the drivers of social entrepreneurial impact: Theoretical development and an exploratory empirical test of SCALERS", in *Journal of Social Entrepreneurship*, vol. 1, no. 1, pp. 126-145.

[7] Bloom, P.N. and Chatterji, A.K. (2009), "Scaling social entrepreneurial impact", in *California management review*, vol. 51, no. 3, pp. 114-133.

[8] Dees, J.G. (2008), *Developing the field of social entrepreneurship*, Center for the Advancement of Social Entrepreneurship, Duke University, Oxford.

[9] Dees, J.G., Anderson, B.B. and Wei-Skillern, J. (2004), "Scaling social impact", in *Stanford Social Innovation Review*, vol. 1, pp. 24–32.

[10] Glaeser, E.L. and Shleifer, A. (2001), "Not-for-profit entrepreneurs", in *Journal of Public Economics*, vol. 81, no. 1, pp. 99-115.

[11] Gugerty, M. (2009), "Signaling virtue: Voluntary accountability programs among nonprofit organizations", in *Policy Sciences*, vol. 42, no. 3, pp. 243-273.

[12] Hackl, V. (2009), *Social Franchising - Social Entrepreneurship Aktivitäten multiplizieren*, St. Gallen.

[13] Hoogendoorn, B., Pennings, E. and Thurik, A. (2010), "What do we know about social entrepreneurship; an analysis of empirical research", in *International Review of Entrepreneurship*, vol. 8, no. 2, pp. 71-112.

[14] Hoogendoorn, B., Zwan, P. and Thurik, A. (2011), *Social entrepreneurship and performance: The role of perceived barriers and risk*, Erasmus Research Institute of Management (ERIM), Rotterdam.

[15] Mair, J. and Marti, I. (2006), "Social entrepreneurship research: A source of explanation, prediction, and delight", in *Journal of World Business*, vol. 41, no. 1, pp. 36-44.

[16] Martin, R.L. and Osberg, S. (2007), "Social entrepreneurship: The case for definition", in *Stanford*

Social Innovation Review, vol. 5, no. 2, pp. 27-39.

[17] Milligan, K. and Schöning, M. (2011), "Taking a realistic approach to impact investing - Observations from the World Econocmic Forum's Global Agenda Council on social innovation", in *Innovations,* vol. SOCAP11: Impact Investing Special Edition, pp. 161-172.

[18] Mirvis, P.H. and Hackett, E.J. (1983), "Work and work force characteristics in the nonprofit sector", in *Monthly Labor Review,* vol. 106, no. 1, pp. 3-12.

[19] Mulgan, G., Tucker, S., Ali, R. and Sanders, B. (2006), *Social Innovation: What is it, why it matters and how it can be accelerated,* SAID Business School, Oxford.

[20] Obermüller, M. (2009), "Mit Social business ein humanes Weltwirtschaftswunder schaffen", in Radermacher, F., Obermüller, M. and Spiegel, P. (eds.), *Global Impact: Der neue Weg zur globalen Verantwortung,* Hanser, München, pp. 117-163.

[21] Pirson, M. and Bloom, G. (2011), "Dancing with Wolves? Social Entrepreneurship Between Promise and Challenge for the Business School and the 21st Century University", Available at SSRN: http://ssrn.com/abstract=1925868.

[22] Roob, N. and Bradach, J.L. (2009), *Scaling What Works: Implications for Philanthropists, Policymakers, and Nonprofit Leaders,* The Bridgespan Group, The Edna McConnel Clark Foundation, New York.

[23] Santos, F. (2009), *A Positive Theory of Social Entrepreneurship,* INSEAD, Barcelona.

[24] Schöning, M. (2007), "Multiplikation durch Franchising", in A.-K. Achleitner, Pöllath, R. and Stahl, E. (eds.), *Finanzierung von Sozialunternehmern,* Schäffer-Poeschel Verlag, Stuttgart, pp. 192-202.

[25] Sharir, M. and Lerner, M. (2006), "Gauging the success of social ventures initiated by individual social entrepreneurs", in *Journal of World Business,* vol. 41, no. 1, pp. 6-20.

[26] Tracey, P. and Jarvis, O. (2007), "Toward a theory of social venture franchising", in *Entrepreneurship Theory and Practice,* vol. 31, no. 5, pp. 667-685.

[27] Uvin, P.S.P. (2000), "Think large and act small: Toward a new paradigm for NGO scaling up", in *World Development,* vol. 28, no. 8, pp. 1409-1419.

[28] Venturesome. (2009), *Access to Capital - A briefing paper,* Charities Aid Foundation.

[29] Waitzer, J.M.P. and Paul, R. (2011), "Scaling Social Impact: When Everybody Contributes, Everybody Wins", in *Innovations: Technology, Governance, Globalization,* vol. 6, no. 2, pp. 143-155.

Part IV: The Market

Social Entrepreneurship in the Market System
Marc Grünhagen & Holger Berg

The Impact of Social Entrepreneurship on Societies
Markus Beckmann

Critical Reflections on Social Entrepreneurship
Pascal Dey & Chris Steyaert

11 Social Entrepreneurship in the Market System

Marc Grünhagen & Holger Berg

University of Wuppertal
Schumpeter School of Business and Economics

Learning goals

Upon completing this chapter, you should be able to accomplish the following:

- Explain the potential role of social entrepreneurship in market economies.

- Recognize the function of social entrepreneurs in addition to commercial entrepreneurs and the state as suppliers of goods and services.

- Explain the scope of activity of social enterprises in relation to their potential for value creation and appropriation.

- Characterize typical areas of activity of social entrepreneurs and provide examples.

11.1   Introduction

This chapter aims to propose a wider economic perspective of what social entrepreneurship is and how its role and functioning may be perceived in a market-based economic system. It relates and contrasts social entrepreneurship to concepts of conventional, i.e., commercial, entrepreneurship and to the state as an intervening force into the market system. By doing so, the potential task of social entrepreneurship are derived, assuming functions that are beneficial to society and which cannot or are not served by commercial entrepreneurship or by the government. It is therefore considered as a complementary economic agent to the other actors in the market system. To this avail, this chapter discusses when social entrepreneurship may be seen as legitimate, how legitimacy may be acquired by social entrepreneurs and what types of legitimacy need to be addressed. Furthermore, deliberations on the potential scope of its domain will be undertaken.

In the context of this book, this chapter therefore provides a classification for social entrepreneurship within the wider framework of economic theory, a task that is currently neglected in the literature on this topic (Santos 2009). Based on a market-system perspective it specifically addresses the economic and social functions of social entrepreneurship. The selected economic view perceives economic action as embedded into a wider social environment and as a part of social relations and institutions (Granovetter 1985).

To achieve these goals, the chapter proceeds as follows: section 2 presents a perspective on the function of social entrepreneurship in the market system, relying on traditional approaches to commercial entrepreneurship, specifically those of Schumpeter and Kirzner. It moreover deliberates the role of social entrepreneurship from a welfare economic perspective based on Pareto's concept of efficiency. With respect to the embeddedness assumption mentioned above, section 3 then positions social entrepreneurship within the social economic context, whereby two distinctive aspects will be discussed: The necessity of legitimacy for the social entrepreneur's purpose in order to gain acceptance and acquire resources on the one hand, and the potential domain of the concept in a market system when compared to commercial entrepreneurship and governmental action on the other. The final section introduces the social enterprise case of the "Committee for Democracy in Information Technology" established by Rodrigo Baggio.

11.2   The Function of Social Entrepreneurship in the Market System

As a first approach to the topic it might be worthwhile to distinguish between the function social entrepreneurship has in a market system when compared to its conventional counterpart. Such a comparison may be necessary as definitions and indeed beliefs about what social entrepreneurship is and what it amounts to differ considerably (Dacin et al., 2010; Zahra et al., 2009). This chapter is thus limited to a functional view of entrepreneurship (see Saßmannshausen, 2010) and will not regard other issues of entrepreneurship research and theory such as behavioural- or traits-based approaches. We will hence concentrate on the effects of the social entrepreneur's endeavours on a (free) market system, and are therefore not interested in specific traits that social entrepreneurs might share in their everyday actions.

Starting with the conventional entrepreneur the three main lines of thinking regarding his or her function were developed by Knight (1921), Kirzner (e.g. 1973, 2009), and Schumpeter (e.g. 1928, 1934). While Knight emphasizes risk-taking as the significant contribution of entrepreneurs to the market system, Kirzner and Schumpeter concentrate on innovative effects. To Kirzner the "alert entrepreneur" discovers price gaps between markets which he then exploits by ways of arbitrage. In doing so, he functions as an "equilibrator" to the markets since his actions will ultimately lead to a price-equilibrium between the originating and the target market (Kirzner, 2009). Schumpeter on the other hand sees the entrepreneur as a "disequilibrator"; in his view the function of the entrepreneur lies in the introduction of new combinations to markets which eventually disrupt or even destroy old market structures (Schumpeter, 1934; 1950). His conceptualization of the entrepreneur is hence one of an innovator who introduces new products, ways of production or organization, utilizes new resources for production or conquers new markets. One may note that the entrepreneur did not stand at the beginning of research for any of these three authors. They were all rather interested in specific phenomena observable in the market (risk-taking, equilibration, development) and found the entrepreneur to be the acting person behind them. Since they address different issues and potential functions, all three approaches stand next to each other in entrepreneurship theory as accepted concepts of the entrepreneur's role in a market system. Moreover, newer approaches exist, that try to combine two or more of these older approaches, especially the ideas of Schumpeter and Kirzner (e.g., Shane, 2003).[22]

---

[22] There have already been attempts to frame the social entrepreneur within these approaches, most notably by Swedberg (2011), who meticulously deducts a Schumpeter-based understanding of the social entrepreneur, and by Zahra et al. (2009) where three models based on Hayek[22] ("The Social Bricoleur"), Kirzner ("The Social Constructionist"), and finally Schumpeter ("The Social Engineer") are devised.

Another discussion circles around the question whether social entrepreneurship takes place in an economic setting or if it is part of non-economic activities. Swedberg (2011) for example distinguishes the non-economic entrepreneurial side of social entrepreneurship from the economic one (see also Neck, Brush and Allen, 2009). The former takes place when a person focuses on initiating social change through the introduction of social innovations. Economic social entrepreneurship on the other side is described as taking place when innovative economic entrepreneurship – in the fashion suggested by Schumpeter – serves a social cause. The entrepreneur's venture yields a capitalist and a social profit, wherein the capitalist profit may serve to further the venture's social impact. This view is consistent with Zahra et al.'s (2009) concept of "total wealth" produced by economically orientated social entrepreneurship. Here, the total performance of social entrepreneurship is differentiated into the creation of social wealth and economic wealth which combined make up for the "total wealth" produced by the enterprise. Zahra et al. (ibid.) propose that entrepreneurial entities may appear on a broad spectrum between the production of social and economic wealth but should express both variables in some gradation to be considered social entrepreneurs. Some scholars find this problematic, since profit maximization and concentration is not necessarily the sole interest of conventional entrepreneurs (e.g., Schramm, 2010) and many conventional enterprises have contributed tremendously to social progress without being referred to as social ventures – Schramm specifically highlights corporations and entrepreneurs that provide all parts of society with affordable and healthy nourishment (ibid.). With regard to this discussion, we will focus on the economic function that entrepreneurship incorporates, as we are interested in the role of the social entrepreneur within a market system. In our approach entrepreneurship will hence be seen as social if it leads to innovation in the social realm through market based operations. Literature on social entrepreneurship often demands that the entrepreneurs pursue major social causes and therein cause considerable social change (e.g., Bornstein, 2004; Dart, 2004; Roberts and Woods, 2005; see also Light, 2006; as well as Dacin et al., 2010 on the subject). However, there is little explanation why this has to be and what social change exactly refers to. Moreover, there is no quantification of what major change is and, consequently, when induced change is large enough to be considered the outcome of social entrepreneurship. Specifically, one question that is raised by this discussion is when exactly a social cause is addressed and if social entrepreneurship only refers to efforts in which the positions of every market participant are embellished, or if it suffices if only some parties profit from the effort and others do not. To elaborate on the latter point, social entrepreneurship is considered in the light of *Pareto-efficiency*. Pareto-efficiency denotes a state where the welfare of no entity can be improved without reducing the welfare state of another entity (Arrow/Debreu, 1954, see also Dean/McMullen, 2007). However, such a state does not indicate that every person is sufficiently amended by the economic status quo, it only postulates that the situation of one person cannot be enhanced without reducing the economic status of a different person (Zahra et al., 2008). Assuming a state of Pareto efficiency in which some actors are in an unfavourable welfare position while others are affluent, entrepreneurial action that favours the former and reduces the income of the latter might well be seen as social entrepreneurship as described above although some market participants are worse off (cf. Martin/Osberg, 2007).[23] From this point of view, social entrepreneurship and the changing of economic and market structures through economic actions does not necessarily foster the welfare of every participant in an economy in a positive way. If one takes a Schumpeterian approach and assumes that entrepreneurial action may indeed lead to considerable destruction of existing structures through innovation, it is rather likely that social entrepreneurship may lead to disadvantages for some members of that economy. Ideally of course, social entrepreneurship leads to *Pareto-superior* states where the disadvantaged are navigated into better positions without affecting anyone else negatively. As an example, such outcomes occur when initiating economic growth from which all parties profit.

A functional microeconomic approach naturally focuses on the entity of the social enterprise. Relying on the traditional approaches to entrepreneurship, a dynamic perspective is preferable. Social entrepreneurship is defined as business models that aim to address a social benefit by *combining* economic market-based operations with a social aim to alleviate the welfare state of a certain target group (Santos, 2009). This approach has several advantages: First, it solves the assumed trade-off relationship between economic and social goals of entrepreneurship proposed in many contributions to social entrepreneurship (cf. Zahra et al., 2009). Social and economic actions are then seen as potentially complimentary rather than conflicting (also see Santos, 2009).[24] Organizations that follow a fair trade approach are a good example here. Disadvantaged farmers in Third World countries benefit from marketing and distribution efforts of trade organizations in the developed world based on a "fair" pricing of their products in contrast to the often exploitive behaviour of other trade organizations. The economic and social aims of fair trade are complimentary because the more successful the fair trade organizations are, the more the farmers profit and the more their social disadvantage is alleviated. Moreover, the proposed understanding allows a clear differentiation between social businesses and charity on one hand and corporate social responsibility (CSR) on the other. As charities do not follow a (market-based) business model by definition, and CSR is not part of a company's original business model, neither concept is included in this understanding of social entrepreneurship. Secondly, from a functional perspective both the Kirznerian and the Schumpeterian approach are commensurable to this view. The Kirznerian entrepreneur alleviates social disadvantage through equilibration within the market system. He or she uses market imperfections to solve perceived deficits in welfare through arbitrage. The aforementioned fair trade concept falls exactly into this category. The Schumpeterian entrepreneur aims to solve perceived social problems through concepts that disrupt existing equilibriums (states that are Pareto-efficient but perceived as socially disadvantageous, also see Santos, 2009) through innovative business models. He or she creatively destroys an existing market system to erect a new one. Mohammad Yunnus' Grameen bank falls into this category. Microlending

---

[23] While other scholars, especially Santos (2009) also argue from a Pareto-based perspective, the reader will see that our argumentation in some parts differs from his conclusions.

[24] Santos is unclear in this point as he both mentions a traded-off relationship and a mere distinction between value creation and appropriation (see Santos 2009, p. 14). Our view is closer the latter concept.

as an innovative banking concept and credit product revolutionised the debt market system of Bangladesh in more than one way: It provided debt capital at lower interest rates (new quality of an existing product), addressed a different target group (women from disadvantaged families) and also introduced a novel concept of securing returns (through peer groups). At the same time, it obliterated the former lending concept which was based on very high interest rates (also see Dowla, 2006 for a more detailed account).

Note that until now the scale of entrepreneurial activity has been ignored. Social entrepreneurship emerges simply by fulfilling the proposed function – this is as another advantage of the approach. Moreover, the concentration on a functional perspective lets the social entrepreneur share a theoretical trait with all other entrepreneurial concepts: The possibility of failure (Dacin et al., 2010). Empirically, an entrepreneur may aim to close a social gap through arbitrage or innovation but this does not mean that he or she succeeds in the endeavour (see also Santos, 2009). Failure however, has two very different forms in social entrepreneurship: Failure in economic performance or failure to address the social need as planned. The first case is the same as for the conventional entrepreneur: The inability to secure sufficient returns and/or to realise sufficient profit leads to a termination of the venture. The second form of failure is more interesting as it is a distinct feature of social enterprises. Indeed, a social venture may not succeed to fulfill its aspired mission, even when it is economically successful. A major reason for this may lie in imperfect markets, which may lack transparency or suffer from bounded rationality, for example. Both economic and/or social failure may be largely caused by the market participants' imperfect information. When a market evolves, participants are not (entirely) able to plan and conduct their actions with perfect forethought; they are – at least partially – "blind" to the outcomes and impacts of their actions (Campbell, 1974). This suggests that the social entrepreneur may err on the perceived problem, on the way a problem has to be mitigated, and on the consequences of impact on the target group. He or she may fail to accomplish their desired goals. The chosen perspective on social entrepreneurship avoids limiting analysis to successful entrepreneurs.[25] A final advantage of the perspective is a possible deviance of (sustainable) success and venture survival (see e.g. Santos, 2009). Like conventional entrepreneurship the view proposed here stresses the act entrepreneurship and the incurred effects. It is hence not necessary for a social enterprise to remain on the market forever or be sustainable for a long time. What is important is the impact of economic entrepreneurial action on social welfare, i.e., the creation of a new or changed system structure.

It is suggested that social entrepreneurship may also be analysed on a more aggregated level. In that case, the outcomes of social entrepreneurship are observed. This approach is based upon Santos' (2009) idea of a holistic value concept. Santos states that the domain of social entrepreneurship lies in value creation processes where value appropriation by the creator – or his or her shareholders respectively – is difficult or impossible. Linking to the approach described above, on an aggregate level, social entrepreneurship occurs when

---

[25] A normative theory for successful social entrepreneurship is of course still useful to the individual and a worthy pursuit. However we would suggest that such a theory would also profit from analyzing failed efforts (Dacin et al. 2010).

activities improve total welfare, meaning that *Pareto-superior* effects occur. Taking a market perspective, this may be observed when social entrepreneurship adds resources (in whichever form) to the market without appropriating – or being able to appropriate for that matter – those additional resources. For example, business models that improve the human capital basis of an economy by training the poor and disadvantaged fall into this category, as do ventures that broaden the capital basis without appropriating this surplus.

A further matter to discuss is the relationship between government intervention, social entrepreneurship and the market system. It is often proposed that the government should intervene where market operations lead to misallocation or unwanted externalities. However, the state is sometimes unable to address specific problems through lack of money, insight, and/or interest, etc. (Santos, 2009). One may thus assume that the simple inability of a government to detect every social gap or deficit could result in need social entrepreneurship and hence be a triggering factor. Here, the Hayekian perspective concerning the advantages of dispersed knowledge in a market based economy comes into bearing (Hayek, 1945). It is the closer proximity of the (local) entrepreneur that allows him or her to act upon a perceived social drawback through entrepreneurial activity. In other cases the state may refrain from action if it does not consider the topics to be of high relevance or fears that addressing them would result in even further problems. A social entrepreneur's deviating perception of the same case may lead to entrepreneurial activities. This is clearly the realm of the Schumpeterian social entrepreneur. And again, it is irrelevant which of the actors is correct. What matters for the social entrepreneur in the market system is that she or he utilizes this system to alleviate a situation that is perceived as socially negative.

11.3   The Socio-Institutional Context of Social Entrepreneurship

As described above, outputs of a social enterprise address social drawbacks or problems, meaning that "the purpose of the social enterprise extends beyond simply revenue generation or profit maximization to include producing goods and services in response to the needs of a community" (Di Domenico et al., 2010, p. 682). Such problems may impair socially-excluded groups of society such as the poor, disabled, discriminated or long-term unemployed (Seelos et al., 2005). Social entrepreneurship fills the gap left by societal institutions failing to address the issues, e.g., state failures to provide welfare to these groups (Aiken, 2006; Bovaird, 2006). Social entrepreneurship thus seems to engage in activities "to provide goods and services..., to develop skills, to create employment, and to foster pathways to integrate socially excluded people...which the market or public sector is either unwilling or unable to provide" (Nicholls, 2006, p.14). This begs the question as to which role the activities of social entrepreneurs have within the market system which, in the above quote, appears to encapsulate first and foremost commercial business activity.

This section argues that it is essential to take a perspective on *the market system* in terms of its *social, cultural, and regulatory embeddedness,* and that it is in this broader context of market economies where the social enterprise has its place in creating social values with economic means (cf. Dart, 2004 for this broad context of social entrepreneurship and Granovetter, 1985 for the general socio-cultural embeddedness of economic action). Within the market system and its wider social environment we address:

- the demand for legitimacy of social enterprises to be able to gain acceptance and obtain resources from societal stakeholders for their activities (11.3.1)

- the perceived scope for social entrepreneurship in market economies and the challenge of scaling novel solutions to social problems by social entrepreneurs (11.3.2).

11.3.1   The Legitimacy of Social Enterprises

In an economic market system the *efficient allocation of resources in face of scarcity* is a pivotal mechanism to produce wealth, for example by supplying needed goods and services to society. And social entrepreneurship has implications on the economic market system particularly through "allocating resources to neglected societal problems" (Santos, 2009, p. 2; Mair and Marti, 2006). However, the Schumpeterian combination of resources (see above) to solve social problems in novel ways will – like any entrepreneurial endeavour – require to obtain these resources from society in the first place (Brush et al., 2001); in particular, for social enterprises to acquire the resources to roll out and scale their social goods and services to other geographies will require them to validate their business models (Santos, 2009). And often on this path social entrepreneurs may face unfavourable normative and regulatory environments for creating social and economic value under resource scarcity (Di Domenico et al., 2010) as external stakeholders will require efforts to be convinced to offer support (Desa, 2011; Dacin et al., 2010).

The *imperative for gaining as well as maintaining acceptance and legitimacy* stem from a number of aspects associated with emerging and young social enterprises: the requirement to assemble and employ external resources to establish and develop the enterprise, the need for acceptance to acquire these resources in face of uncertain future performance of the venture and the request for conforming to societal norms and institutions (for an overview of the legitimacy of social entrepreneurship see Dart, 2004 and Nicholls, 2010):

- First of all, legitimacy will be required in order to attract resources from society (and the market system within it) in competition to alternative uses of resources. In this respect Parsons (1960, pp. 175) clarified that "the utilization of resources from a larger social system, that could be allocated elsewhere, must be accepted as legitimate by members of that larger system".

- In social as well as in general entrepreneurship obtaining acceptance is critical because of concerns about future performance of new entrepreneurial organizations (Brush et al., 2001), in particular when the products and services offered are novel (for example social innovation). The demand for legitimacy in entrepreneurship exists because of the

risk of failing to achieve the desired social and economic outcomes (for the issue of social entrepreneurial failure also see Massarsky and Beinhacker, 2002). Social entrepreneurs may feel "resource-based pressures to extant sector- or society-level normative
frames of reference in order to survive and prosper" (Nicholls, 2010, pp. 613). For example, consider the introduction of micro-lending in Bangladesh and the offers of mi-
cro-loans from the Grameen Bank. They were faced with (and perhaps there still are)
questions about the general efficiency and impact of microfinance and, even put unintended pressure of the communities on the women obtaining loans, contradicting the
idea of empowering them (Phills et al., 2008). Apparently, the initial loans were not in
line with local culture and norms, resulting in adverse effects that had to be remedied
over time by adjusting the loan packages.

■ The need for entrepreneurs and organizations to demonstrate institutional conformity
will be stakeholder- and domain-specific (Suchman, 1995) and there may be social as
well as economic demands regarding both the accountability of social entrepreneurs as
well as social enterprises as emergent organizations (Nicholls and Cho, 2006). Members
of society may only want to offer resources like money or their work (be it as employees
or volunteers) if they value the social vision and goals of the enterprise. Moreover, there
may be questions about the accountability of social entrepreneurs and the quality of
products and service. In particular, it has to be kept in mind that social entrepreneurs
will not be the only suppliers. Namely, the goods offered by social entrepreneurs may
also be provided alternatively by the state or regular for-profit businesses. In this respect, the business model of social entrepreneurs competes with alternative modes of
supply (Zahra et al., 2009). Economically, in view of competing forms of goods' supply
social entrepreneurs may need to address concerns about the "efficiency of the allocation process they use in creating the public good" (ibid., p.12). In their pursuit to create
economic and social wealth, social enterprises need acceptance to acquire resource support in competition to state welfare production and traditional for-profit business models. Section 3.2 below will sketch out the room for and purpose of social entrepreneurship in a market economy in the context of other forms of supply of goods and services.
Before this, the remainder of this section will develop a differentiated understanding of
organizational legitimacy of social enterprises. In particular, different forms of legitimacy will be addressed.

Within organizational sociology and institutional theory *organizational legitimacy* has been
defined as "a generalized perception or assumption that the actions of an entity are socially
desirable, proper or appropriate within some socially constructed system of norms, value,
beliefs and definitions" (Suchman, 1995, p. 574). The legitimacy of new enterprises rests in
the views of society based on existing societal normative rules and thus "ultimately exists
in the eye of the beholder" (Zimmerman and Zeitz, 2002, p. 415). In other words, it will be
society members themselves who hold beliefs and views about a new enterprise organization as to whether it is useful and proper. For example, a social enterprise that offers elementary education to the young may be considered as valuable and legitimate because the
state does not provide that education in an adequate manner. Even though legitimacy constitutes a generalized perception across audiences, there are different dimensions and *forms*

of legitimacy social enterprises may establish. As depicted in table 1 below, there are different categorisations based on regulatory, normative, and cognitive frames of reference. This
chapter follows the seminal differentiation in Suchman (1995), which is the most widely
used in sociology and economics, distinguishing between the *cognitive, pragmatic, and moral
legitimacy* of organizations. The latter forms of legitimacy are more evaluative while the
former, i.e. cognitive acceptance, refers to the comprehensibility and taken-for-grantedness
of an organization in society. *Cognitive legitimacy* is important primarily in the early stages
of a social enterprise which offers novel products or services to cater for social needs which
may be difficult to grasp in the first place. Consider the example of "Dialogue in the Dark"
founded in 1988 by the (later) Ashoka Fellow Andreas Heinecke (see the case in this book)
or the early days of micro-lending. Today, these concepts and the social ideas behind them
are universally known, but in the beginning it might have been not so clear what these
concepts actually are and how they function to address neglected social needs (i.e., suffering from an initial liability of newness; originally Stinchcombe, 1965, in contemporary entrepreneurship and non-profit organizations see, e.g., Hager et al., 2004). In addition to
merely achieving comprehensibility of what they do and offer, social enterprises will also
need to be evaluated positively in terms of the immediate interests of their potential stakeholders and in consonance with the social, regulatory and cultural norms of the societies
they operate in.

Table 11.1   Forms of Legitimacy of Social Enterprises

Source	Forms of Legitimacy
Scott (2001)	*normative legitimacy:* compliance with relevant social expectations *regulative legitimacy:* conformance with legal rules
Aldrich (1999); Aldrich & Martinez (2003)	*socio-political legitimacy:* moral conformity with cultural norms and values; regulatory conformance with governmental rules and regulations
Suchman (1995)	*pragmatic legitimacy:* evaluation of ressource efficiency and organizational incentives by direct stakeholders; *moral legitimacy:* normative evaluation of organizational characteristics and activities *cognitive legitimacy:* comprehensibility and taken-for-grantedness of organizational features

Own table

Pragmatic legitimacy reflects the support of an organization and its actions based on their
"expected value to a particular set of constituents" (Suchman, 1995, p. 578) like the state,
customers, investors, and employees as immediate stakeholders. In other words it is ex-
change-based in that pragmatic acceptance "denotes an attribution of social acceptability by
stakeholder groups if an activity provides them with anything of value" (Dart, 2004, p. 417).
For example, a state institution or foundation might value the initiative of a social enter-

prise because it caters for social problems and groups of society in an innovative way, which would otherwise have to be supported by state aid (ibid.). Or consider investors and sponsors of a social enterprise, who – though not striving for maximum return – may still demand for cost recovery or benefits like public attention and publicity. Because of the expectations to receive something in exchange for any support offered, pragmatic acceptance may be fairly fragile (Dart, 2004), in particular when social enterprises fail to produce desired social (and economic) outcomes.

In contrast, *moral legitimacy* is more sociotropic by evaluating the appropriateness of organizational characteristics and actions relative to the norm and value systems of groups of society (Suchman, 1995). This dimension of legitimating an entrepreneurial organization seems easier to achieve for social enterprises because of their focus to achieve the public good. However, as noted by Zahra et al. (2009) social enterprises still need to be considered appropriate in the light of existing public instruments and institutions of social policy-making. With regard to this, Dart (2004, p. 419) supposes that *"given our contemporary social fascination with market-based solutions and mechanisms, social enterprise is likely to both retain and expand its moral legitimacy"* [emphasis added]. From 2004 onwards, the world has evolved in ways which may both moderate and emphasize this prognosis regarding the role of social enterprises in the market system. For example, the recent financial crisis has made people less inclined to bank on market-based solutions to address problems and needs of society. And at the same time the crisis has put substantial pressures on public budgets to continuously fund areas like social security, health care, and education. Overall, this makes alternative modes like social entrepreneurship look more acceptable and welcome by society as social entrepreneurs offer goods in addition to supply by the state and private commercial enterprises. This will be discussed further in the next section (11.3.2).

It is not necessary to go into detail on how social entrepreneurs may go about their legitimizing action to establish their social enterprise and attract resources. It is, however, useful to understand that there are two strands of theory in this regard:

- the *institutional view* which considers legitimacy to be conferred by external members of society and

- an *agency perspective* regarding legitimacy as something to be actively acquired and achieved by organizations (cf. Scott 2001; Dart 2004; Nicholls 2010; Desa 2011).

In the prior view, the legitimating options (Suchman, 1995) need to *conform* to external institutional demands to win support. The latter perspective embraces activities of organizations and entrepreneurs to build legitimacy, e.g., through public relations. They aim at generating organizational legitimating capital and *manipulating* the views society holds about them. Also, social enterprises may actively build relationships and refer to industry legitimacy capital together with other social entrepreneurs and players (see Lounsbury and Glynn, 2001 for these sources of domain-level capital (industry, individual firm) in cultural and social entrepreneurship). For example, in the domain of social entrepreneurship, institutions like the Skoll foundation, fellowship organizations like Ashoka, the Schwab foundation or others, as well as sector-conferences, publications, media events, and competitions have raised awareness and acceptance of social entrepreneurs and entrepreneurship in the public over the last two decades (more examples may be found in Nicholls, 2010 discussing the legitimacy of the entire field of social entrepreneurship in depth).

A final legitimising option of interest when striving for the dual creation of social and economic value, is the *selection* of specific groups or constituents of society for their support. Here, entrepreneurs turn to those stakeholders which value the offers of the organization. For example, to raise funding, a social enterprise may specifically turn to philanthropic investors instead of commercial investors or banks, because these financiers value the social benefits created by the enterprise (for the range of potential social financiers see chapter 8). Or in the area of personnel, social entrepreneurs may seek volunteers who are committed to the social vision of the organization instead of hiring paid employees.

The resource base of social entrepreneurs is specific and they may not get access to the full scale of resources a market economy has on offer (e.g., in terms of funding sources). Here, social entrepreneurs often make do with those they can persuade, and also improvise with the resources at hand, acting as *bricolageurs* (Zahra et al., 2009; also see the study of Di Domenico et al., 2010 exploring the resource acquisition and management of social enterprises in practice). Compared to commercial entrepreneurship, potential differences in resource composition and access stem from the unique mode of *value creation* and *value appropriation* in social enterprises. In particular their high level of external social value creation but (relatively) low scope for value appropriation might make it more difficult to establish and grow social enterprises. In particular, this may be in terms of finding employees and financial investors who are attracted by salaries and economic returns. It will be difficult for social enterprises to appropriate such returns and, in turn, to offer appropriated proceeds to employees and investors as immediate stakeholders in exchange for their pragmatic support (Santos, 2009, p. 20). These specific forms of *initial legitimising and resource acquisition* and the *process of value generation and distribution through resource allocation* offer a lens for defining the scope for social entrepreneurship in the market system.

11.3.2   The Scope for Social Entrepreneurship in the Market Economy

To derive the possible function of social entrepreneurship in a market system which also includes commercial business and state action requires

- differentiating between economic *value creation and value appropriation* and

- discussing events of *market (and state) failure* in producing societal wealth as an opportunity for social enterprises to step in and remedy such failures.

First of all, we follow a holistic notion of value creation (as in Santos, 2009). In this sense value creation constitutes an increase in the aggregate utility of societal actors' individual utility functions. In consonance with the above, this encapsulates both economic *and* social value generation (rather than defining a dichotomy or trade-off between the two). In this sense, economic action increases societal wealth. However, when defining the role of social entrepreneurs in the market place it is useful to concentrate on economic value.

While there does not need to be a dichotomy between final economic and social value creation, a differentiation between the *creation and appropriation of economic value* is critical in
understanding what different market actors are able to supply in terms of goods and services to society. Appropriation reflects the share of the created economic value that the
enterprise is able to capture for itself, e.g., as a financial return. The extent of value appropriation and creation will vary across different areas of the overall supply of goods and
services. This heterogeneity in creating and appropriating value brings about different
types of market actions in the market system with social entrepreneurship among them
(**Figure 11.1**; adapted from Santos, 2009):

Figure 11.1   Economic Value Distribution and Market Activities

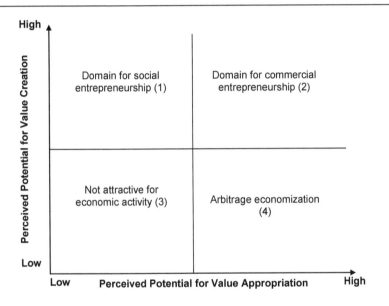

Own illustration based on Santos (2009)

The traditional domain for commercial entrepreneurship and business activity in the market place is in areas where there is substantial value creation (as reflected by corresponding
consumer demand) and where this value can be appropriated by the business and returned
to its owners, for example in markets for consumer products like sportswear or electronics
(2). Here, for-profit entrepreneurial businesses will grow and market incentives will drive
efficient supply. In contrast, areas with few opportunities for value creation and appropriation are unlikely to attract economic activity (3). And domains with little potential for value
creation but high chances for value appropriation may attract speculators seeking arbitrage
opportunities which get eliminated over time or are ruled out by state legislation (4); examples are benefits from price inefficiencies in financial markets or profits from negative externalities like environmentally-harmful industrial activities.

Overall, from the viewpoint of society the market functions to supply products and services for private consumers and paying customers. However, there will also be services and products which are in high demand by society – and which would produce substantial societal value – but will be undersupplied by commercial market participants because they perceive a low potential for value appropriation and profit generation through regular business activity (1). In particular, in such situations it will be difficult for business to acquire resources from resource owners who expect an economic return to the production of such goods and services (e.g., financial or strategic investors). The role which social entrepreneurship plays can be defined when addressing why the commercial market may fail to make sufficient offers in this context.

The *failure of markets* to allocate resources and, in turn, goods and services efficiently can have a number of reasons, e.g., non-competitiveness, asymmetric information distribution, unaccounted externalities, and public goods (e.g., Stiglitz, 1989 or, in relation to social entrepreneurship, Nicholls, 2006). In the situation in quadrant (1) above markets may not fulfil societal demand because of low potential for value appropriation. There may be an undersupply by for-profit businesses of goods that are non-rival or non-excludable in consumption (i.e., public), e.g., some environmental or information goods (Rangan et al., 2006). Note that – though not completely non-excludable or -rivalrous – goods and services in typical fields of activity of social entrepreneurs like education or health do feature partial non-exclusivity and externalities. On account of such positive externalities where others do benefit (e.g., vaccination or employability programs) full-scale value appropriation is difficult. In addition, there may also be the issue that target groups, who need a product or service, are unable to pay for it, e.g., education or health services (Santos, 2009). It is in these areas where substantial societal values may be generated – but the low ability of appropriation hampers traditional commercial supply – that social entrepreneurs can unfold their activities. Due to their primary focus on generating social value they are able to internalise positive externalities when creating the public good. However, the *government* could also try to foster the internalisation of such externalities in the rationale of for-profit economic agents in sectors like education or healthcare. This may be done for example by offering monetary incentives for businesses so as to stimulate service offers to social target groups who cannot afford to pay for themselves (e.g. through subsidies or a voucher-program). Alternatively, the state could even provide goods and services. However, sometimes the state neither offers incentives for business nor provides goods itself. This may be due funding or other resource constraints, or conflicts with other duties and priorities on the political agenda (Santos, 2009; Dart, 2004; for a broader discussion of government failure versus market failure see, e.g., Winston, 2006).

Having described supply-side gaps by commercial market agents as well as the state, the function of social entrepreneurship in a modern market economy can finally be appreciated in terms of *(a) additional supply, (b) innovation and (c) welfare extension.*

(a) As described above, in a market economy, social entrepreneurship can produce goods or services to society and create additional value in areas of undersupply by commercial businesses or state (closing the gap in quadrant (1) in figure 1 above). The unwillingness or inability of business and governmental actors to supply may stem from perceived limits for value appropriation (in case of the former) and scarce public resources to tackle neglected externalities (Santos, 2009) (in case of the latter).

(b) However, there is more to the role of social entrepreneurship than merely supplying goods or services. As businesses and state lack activity to address societal needs in some areas, social entrepreneurs take on an innovation function in exploring novel solutions to unmet social needs. Whether social enterprises perform this function efficiently and whether there will be demand for their offers is evaluated by societal resource owners and consumers as described in the discussion of the imperative for legitimacy (cf. 3.1). Note that this is a form of entrepreneurial hypothesis-testing (Kerber, 1997) where social entrepreneurs take on risks and could fail as introduced above. Put it another way, social entrepreneurs will try out whether their new products and services will be valued and demanded by society. This exploration and innovation function is particularly important since state offers to fulfill education, health care and other needs of society will be suboptimal in face of imperfect government knowledge. To propel such innovation by social entrepreneurs at the market level, the state may take on an instrumental support function towards social entrepreneurship in two ways: first, providing a facilitating legislative framework to innovating social entrepreneurs and second, relieving information asymmetries and generating economies of scale.

Flanking social entrepreneurial activities by providing an institutional framework is instrumental because of the need for legitimacy of innovating social entrepreneurs. A good example reported in Santos (2009) is the French social enterprise Unis-Cité. It offers opportunities to the French youth to engage in social projects as a civic service. These opportunities help young people from diverse cultural backgrounds to develop skills and knowledge relevant to the French labour market which suffers from considerable youth unemployment and integration problems. The government started to support the Unis-Cité initiative after the youth revolts in France in 2006, offering a legal basis for this volunteer social work as well as providing substantial funding. This support catalysed the growth of Unis-Cité considerably and fostered the nation-wide roll out beyond small-scale pilot and follow-up projects. Beyond the provision of supportive legislative frameworks by the government, social entrepreneurs themselves may even contribute to alleviate problems arising from (initially) weak institutional frameworks, e.g., in terms of property rights or capital market institutionalisation in the case of micro-lending in developing economies (De Soto, 2000). It may even be that legislation evolves around the positive externalities addressed by social pioneers as institutional entrepreneurs. Government policy-makers can also help to alleviate information asymmetries and resource shortages particularly in novel areas of social entrepreneurship. For example, public institutions can play a role in initiating networks or establishing foundations in the field of social entrepreneurship (see Nicholls, 2010, who discusses a range of governmental contributions to building and legitimating the field). In addition to enabling reciprocal information and resource exchange under the roof of social foundations or programs, the government itself can provide financial resource support. This can aim at assisting social enterprises in reaching a threshold size or in scaling the geographical presence of their projects. Often, government action will take the form of public-private partnerships. This kind of state intervention to promote entrepreneurship ideally concentrates on cases of market failure, e.g., cases of neglected positive externalities or information asymmetries (cf. Grünhagen, Koch and Saßmannshausen, 2005).

(c) As discussed in section 2. above, social entrepreneurship has a particularly important function when providing Pareto-superior effects in terms of improved overall resource efficiency and welfare. Often, social entrepreneurs will be active in areas where they improve health care, develop skills of people and create employment, or they establish paths to integrate socially-excluded groups of society (cf. Nicholls, 2006); examples are "Dialogue in the Dark" or the case of "CDI Committee for Democracy in Information Technology" in section 4. below. In these to cases the social and economic action of the entrepreneurs particularly helps to add human capital to the production function of economies and create additional wealth. In general, however, there are many ways in which social entrepreneurs can be instrumental in generating welfare. Whether a social entrepreneur identified an efficient way to do so will be evaluated and legitimated by societal resource holders themselves. One example of a social entrepreneur who has sensed social demand from excluded groups of society for a new service is the case of Rodrigo Baggio and his Committee for Democracy in Information Technology (CDI). The mini-case shows how a social enterprise has introduced social service innovation, in this case IT education and access, to a market where other actors – at least initially – did not fulfill demand. At the same time, the case leads to a discussion from a market perspective on what roles CDI as a social enterprise, commercial businesses, and the government may be tasked with.

11.4   Case Study

Baggio and the Committee for Democracy in Information Technology (CDI)
Around the world computers and the internet are used every second of the day – but not by everybody on the planet.[26] In what is often coined the "digital divide", there are people who are excluded from the use of information and communication technology, both in developing economies as well as in developed economies, for example immigrants, the disabled and the poor. The Committee for Democracy in Information Technology – CDI – is a social enterprise striving to help and serve such social groups, in particular young people, and their demand for IT infrastructure and skills – but there is more to it. It all began in 1995 when Rodrigo Baggio, a Brazilian IT consultant, founded the first Information Technology and Citizen Rights School of CDI in the Santa Marta favela of Rio de Janeiro. Rodrigo Baggio envisioned the heart of CDI to be in empowering people to become active citizens in their communities through information and communication technology: "One must believe in the power of communities to transform their social reality by mastering new information and communication technologies." CDI not only provides computer and communication infrastructure, but makes long-lasting efforts to educate and support people in their life.

Since the mission of CDI is not about IT alone, the CDI schools or community centres take steps towards the social inclusion of low-income communities. Correspondingly, every new CDI school is build around solving challenges and developing entrepreneurial ideas in one's community through information technology, for example by offering a free or low-cost internet access through an internet café or planning a PR campaign against child abuse in the community. As school students develop new competences around IT and communication technologies they engage in economic and entrepreneurial activities, address pressing social problems, and increase their own employability. With CDI providing the computer and other hard- and software, the local community is taken further on board, running and administering the school and providing school buildings and facilities. In its education mission CDI follows a train-the-teacher concept, closely collaborating with local volunteers and educators from the community. The students of the schools take a course to develop computer and software skills and work on a community project at the same time. Today, CDI has a budget of more than 5 million USD per year. Funding is a mix of small, symbolic course fees to pay the teachers and donations from "maintainers" and "supporters" that make contributions in money or materials. Overall, CDI taps multiple funding sources, aiming to include public support and partnering with other foundations which help specific disadvantaged groups like disabled and chronically ill people, prisoners and drug addicts.

---

[26]   This mini-case has been prepared for class discussion of CDI from an economics perspective. It is not intended to prefer a specific form of supply of IT education to other forms such as public education policy. For preparing the case the authors have used material from earlier works, in particular the CDI cases written by J. Mair and C. Seelos at IESE and O. Kayser and F. Santos at INSEAD, which, however, focus more on issues of the entrepreneurial management of CDI's expansion. See http://cdiglobal.org/.

When establishing the first school, Baggio received requests from other communities inquiring about the concept as well as donations of computers from businesses. Building on the success of opening the first school, he chose a social franchise concept to grow and establish more schools throughout Brazil and, later, internationally. Local communities send proposals for new schools to CDI, making suggestions what kind of community work may be facilitated by information technology. CDI then co-operates with the community in training (both technical and educational), fund raising, and in the formation of a new school. Over time, CDI has established a network of more than 700 information technology and citizen rights schools, operating across Brazil and in several Latin American countries. CDI has created a range of direct and indirect impacts on society, both socially and economically (see the impact section on CDI's global website: http://cdiglobal.org/). For example, more than 50,000 students have graduated from the schools, increasing their chances for employment. Moreover, many school teachers and educators have been trained, community projects have been developed, and many communities got access to computers and the internet.

As often is the case with successful pioneering entrepreneurs, the success of Baggio and CDI as a social enterprise also attracted attention and competition in Brazil. In particular, the Brazilian government initiated its own policies to fight digital exclusion among poor people in the first decade of the new millennium. This initiative may have developed because Baggio himself raised awareness towards the drawbacks of the digital divide for the Brazilian society. Most prominently, thousands of computer centres (so called "Telecentros Comunitarios") have been established with public funds. The telecentros offer computer and peripheral equipment free to use, for example to search the internet or to write and print documents, as well as IT training courses similar to CDI. In addition, commercial internet cafes and computer businesses now target low-income households which cannot afford a personal computer at home. While not building computer skills and developing community projects in the way CDI does, these businesses still supply competitive computer and internet access at low cost. The fact, that now both the government and private businesses have entered into the supply function, poses interesting questions with regard to the future role CDI may play as a social enterprise in the market segment of IT training and access provision for low-income households.

Questions:

1. Consult the impact section of CDI's website at http://cdiglobal.org/ and discuss the positive externalities and values created by Rodrigo Baggio and his social enterprise. Try to develop a concept as to how the direct and indirect impact created by CDI may be accounted for. In how far is it difficult for commercial for-profit businesses to create this value and impact on individuals and communities?

2. Sketch out the innovator role played by Rodrigo Baggio and find examples of other social entrepreneurs and their function in addressing social needs in a novel way. How did the government react in these examples?

3. Becoming aware of the problem of digital exclusion in Brazil, the government developed its own policy program to provide low-income and rural households with computer access and IT education through public sources. Do you think that there may be negative crowding-out effect on social and commercial entrepreneurs from the private sector? What could have been alternative paths for the government to combat digital exclusion?

4. Rodrigo Baggio scaled his social entrepreneurial idea through a bottom-up franchise concept. What would have been alternative ways to grow CDI? In the development of alternative expansion concepts, also consider the challenges and approaches to gaining organizational legitimacy for CDI. While demands for moral acceptance may be less difficult to meet, how can pragmatic legitimacy be build in terms of portraying an efficient use of donated money and computers?

11.5   Further Reading

[1] Nicholls, A. (2010), "The Legitimacy of Social Entrepreneurship: Reflexive Isomorphism in a Pre-Paradigmatic Field", in *Entrepreneurship Theory and Practice*, vol. 34, no. 4, pp. 611-633.
[2] Santos, F.M. (2009), "A Positive Theory of Social Entrepreneurship", INSEAD Faculty & Research Working Paper, 2009/23/EFE/ISIC.
[3] Swedberg, R. (2011), "Schumpeter's full model of entrepreneurship: economic, non-economic and social entrepreneurship", in Ziegler, R. (ed.), *An introduction to social entrepreneurship*, Edward Elgar, Cheltenham, pp. 77-106.
[4] Zahra, S.A., Gedajlovic, E., Neubaum, D.O. and Shulman, J.M. (2009), "A typology of social entrepreneurs: Motives, search processes and ethical challenges", in *Journal of Business Venturing*, vol. 24, no. 5, pp. 519-532.

11.6   Bibliography

[1] Aiken, M. (2006), "Towards market or state? Tensions and opportunities in the evolutionary path of three types of UK Social Enterprise", in Nyssens, M. (ed.), *Towards market or state? Tensions and opportunities in the evolutionary path of three UK social enterprises*, Routledge, London, pp. 259-271.
[2] Aldrich, H.E., Martinez, M.A. (2003), "Entrepreneurship as social construction: a multi-level evolutionary approach", in Acs, Z.J. and Audretsch, D.B. (eds.), *Handbook of entrepreneurship research – an interdisciplinary survey and introduction*, Boston, Kluwer, pp. 359-401.
[3] Aldrich, H.E. (1999), *Organizations evolving*, Sage, Thousand Oaks.
[4] Arrow, K., Debreu, D.G. (1954). "Existence of equilibrium for a competitive economy", in *Econometrica*, vol. 22, pp. 265-290.
[5] Bornstein, D. (2004), *How to change the world: social entrepreneurs and the power of new ideas*, Oxford University Press, Oxford.
[6] Bovaird, T. (2006), "Developing new relationships with the 'market' in the procurement of public services", in *Public Administration*, vol. 84, no. 1, pp. 81–102.
[7] Brush, C.G., Greene, P.G., Hart, M.M. and Haller, H.S. (2001), "From initial idea to unique advantage: the entrepreneurial challenge of constructing a resource base", in *Academy of Management Executive*, vol. 15, no. 1, pp. 64-81.
[8] Campbell, D.T. (1974), "Evolutionary Epistemology", in Schilpp, P.A. (ed.), *The philosophy of Karl Popper*, vol. 1., Open Court ,La Salle, pp. 413-463.
[9] Dacin, P.A, Dacin, T.M. and Matear, M. (2010), "Social Entrepreneurship: Why We Don't Need a New Theory and How We Move Forward From Here", in *Academy of Management Perspectives*, vol. 23, no. 3, pp. 37-57.
[10] Dart, R. (2004), "The Legitimacy of Social Enterprise", in *Nonprofit Management & Leadership*, vol. 14, no. 4, pp. 411-424.
[11] Dean, T.J., McMullen, J.S. (2007), "Toward a theory of sustainable entrepreneurship: Reducing environmental degradation through entrepreneurial action", in *Journal of Business Venturing*, vol. 22, pp. 50–76.
[12] Desa, G. (2011), "Resource Mobilization in International Social Entrepreneurship: Bricolage as a Mechanism of Institutional Transformation", in *Entrepreneurship Theory and Practice*, online: http://onlinelibrary.wiley.com/doi/10.1111/j.1540-6520.2010.00430.x/pdf, accessed date: 31/10/2011.
[13] De Soto, H. (2000), *The Mystery of Capital*. Black Swan, London.
[14] Di Domenico, M.L., Haugh, H. and Tracey, P. (2010), "Social Bricolage: Theorizing Social Value Creation in Social Enterprises", in *Entrepreneurship Theory and Practice*, vol. 34, no. 4, pp. 681-703.
[15] Dowla, A. (2006), "In credit we trust: Building social capital by Grameen Bank in Bangladesh", in *Journal of Socio-Economics*, vol. 35, no. 1, pp. 102-122.

[16] Granovetter, M. (1985), "Economic Action and Social Structure: The Problem of Embeddedness", in *American Journal of Sociology*, vol. 91, no. 3, pp. 481-510.

[17] Grünhagen, M., Koch, L.T. and Saßmannshausen, S.P. (2005), "Kooperation in EXIST-Gründungsförderungsnetzwerken – eine explorative Untersuchung zur Bedeutung von Promotorenfunktionen", in Achleitner, A.-K., Klandt, H. and Voigt, K.I. (eds.), *Jahrbuch Entrepreneurship - Gründungsforschung und Gründungsmanagement 2004/2005*, Berlin: Springer, pp. 319-338.

[18] Hager, M.A., Galaskiewicz, J. and Larson, J.A. (2004), "Structural embeddedness and the liability of newness among non-profit organizations", in *Public Management Review*, vol. 6, no. 2, pp. 159-188.

[19] Hayek, F.A. (1945), "The Use of Knowledge in Society", in *American Economic Review*, vol. 35, no. 4, pp. 519-530.

[20] Kerber, W. (1997), "Wettbewerb als Hypothesentest: Eine evolutorische Konzeption wissenschaffenden Wettbewerbs", in Delhaes, K.v. and Fehl, U. (eds.), *Dimensionen des Wettbewerbs*, Lucius & Lucius, Stuttgart, pp. 31-78.

[21] Kirzner, I.M. (2009), "The Alert and Creative Entrepreneur: A Clarification", in *Small Business Economics*, vol. 32, no. 2, pp. 145-152.

[22] Kirzner, I.M. (1973), *Competition and Entrepreneurship*, University of Chicago Press, Chicago.

[23] Knight, F.H. (1921), *Risk, Uncertainty and Profit*, Kelley, Boston and New York.

[24] Light, P.C. (2006), "Reshaping Social Entrepreneurship", in *Stanford Social Innovation Review*, fall 2006, pp. 45-51.

[25] Lounsbury, M., Glynn, M.A. (2001), "Cultural entrepreneurship: stories, legitimacy, and the acquisition of resources", in *Strategic Management Journal*, vol. 22, pp. 545-564.

[26] Mair, J., Marti, I. (2006), "Social entrepreneurship research: A source of explanation, prediction, and delight", *in Journal of World Business*, vol. 41, no. 1, pp. 36-44.

[27] Martin, R. J., Osberg, S. (2007), "Social entrepreneurship: The case for a definition", in *Stanford Social Innovation Review*, spring 2007, pp. 29–39.

[28] Massarsky, C., Beinhacker, S. (2002), *Enterprising Nonprofits: Revenue Generation in the Nonprofit Sector*, Goldman Sachs Partnership on Nonprofit Ventures, Yale School of Management, New Haven, Conn.

[29] Neck, H., Brush C. and Allen, E. (2009), "The landscape of Social Entrepreneurship", in *Business Horizons*, vol. 52, no. 1, pp. 13-19.

[30] Nicholls, A. (2010), "The Legitimacy of Social Entrepreneurship: Reflexive Isomorphism in a Pre-Paradigmatic Field", in *Entrepreneurship Theory and Practice*, vol. 34, no. 4, pp. 611-633.

[31] Nicholls, A. (2006), "Introduction", in Nicholls, A. (ed.), *Social Entrepreneurship: new models of sustainable social change*, Oxford, pp. 1-37.

[32] Nicholls, A., Cho, A.H. (2006), "Social Entrepreneurship: the structuration of a new field", in Nicholls, A. (ed.), *Social Entrepreneurship – new models of sustainable social change*, Oxford, pp. 99-118.

[33] Parsons, T. (1960), *Structure and process in modern societies*, Free Press, New York.

[34] Phills Jr., J.A., Deigelmeier, K. and Miller, D.T. (2008), "Rediscovering Social Innovation", in *Stanford Social Innovation Review*, Fall 2008, pp. 34-43.

[35] Rangan, S., Samii, R. and Van Wassenhove, L.N. (2006), "Constructive Partnerships: When Alliances between Private Firms and Public Actors Can Enable Creative Strategies", in *Academy of Management Review*, vol. 31, no. 3, pp. 738-751.

[36] Roberts, D., Woods, C. (2005), "Changing the world on a shoestring: The concept of social entrepreneurship", in *University of Auckland Business Review*, vol. 11, no. 1, pp. 45–51.

[37] Santos, F.M. (2009), "A Positive Theory of Social Entrepreneurship", INSEAD Faculty & Research Working Paper, 2009/23/EFE/ISIC.

[38] Saßmannshausen, S.P. (2011, forthcoming), Entrepreneurship-Forschung – Fach oder Modetrend? Evolutorisch-wissenschaftssystemtheoretische und bibliometrisch-empirische Analysen, (Zugleich Dissertation Bergische Universität Wuppertal, Schumpeter School of Business and Economics 2010), Köln, Lohmar: Eul Verlag (Reihe Entrepreneurship-Monographien).

[39] Schramm, C. (2010), "All Entrepreneurship is Social", in *Stanford Social Innovation Review*, spring 2010, pp. 20-22.

[40] Scott, W.R. (2001), *Institutions and Organizations*, 2nd ed., Sage, Thousand Oaks.

[41] Schumpeter, J.A. (1950), *Capitalism, Socialism and Democracy*, 3rd ed., Harper Torch Books, New York.

[42] Schumpeter, J.A. (1934), *The Theory of Economic Development*, Transaction Publishers, New Brunswick, London.

[43] Schumpeter, J.A. (1928), "Unternehmer", *Handwörterbuch der Staatswissenschaften*, 4th ed., vol. 8, Jena, pp. 476-487.

[44] Seelos, C., Mair, J. (2005), "Social Entrepreneurship: Creating new business models to serve the poor", in *Business Horizons*, vol. 48, pp. 241-246.

[45] Shane, S.A. (2003), A General Theory of Entrepreneurship – The Individual-Opportunity Nexus, Edward Elgar, Cheltenham.

[46] Stiglitz, J.E. (1989), "Markets, Market Failures, and Development", in *American Economic Review*, vol. 79, no. 2, pp. 197-203.

[47] Suchman, M.C. (1995), "Managing legitimacy: strategic and institutional approaches", in *Academy of Management Review*, vol. 20, no.3, pp. 571-610.

[48] Swedberg, R. (2011), "Schumpeter's full model of entrepreneurship: economic, non-economic and social entrepreneurship", in Ziegler, R. (ed.), *An introduction to social entrepreneurship*, Edward Elgar, Cheltenham, pp. 77-106.

[49] Winston, C. (2006), *Government Failure versus Market Failure: Microeconomics Policy Research and Government Performance*. Brookings Institution Press, Washington D. C.

[50] Zahra, S.A., Gedajlovic, E., Neubaum, D.O. and Shulman, J.M. (2009), "A typology of social entrepreneurs: Motives, search processes and ethical challenges", in *Journal of Business Venturing*, vol. 24, issue 5, pp. 519-532.

[51] Zahra, S.A. Rawhouser, H.N., Bhawe, N., Neubaum, D.O. and Hayton, J.C. (2008), "Globalization of Social Entrepreneurship", in *Strategic Entrepreneurship Journal*, vol. 2, no. 2, pp. 117–131.

[52] Zimmerman, M., Zeitz, G. (2002), "Beyond survival: achieving new venture growth by building legitimacy", in *Academy of Management Review*, vol. 27, no. 3, pp. 414-432.

12 The Impact of Social Entrepreneurship on Societies

Markus Beckmann

Leuphana University of Lüneburg
Centre for Sustainability Management

Learning goals

Upon completing this chapter, you should be able to accomplish the following:

- Distinguish between an organizational and a societal perspective on social entrepreneurship and social business.

- Discuss social entrepreneurship as an alternative instrument for solving social problems and addressing social needs.

- Explain the difference between a static and a dynamic perspective on impact.

- Compare the contribution of social entrepreneurship with the potential of charitable NGOs and aid, for-profit companies, and government provision.

- Describe the conditions under which governments, aid, and for-profit markets can best deliver static impact.

- Explain the dynamic impact of social entrepreneurship for systemic learning.

12.1   Introduction

Social entrepreneurship has created high expectations. It is welcomed as a new approach to overcoming poverty and social exclusion in the developing world (Seelos and Mair, 2005). It is heralded as a new mechanism for solving social ills and satisfying human and ecological needs in the developed world (Mawson, 2008). And, indeed, there are impressive examples of how social entrepreneurs around the world have come up with innovative and far-reaching solutions to hitherto unmet social and ecological challenges (Bornstein, 2004; Elkington and Hartigan, 2008). For many, social entrepreneurship promises a new "hope for sustainable development" (Seelos and Mair, 2009). Others argue that social entrepreneurship and the concept of social business hold the key to building a new kind of capitalism (Yunus, 2007; 2010).

It is not hard to see how individual social entrepreneurs have created considerable social change in their specific fields, but questions remain as to the overall impact that social entrepreneurship can have on entire economies and societies. What is different about social entrepreneurship compared to other approaches like charitable NGOs, markets, or public government provision? What is it that social entrepreneurship can offer for developing countries and for the future development of capitalism? In short, how does social entrepreneurship impact economies?

To answer these questions, this chapter takes two perspectives on the impact of social entrepreneurship. The first one is a *static* perspective. Seen from this viewpoint, the impact of social entrepreneurship has to do with the solutions, goods, and services that social entrepreneurs themselves deliver at a given point in time. The second perspective is a *dynamic* one. From this vantage point, impact is viewed in light of how social entrepreneurs change their environment so that not only they but also other actors begin to provide solutions and offer much needed goods and services. Static impact is, in other words, about efficiency; dynamic impact focuses on innovation.

Distinguishing between static and dynamic impact allows delineating more rigorously the systematic role and relevance of social entrepreneurship. Social entrepreneurship, according to the central argument developed here, is important both for its static *and* its dynamic impact. Systematically, however, it is particularly the dynamic impact that defines the contribution of social entrepreneurship. Social entrepreneurs are change agents who institute new patterns of value creation that other actors may adopt, ultimately realizing an even higher static impact. The impact of social entrepreneurship is thus, above all, a transformative one.

This argument will be developed in five steps. Section 12.2 highlights the need to take a societal perspective when talking about impact. Section 12.3 compares the static impact potential of social entrepreneurship with that of charitable NGOs, for-profit companies, and government provision. By analogy, Section 12.4 develops such a comparison with regard to dynamic impact. Section 12.5 offers a short conclusion, followed by a case study in Section 12.6.

12.2   A Societal Perspective on Impact

In his controversial essay, Milton Friedman (1970) argued that the "social responsibility of business is to increase its profits." According to this perspective, the purpose of business is to maximize profits. In contrast, social entrepreneurship and social business are defined as ventures intended not to maximize profits but social impact. Consequently, the position of social business proponents such as Nobel laureate Muhammad Yunus might be stated as the "social responsibility of business is to address social needs."[27]

These two positions appear to be radically different, at least at first glance, and this difference is sometimes used as a key argument in support of the idea that social business entrepreneurship is in a superior position to achieve social impact. In their presentations on the concept of social business, the Grameen group illustrates this point as shown in **Figure 12.1**. Building on the distinction between ends and means, **Figure 12.1** provides a useful starting point for comparing charitable non-governmental organizations (NGOs), traditional for-profit companies, and the social business approach.[28]

Figure 12.1   The Means and Ends of NGOs, Social Business, and Traditional Business

Own illustration based on Grameen Creative Lab (2010)

---

[27] The Grameen Creative Lab, a think tank of the Grameen social business group, puts it this way: "Unlike traditional business, social business operates for the benefit of addressing social needs that enable societies to function more efficiently." See "The Social Business Concept" at http://www.grameencreativelab.com/a-concept-to-eradicate-poverty/the-concept.html.   accessed date: 01/11/2011.

[28] The concepts of social business and social entrepreneurship are not exact equivalents, of course, but for the sake of brevity, they will be treated as synonymous here because both have a social mission and both typically try to achieve financial sustainability in the long term.

According to Grameen, social business combines the best of both worlds: it not only seeks to maximize social impact like an NGO; it is also financially self-sustainable like a for-profit company and thus independent of donations. As a result, it links the social ends of NGOs with the means of business and is thus able to have far greater impact than either on their own.

The Grameen illustration helps point out the differences regarding means and ends for NGOs, social enterprises, and for-profit companies, but it is less helpful in assessing the potential and actual impact of these different approaches as it is a purely *internal* perspective of the organizations. Yet, when talking about societal impact, the relevant perspective is a societal one. **Figure 12.2** clarifies this difference.

Looking at things from a societal perspective makes it possible to reconcile the seeming contradiction between the Friedman and Yunus positions. Yunus takes an organizational perspective and then suggests defining a social purpose directly as the organizational end. Friedman takes a societal perspective and argues that the profit-motive as an organizational end can be a powerful means for indirectly achieving diverse societal needs.[29] Thus, Yunus and Friedman are arguing at two different levels (**Figure 12.2**). Yunus highlights the *differences* between NGOs, social business, and for-profit companies; the societal perspective emphasizes a very important *commonality* in that each of the three organizational forms can be an instrument for addressing social needs. When looking at the issue of impact, NGOs, social enterprises, and for-profit companies are thus not competing ends but alternative means for meeting manifold social needs.

Figure 12.2   A Societal Perspective on Means and Ends

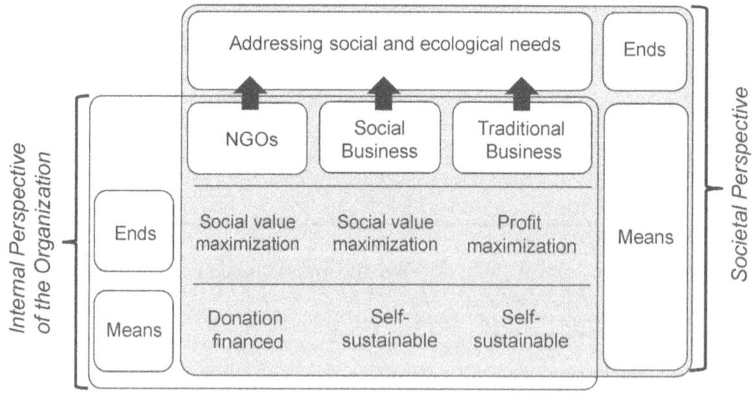

Own illustration

---

[29]   Friedman (2005) makes this explicit when he states: "Maximizing profit is an end from the private point of view; it is a means from the social point of view."

A societal perspective on the issue of impact reveals two insights. First, just because a social entrepreneurship venture has a social purpose does not mean that it automatically has a stronger social impact than a comparable for-profit business. Second, just because a social enterprise actually earns money does not necessarily mean that it is a better solution to a problem than a charitable NGO financed by donations. The societal perspective highlights that each organizational approach uses a different instrument—a specific tool—for addressing societal needs. A tool, however, does not have an intrinsic impact nor is it intrinsically superior to another type of tool. What is the intrinsic impact or superiority of a hammer? The answer depends on the problem: Do you want to nail something to the wall or do you want to cut a piece of cloth? It also depends on other circumstances or conditions of use, for example, on whether you have nails or only screws. Finally, it depends on the alternatives. If you want to cut a piece of cloth, a pair of scissors is probably better than a knife; however, a knife would be superior to a hammer, if those were the only tools available.

This analogy illustrates that social entrepreneurship can be seen as a "tool" to address social needs. How powerful the impact of this tool is will depend on

- the problem to be solved,
- the conditions under which it will be used, and
- the alternatives.

The next section compares charitable NGOs, for-profit companies, government provision, and social entrepreneurship as alternative tools for addressing social needs. By looking at different problems and different boundary conditions, the discussion provides a better understanding of the potential static impact of social entrepreneurship on economies and society at large.

12.3   Static Impact and Social Entrepreneurship

In this section, the static impact of social entrepreneurship is explored by focusing on a given point in time and discovering what social entrepreneurship can contribute in different problem settings. To this end, a rough and generic overview of the potential impact of other problem-solving approaches serves as a benchmark against which to compare the specific static impact that social entrepreneurship can have. Comparing social entrepreneurship with the idealized solutions of charitable NGOs, the state, and for-profit companies, the key claim is that social entrepreneurship is often an important second-best solution in areas where first-best solutions fail.

12.3.1   Static Impact of Charitable NGOs and Aid vs. Social Entrepreneurship

As illustrated by **Figure 12.1**, a major difference between traditional NGOs and social entrepreneurship is financing. Many social entrepreneurship ventures try to achieve financial sustainability over time; many NGOs rely systematically on donations. Depending on the problem context, both have certain advantages.

Donations are a fairly pure form of unilateral solidarity and altruism. The donor gives money or other inputs without receiving a material payment in return. How well does this principle work in different problem contexts?

Figure 12.3 presents a typology that illustrates under which conditions the solidarity principle can be particularly effective and where it is less so. The vertical dimension distinguishes between one-time problems that can be solved more or less at one given point in time and permanent problems that require continuous contributions. The horizontal dimension differentiates between problems that occur in small groups where people have strong face-to-face relations and problems that arise in complex and anonymous societies. This typology shows how the principle of solidarity has more potential to solve some problems than others.

Figure 12.3   The Impact of Solidarity

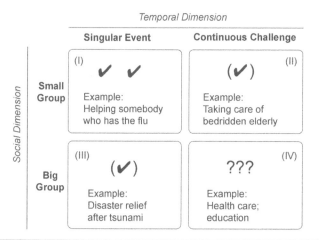

Own illustration inspired by a presentation by Andreas Suchanek

Box I of **Figure 12.3** illustrates a one-time problem in a small group: a friend or a neighbor who has the flu and needs help. In this situation, many people will be willing to go grocery shopping or walk the dog for a day or two. The situation in Box II, however, is more difficult. Again, someone is ill, but permanently—perhaps an elderly person who is bedridden after a stroke and needs care continuously. In a small group with strong social ties, such as a family, it might still be possible to meet this challenge, but it will grow increasingly difficult and stressful with time, and in some cases there will be no family or volunteers willing to provide long-term help. Box III looks at one-time, singular problems that affect people outside their personal world, maybe even abroad. In these exceptional cases, many people are willing to make a one-time donation. Take the example of the tsunami disaster in Indonesia or the devastating earthquake in Haiti: millions of North Americans and Europeans willingly gave billions of dollars to help. In such cases, solidarity can be a powerful motive. The situation changes, however, in Box IV. This box also contains problems that affect other people outside one's personal realm or even in faraway places, but these problems require a continuous solution. In this situation, spontaneous solidarity is rarely sustainable. Some people might be willing to give some money, but it will be hard to mobilize many people to make long-term financial commitments to people they do not know, especially when the results of their generosity will be a long time coming.

The typology in **Figure 12.3** highlights an important difference between the potential static impact of social entrepreneurship compared to that of charitable NGOs. Donation-based NGOs can be particularly powerful in the case of single-event or highly specific problems. In cases like the tsunami disaster, for example, NGOs provided the organizational infrastructure for large-scale solidarity. Without their mediation, individual donors in, say, Germany, would have found it very difficult to help the people suffering that crisis. In contrast, for that particular point in time, a social entrepreneurship venture built on a complex business model probably would not have had the same impact in terms of providing immediate short-term relief.

Compared with charitable NGOs, therefore, social entrepreneurship might have less of a static impact when it comes to providing short-term relief. Yet, this is not what the genuine domain of social entrepreneurship is about. Social entrepreneurship is about innovating self-sustainable solutions to large-scale social problems. Put differently, social entrepreneurship is about long-term solutions with the potential to have an impact on big social groups. The systematic domain of social entrepreneurship is thus found in Box IV.

Box IV of **Figure 12.3** contains problems that require a continuous, or at least long-term, solution. Consider the case of providing education or fundamental health services. Similar to the problems in Box III, an organizational infrastructure will be necessary to effectively provide these, but an organized one-time intervention such as erecting a school building or a donation-based solution that depends on outside inputs would simply be neither sufficient nor sustainable. The permanent character of such challenges requires a *systemic* solution that can be self-sustaining.

Despite some efforts by charitable NGOs to solve the sort of problems found in Box IV of **Figure 12.3**, the static delivery of systemic solutions is a domain where the relevant alternatives for social entrepreneurship are the public provision of goods and services as well as the market delivery by for-profit firms. To further assess the static impact of social entrepreneurship, the next two sections look at these alternative problem-solving arrangements.

12.3.2   Static Impact of For-Profit Companies vs. Social Entrepreneurship

As illustrated by **Figure 12.2**, for-profit firms can be instruments for addressing important social needs. Indeed, the growth of capitalist markets over the last 150 years shows that a functional institutional framework can harness the pursuit of profit and self-interest for highly desirable social results, such as innovation, new jobs, growth, and better and cheaper products and services (Baumol, 2002). In fact, under appropriate institutions, profits signal that a company has successfully created value. That is, in a functioning market system, a company can make a profit only if customers are willing to pay more for its product than it spent to produce it. Profits are then an epiphenomenon of successful value creation, a signal that the firm is giving more to society than it is taking from it. Seen this way, profits motivate companies to fulfill their raison d'être as societal actors: to organize the creation of value (Jensen, 2002). Given appropriate institutions and functioning markets, there are a number of reasons why traditional for-profit ventures can have a stronger societal impact in terms of delivering much-needed goods and services than mission-driven social entrepreneurship ventures.

First, if (and only if!) profits are an indicator of value creation, they send a strong signal as to whether a company is fulfilling its societal purpose by rewarding successful value creators and punishing those companies that realize losses, meaning that they actually destroy societal value because they consume resources of more value than what they produce. Second, from an internal firm perspective, profit expectations provide a way of deciding between alternative investments and strategies. Third, profits show investors the areas with the largest potential for value creation and thus direct scarce resources into a more valuable use. Social investors and social entrepreneurs have begun to develop methods for performance measurement, but to date these indicators are highly ambiguous and hard to understand compared to a simple profit measure.

In short, when looking at the efficiency of social entrepreneurship in achieving static impact, it might often be only a *second-best solution*. For-profit firms may very well be the first-best-solution in certain cases because they can deliver needed goods and services more efficiently, can take advantage of economies of scale, and are more sustainable financially. However, the potential superiority of profit-driven companies hinges on a number of critical conditions. If and only if markets have a perfect institutional framework with no market failure will the profit-driven invisible hand lead to the first-best solution with a necessarily stronger static impact than the visible hand of the social entrepreneur. Under such idealized conditions, there are no negative or positive externalities, property rights are perfectly defined, complete private contracts are possible and can be sanctioned by functioning institutions of the rule of law, and, finally, there is no exclusion of underprivileged groups so that everybody has free access to markets, capital, education, and legal justice.

Real life is often far from ideal, however, and in the presence of market failures or shortcomings, for-profits may fail to realize their potential as first-best solutions. In these situations, social entrepreneurship can be an important second-best solution by providing much needed goods and services that internalize externalities, by providing access for the excluded, and by creating value where for-profits cannot or do not (Santos, 2009). Compared to the real-life alternatives, social entrepreneurship is the best "tool" for the job; however, compared to ideal and properly functioning for-profit markets, social entrepreneurship remains a second-best solution.

12.3.3   Static Impact of Government Provision vs. Social Entrepreneurship

Markets are a powerful instrument for providing private goods and services, but there are important social needs that markets do not meet as well. Most importantly, markets are not very suitable for providing public goods. In economics, public goods are defined as goods that are non-rival and non-excludable. Non-rivalry means that if someone consumes a public good, it does not mean that no one else can. Non-excludability means that everyone can enjoy the good. Take the case of eradicating malaria, which is an example of both. The fact that one person benefits from this public health good does not reduce the availability of "eradication of malaria" for somebody else (non-rivalry). At the same time, it is hardly possible to exclude somebody who lives in this country from enjoying the benefits of eradicating malaria (non-excludability).

Non-rivalry and non-excludability appear to be excellent characteristics: everybody benefits from the public good and nobody can be excluded. However, the problem is that these two characteristics render the market provision of public goods difficult, if not impossible. If no one can be excluded from enjoying the benefits of a public good, nobody will be willing to pay for it. As a consequence, functioning markets for these products will not evolve.

Many of the most pressing problems in Box IV of **Figure 12.3** involve the challenge of providing such public goods, including providing communities with infrastructure, education, public health services, basic research, a functioning legal system, peace, stability, to name just a few.

The arguably most powerful instrument that societies have developed for systematically organizing the provision of such public goods is the state, its government, and related public-sector institutions.

First, the state is a powerful means of overcoming the problem of free-riding. Providing public goods for a community requires effective collective action. Only if everybody contributes their share, can the optimal level of public goods be provided. Yet, every individual has an incentive to free-ride on the contributions of others. In this situation, the state can be used to make contributions to the public good mandatory. For example, the state can tax citizens to collect those resources necessary to finance socially desirable public goods. Note that this does not necessarily mean that the state itself needs to *produce* these goods; instead, it can also regulate and finance an arrangement that delegates this task to other actors (e.g., private firms, NGOs).

Second, given functioning and efficient public bureaucracies, the state can draw on a so-phisticated infrastructure that already exists and that allows realizing economies of scale and scope. Take, for example, the field of public health. Once there is an infrastructure to organize and finance the vaccination of children against, say, polio, in one place, the same publicly financed agency can take this service to many other places and can also be used to carry out other health-related services, such as vaccinations against measles or providing medical checkups.

Third, in democratic states, the citizens can hold the government accountable for its suc-cess, or lack thereof, in delivering public goods. People can vote ineffective governments out of office and let the public authorities know which public goods are actually needed. The democratic process provides feedback that directs scarce resources into their best usage from a societal perspective.

Thus, given a functioning state with efficient institutions and democratic accountability, government can have a much stronger impact in terms of providing public goods than can social entrepreneurship. Compared to a functioning state, social entrepreneurs do not have systematic means to organize collective action for an entire society, they cannot easily draw on a comparable existing and sophisticated infrastructure, and they do not necessarily have well-established feedback-mechanisms for democratic accountability.

In short, when looking at the efficiency of social entrepreneurship for delivering public goods and services at a given point in time, social entrepreneurship may well be only a *second-best solution*. Ideally, a functioning public sector has the most potential to be the first-best solution. Yet, just as in the case of for-profit markets, this potential superiority of the public sector as an instrument for providing public goods hinges on a set of demanding and critical conditions. To start with, there must be a well-functioning state, a fair and effec-tive tax system, and no corruption. Furthermore, for democratic accountability to work as intended, the majority should not be allowed to ignore the needs of a minority, and all citizens must be well informed and have full political rights.

In many countries, not only but particularly in the developing world, these idealized condi-tions are far from being realized. In these situations, social entrepreneurship can be an important second-best solution. In the face of government failure, social entrepreneurs can create alternative solutions that generate awareness of unaddressed needs, organize collec-tive action to bring together critical resources, and actually provide the much-needed goods and services. Compared to the relevant alternatives at that given point in time, this static impact of social entrepreneurship is highly important, if not critical, for the lives of many. Compared to the idealized potential of a functioning systemic public-sector solution, how-ever, social entrepreneurship often remains a second-best solution.

12.3.4   Social Entrepreneurship as a Second-Best Solution in Terms of Static Impact

In his books on social business, Muhammad Yunus (2007, 2010) proposes a distinction between two types of social business that social entrepreneurs can build to address pressing societal needs. This distinction allows substantiating the claim made in this chapter that social entrepreneurship is an important second-best alternative to the ideal first-best solutions of for-profit markets and government provision. Yunus's social business Type I can be seen as a substitute for a functioning market solution; the Type II social business is a second-best alternative to an idealized government solution.

According to Yunus, a *Type I social business* focuses on providing a product with a specific social, ethical, or environmental goal. Profits the social business generates are then used to scale and improve delivery of this product. A prominent example is Grameen Danone, a joint venture started in 2006 in Bangladesh that distributes Shakti doi, a yogurt fortified with many of the key nutrients typically absent in the diet of children in rural communities.

The Type I social business model can be interpreted as a substitute for fully developed for-profit markets. In the Shakti doi case, there are a number of reasons why for-profit markets fail to provide products that satisfy poor people's nutritional needs, including the low purchasing power of the villagers as well as their limited knowledge about the benefits of enriched nutrition. Consequently, social entrepreneurship can have an important social impact. Grameen Danone increases nutritional quality, consequently improves children's health, and thus enhances their future chances. All good, but how does this social business solution fare from a static impact perspective? If the status quo continues, does this solution really offer the most efficient and effective impact possible? This is of course a question of relevant alternatives. Since high-quality foods are a private good, the systematic benchmark is fully developed for profit-markets. The alternative scenario is that all villagers know and appreciate the value of enriched nutrition as well as have purchasing power and thus access to these markets. Given competitive markets, a diversity of for-profit firms could then enter this market, bring in the resources to scale a systemic solution countrywide, and compete both in terms of lower prices and better quality. In the absence of such fully developed markets, however, a social business approach can provide a valuable second-best alternative.

Let us now turn to Yunus's concept of a *Type II social business*. A Type II social business does not aim to achieve impact primarily through its products. Rather, it is a profit-maximizing business that uses all its net profits to address important social needs in a local community. Profits are thus not issued as private dividends but are directed into local development activity.

A prominent example of a Type II social business is Otto Grameen, a joint venture between the German retailer Otto and the Bangladeshi Grameen group. The idea behind Otto Grameen is to establish textile factories in Bangladeshi villages that produce T-shirts and other garments for the lucrative European market. The profits of this textile company go to the

Otto Grameen Trust, which uses them to provide social services to the local poor, such as access to health care or basic education (Yunus, 2010). The idea is that, ultimately, "each Otto Grameen factory might anchor an 'Otto Grameen village' in which everyone enjoys a higher standard of living thanks to the company's presence in the community" (Yunus, 2010, p. 185).

This Type II social business model can be interpreted as a second-best alternative to a functioning government provision of public goods. As the local governments cannot provide public goods such as health care or education, Otto Grameen, as a social entrepreneurship venture, takes over and provides these services. With regard to this public good challenge, the paradigmatic benchmark is a functioning local government that provides access to education, health services, and other infrastructure. If such efficient, effective, and democratically accountable local government institutions existed, this solution could very well have a much higher social impact than that of Otto Grameen. Note the relevant alternative here: if Otto Grameen realized and issued private profits, they could be taxed by the local government and thus contribute to publicly funding the provision of social services. Yet, in the absence of such an ideal, functioning public sector, Type II social businesses like Otto Grameen may offer a much-needed and effective second-best alternative.

12.4   Dynamic Impact and Social Entrepreneurship

The previous section looked at the comparative potential of social entrepreneurship for having a static impact on society, with "static" meaning that the analysis looked at a given problem setting, treated the situation as fixed without considering potential dynamic effects changing the situation over time, and then asked about the direct impact that social entrepreneurs had on their immediate beneficiaries in that given moment.

We now shift from a static perspective to a dynamic one, focusing on how social entrepreneurship affects the dynamic evolution of how societies deal with social challenges. Instead of merely emphasizing direct effects of activities on immediate beneficiaries in a given moment, dynamic impact also involves the indirect effects that derive from changing the entire field and leading other actors to adopt new solutions over time. Static impact focuses on efficiency; dynamic impact highlights the importance of innovation.

The key claim of this section is that social entrepreneurship has often a systematic and important comparative advantage for creating a dynamic impact. To substantiate this claim, we again compare the potential of charitable NGOs, for-profit companies, and government provision to solve problems with the transformative capacity of social entrepreneurship.

12.4.1   Dynamic Impact of Charitable NGOs and Aid vs. Social Entrepreneurship

Section 12.3.1 argued that—from a static perspective—philanthropic NGOs are particularly well equipped to organize issue-specific solidarity for a relatively short time period. Of course, they can, and do, also start processes of systemic social change. In fact, many long-term aid projects are based on the idea of "helping others to help themselves" and often have an important dynamic impact on their environment.

Social entrepreneurship, however, offers a number of systematic comparative advantages when it comes to innovative and sustainable solutions to societal problems. This argument applies to the charitable NGO approach generally, but this section highlights these advantages by comparing social entrepreneurship to the more specific case of philanthropic NGOs that work as aid organizations in developing countries.

First, a scalable and systemic solution to a persistent problem requires a sustainable basis. It needs to be self-sufficient and independent in the long run. The very concept of aid, however, implies a certain degree of dependence. Development aid, in particular, tends to rely on outside inputs to solve a local problem. To be sure, transfer-based aid projects might well be able to develop a solution that is ultimately self-sustainable, but the obstacles that must be overcome to accomplish this are formidable.

In contrast, as illustrated in **Figure 12.1**, a key idea of social entrepreneurship, and social business in particular, is to aim for self-sufficiency. Social entrepreneurs seek innovative solutions or business models that mobilize the needed resources from within the system. Instead of relying on outside inputs such as aid transfers, social entrepreneurs activate and empower their constituents to contribute diverse resources that sustain the enterprise. As a result, such self-sustainable solutions are much easier to scale onto a systemic level—be it through for-profit companies copying innovative approaches to value creation or through government institutions that adopt successful social entrepreneurial solutions.

Second, innovative and transformative solutions do not just fall out of the sky; they are the result of constant processes of trial and error. These learning processes are only fully effective if they build on rich feedback to analyze what works well and what can be improved. Aid projects that hand out transfers can find it difficult to obtain such feedback. Of course, many aid organizations try to evaluate their work through feedback, but if the aid beneficiaries are receiving help completely for free, they have very little incentive to complain or make suggestions for improvement. In short, comprehensive and unbiased feedback is a rare commodity for aid organizations.

Social entrepreneurs are not immune from the problem of receiving rich feedback. In fact, measuring impact is one of the most demanding challenges faced by both social entrepreneurship researchers and practitioners. Nevertheless, the social entrepreneurship approach can draw on feedback channels that are closed to traditional aid organizations. Social entrepreneurs often manage to empower their stakeholders and integrate them into the process of value creation. In social enterprises such as Dialogue in the Dark (www.dialogue-in-the-dark.com) or Specialisterne (specialisterne.com), differently abled people, for example, the blind or autistic, contribute as valuable experts. Thus, if people provide important resources—be it a price they pay, their labor or expertise, their activism or community support—they are likely to experience a higher degree of involvement and ownership and be more willing to provide valuable feedback. The cooperation at arm's length between a social entrepreneur and its stakeholders is an important feedback channel.

Third, providing aid runs the risk of crowding out desirable systemic solutions that local governments or the market could provide. Take the case of an NGO that delivers basic health services in a developing country. If foreign aid finances these services, the local government might have fewer incentives to build a functioning health system itself. Even worse, aid transfers can create perverse incentives. If corrupt governments benefit from outside aid monies, it creates an incentive to prolong or even create crisis situations. Similarly, aid can destroy local markets. If charitable NGOs hand out, say, food for free, local farmers may be forced out of business. In all these instances, aid runs the risk of providing a short-term cure for the symptoms of a social problem while actually perpetuating or even exacerbating its causes.

Again, social entrepreneurs are not immune from these problems. However, a number of social entrepreneurship characteristics reduce the risks significantly. To start with, social entrepreneurship tries to mobilize resources within a system instead of relying primarily on outside charitable donations, which reduces the problem of corruption. Also, social entrepreneurs often seek to activate new market mechanisms, thus developing markets rather than crowding them out. In effect, they often provide the blueprint for an innovation that for-profit firms later adopt. Finally, social entrepreneurs are in a better position to induce governments to improve their performance. For example, they can provide "proof" that a new approach actually works and need not create additional costs for the public but even net savings. This claim is supported by evidence that half the social entrepreneurs supported by Ashoka report having influenced national legislation within the first five years after creating their organization (Sen, 2007).

12.4.2 Dynamic Impact of For-Profit Companies vs. Social Entrepreneurship

For-profit companies are remarkable at creating shock waves of creative destruction in the economy and in society at large. In fact, their dynamic impact on our lives is immense. Just take the pace of innovation in the fields of mobility, information technology, pharmaceuticals, or communication. Even in failed states like Somalia, poor people have an astonishing degree of access to long-distance telecommunication thanks to cell-phone technology and pre-paid billing mechanisms.

Nonetheless, there are many problems for-profit companies have failed to solve and mission-driven social entrepreneurs often have a comparative advantage for developing inclusive market solutions, for at least three reasons.

First, social change takes time, and so do properly functioning markets. If a new market is the solution to a problem, it is hardly feasible to create one overnight and start making profit immediately. Social entrepreneurs, on the other time, have the luxury of investing over a much longer-term time horizon than do for-profit companies who need to realize a return on their investments in a rather short period of time. Social entrepreneurs can work with "patient capital" that allows them to invest in much riskier, uncertain, and long-term approaches. These new approaches, however, have a high potential to overcome deadlocks, innovate new markets, and achieve a new equilibrium.

Second, social entrepreneurs tend to be stubbornly committed to a specific problem. It is not that for-profit companies never try to address social needs; they can and do choose a social challenge as a starting point for thinking about new business opportunities. And if the company finds a solution to this problem that enables it to create and capture enough value to make a substantial profit, the company will push this development further. If, however, the project disappoints the company's expectations, the firm will sooner or later stop searching for a solution and move on to the next promising challenge. In contrast, social entrepreneurs tend to care deeply about the very specific problem at hand. If one strategy for solving it fails, the social entrepreneur, instead of abandoning the problem, tests a new solution.

Third, thanks to their specific mission, social entrepreneurs have access to critical resources, such as trust, that for-profit companies cannot access as easily. Social entrepreneurs often cooperate with existing NGOs, community networks, or foundations. They can mobilize important non-monetary resources, such as volunteers. But perhaps their most important advantage, as compared to a traditional for-profit firm, is their reputation for being trustworthy, credible, and legitimate. This is important as many markets fail because due information asymmetries. Take a new medicine that is unfamiliar to the people in a community. A for-profit firm might find it hard to develop this new market if it lacks the credibility and trust to explain the benefits of the new medicine. In contrast, a social business will find it much easier to convince the community that its new product is not intended to make a private profit but that it actually benefits the consumer and delivers value. Social business approaches can thus address lack of transparency, reduce information asymmetries, and develop underdeveloped markets. Once transparency has increased and consumers come to understand the value of the novel products and services, other players, such as for-profit firms, can enter the new market and further increase the overall impact of the innovation.

12.4.3   Dynamic Impact of Government Provision vs. Social Entrepreneurship

Governments and public authorities can certainly have a dynamic impact by innovating new forms of delivering public goods. In comparison, however, social entrepreneurship can build on at least the following three advantages to innovate new approaches and create dynamic impact.

First, dynamic impact is significantly related to successful learning processes. As Douglas North (2005) put it, the "adaptive efficiency" of such learning depends not only on the amount and variety of trial and error experimentation, but also on the feedback loops that allow learning from failure. Unfortunately, governments face substantial barriers to adaptive efficiency. On the one hand, government and public authorities tend to be highly centralized with a unified bureaucracy, which is valuable for diffusing a tested and well-working solution on a broad scale, but is not very conducive to experimentation. On the other hand, simple experimentation—trial and error—even were it possible, is not enough. The results of experimentation and especially the failures need to feed back into the decision-making process. The typical feedback mechanism for governments, however, is rather crude: elections and polls can indicate the population's general approval or disapproval, but can hardly provide specific feedback for any single experiment, much less one that must be repeated over and over again.

In contrast to top-down government provision, the bottom-up concept of social entrepreneurship can increase adaptive efficiency by mobilizing decentralized experimentation and feedback. On the one hand, social entrepreneurs can start many different ventures using different models, that is, they are not constrained by an existing and well-entrenched system for doing things. On the other hand, social entrepreneurs receive more direct feedback from their beneficiaries, who, as discussed above, are often integrated and play an active role in the value creation process.

Second, many societal problems are local or affect only specific minorities. Governments, however, especially at the national level, although capable of providing uniform solutions for the general public, are less able, and very often less willing, to respond to local needs or the needs of minorities, especially when not doing so does not have much of an effect on the outcome of an election. Social entrepreneurship, on the other hand, being not at all dependent on the vote, can be more receptive to minorities, ultimately increasing their visibility. By innovating solutions that show how catering to these minority needs also benefits the majority, they can mainstream new ideas and influence the public sector in the long term.

Third, innovation requires taking risks. The public providers of social services, however, have a tendency to be risk-averse, and for good reason: they are spending the taxpayers' money. In fact, public authorities often only provide funding for a solution that has already been "proved" to work for fear of being criticized for wasting taxpayer money. As a consequence, the public sector has preference for the status quo—solutions already known and tested. Social entrepreneurs, in contrast, are able to test much riskier and innovative approaches. Once these solutions demonstrate their effectiveness and deliver the "proof of concept," other actors, including the public sector, can adopt them. Social entrepreneurship can thus achieve a potentially high dynamic impact over time.

12.5   Conclusion

Social entrepreneurship is often seen as unique because of the specific organizational ends that motivate it and the organizational means it uses. Yet, impact is not about intentions or input but about outcomes. Seen from a societal perspective, the specific organizational approach of social entrepreneurship is therefore not an end in itself, but an alternative means—one instrument among others—to solve social problems. It is the problem itself that determines which of these instruments will most effectively solve it.

Charitable NGOs are particularly powerful in mobilizing altruistic donations to provide relief for short-term, singular problem situations. Long-term, broad-scale problems need a more systemic solution. This is the domain of for-profit markets, government provision, and social entrepreneurship. In an ideal perfectly competitive market, for-profit firms are the first-best solution in terms of providing private goods. Similarly, efficient and well-functioning governments offer a first-best solution for providing public goods. Compared to these idealized solutions, social entrepreneurship is only a second-best solution. Yet, in those areas where the first-best solutions are absent or failing, this second-best choice is highly important. This is especially true in developing countries where social entrepreneurs can play an important role in compensating market and government failures.

While the static impact of social entrepreneurship is important in those areas where first-best systemic solutions are still absent, it has the potential to create an even higher dynamic impact. Compared to charitable aid, for-profit companies, and government provision, social entrepreneurs are in a special position to innovate solutions for a variety of otherwise neglected problems. Once these innovations have proven successful, they can be adopted by other actors, with the eventual result that the innovation has an even higher static impact. Thus, even though social entrepreneurship and social business might not be the future *of* capitalism, they are extremely important *for* the future of capitalism. In light of the complex and manifold challenges facing societies around the world, social entrepreneurship is a powerful transformative force whose static and dynamic impact does create "hope for sustainable development."

12.6   Case Study

Micro-credit programs are an important innovation. They address the problem of credit rationing that leaves many poor people in developing countries without access to the credit that could enable them to make productive investments and rise out of poverty.

Today, both for-profit and social business companies operate in the field of micro finance. In fact, micro finance has become a huge and growing market. Initially, however, this market did not exist due to market failures. Because of their poverty, poor people did not have the collateral that would make them eligible for credit. As a consequence, for-profit banks did not see a prospect for profits and neglected the poor as potential customers. Excluded from the benefits of financial markets, the poor could not participate in many transactions that would actually have been productive for both sides.

Driven by the mission to overcome this sort of exclusion, Muhammad Yunus founded the Grameen Bank in 1983 as a financially sustainable social business that would provide credit to the poor. A key innovation of his micro-credit approach are "credit-rings." Instead of pledging collateral to individual borrowers, groups of borrowers—mainly women—are formed, the members of which are jointly liable and thus have an incentive to monitor each other. Furthermore, because it was a social business, as opposed to a strictly for-profit one, Grameen gained access to rural social networks and thus created understanding and legitimacy for the idea of credit-rings and micro credits.

The social business approach thus played a crucial role in developing the micro-finance market. In effect, it had a remarkable *dynamic* impact. Over the years, thousands of new micro-finance institutions all over the world diffused the idea of micro credits. In Mexico, José Ignacio Avalos Hernández adopted the idea of micro finance in 1990 and transformed his charitable NGO into the micro-finance institution Compartamos, which is aimed at combating widespread poverty. As a non-profit, Compartamos significantly contributed to developing the local market for micro finance. Then, in 2000, it was legally converted into a for-profit bank and grew rapidly. Six years later, in 2006, Compartamos went public and became a privately held for-profit corporation that continued to grow massively. In 2010, Compartamos had annual revenues of about $493 million, with growth rates of about 30%. Grameen's annual revenue, by way of comparison, is about $177 million.

Compartamos's transformation into a for-profit has been harshly criticized by social business proponents. The criticism touches on the general question of whether a for-profit or a social business approach is the superior instrument for providing micro credits. While this question is far too complex to be answered easily, the distinction between dynamic and static impact can perhaps shed some light on the inquiry.

In terms of dynamic impact, social entrepreneurs such as Yunus and the early Avalos Hernández played a critical role in overcoming market failures and creating financial innovations. Once these markets had emerged, however, for-profit banks like Compartamos entered the market. Proponents of the for-profit approach could argue that these for-profits take static impact to a new level. For-profit competition increases efficiency, attracts additional capital, thus making more loans available, and ultimately drives down interest rates, which are still very high in micro finance in general. From this perspective, the fact that Compartamos has tripled its revenues in comparison to Grameen shows that for-profit companies can be powerful engines of static impact.

On the other hand, social business proponents could argue that the for-profit approach is flawed based on remaining market failures in the domain of micro finance. Many poor people are economically illiterate and cannot make fully informed decisions. They are often in situations of dire urgency that easily could be exploited. Also, credit-rings can create social pressure sufficient to drive people to commit suicide when they cannot repay the loans. These problems create the need for further innovations guided by a strong social mission—a challenge social business might be better positioned to address than for-profits.

Questions:

1. Why did for-profit markets fail and lead to credit rationing before the concept of micro credit? Why was social business important in overcoming these problems?

2. What are the benefits of a for-profit micro-finance solution? Under what conditions?

3. What are the benefits for a social business solution? Under what conditions?

4. "In the long run, the poor should not need to rely on social business services but should be able to freely choose between for-profit firms that compete to serve them as valued customers." Do you agree or disagree? Are the micro credits provided by social businesses the future of financial markets—or a transitory step in economic development?

12.7   Further Reading

[1]   Armendáriz, B. and Morduch, J. J. (2007), *The Economics of Microfinance*, MIT Press, Cambridge.
[2]   Baumol, W.J. (2002), *The free-Market Innovation Machine. Analyzing the Growth Miracle of Capitalism*, Princeton University Press, Princeton.
[3]   Easterly, W.R. (2006), *The White Man's Burden: Why the West's Efforts to Aid the Rest Have Done So Much Ill and So Little Good*, Oxford University Press, Oxford.
[4]   Yunus, M. (2010), *Building Social Business: The New Kind of Capitalism that Serves Humanity's Most Pressing Needs*, Public Affairs, New York.

12.8   Bibliography

[1]   Bornstein, D. (2004), *How to Change the World: Social Entrepreneurs and the Power of New Ideas*, Oxford University Press, Oxford, UK.
[2]   Elkington, J. and Hartigan, P. (2008), *The Power of Unreasonable People: How Social Entrepreneurs Create Markets and Change the World*, Harvard Business Press, Boston, MA.
[3]   Friedman, M. (1970), "The social responsibility of business is to increase its profits", in *New York Times Magazine*, September 13, pp. 32–33, pp. 122–126.
[4]   Friedman, M. (2005), Making philanthropy out of obscenity, in *Reason*, October 2005, online: http://www.pitt.edu/~woon/courses/reason.pdf, accessed date: 02/11/2011.
[5]   Grameen   Creative   Lab   (2010),   Social   Business   Lab,   online: http://desautels-events.mcgill.ca/yunus/Final_ Social_Business_Lab_Program.pdf, accessed date: 02/11/2011.
[6]   Jensen, M. C. (2002), Value maximization, stakeholder theory, and the corporate objective function, in *Business Ethics Quarterly*, vol. 12, no. 2, pp. 235–256.
[7]   Mawson, A. (2008), *The Social Entrepreneur: Making Communities Work*, Atlantic Books, London.
[8]   North, D.C. (2005), *Understanding the Process of Economic Change*, Princeton University Press, Princeton, NJ.
[9]   Santos, F. (2009), A positive theory of social entrepreneurship, *INSEAD Working Paper*.
[10] Seelos, C. and Mair, J. (2005), "Social entrepreneurship: Creating new business models to serve the poor", in *Business Horizons*, vol. 48, no. 3, pp. 241–246.
[11] Seelos, C. and Mair, J. (2009), "Hope for sustainable development: How social entrepreneurs make it happen", in Ziegler, R. (ed.), *An Introduction to Social Entrepreneurship: Voices, Preconditions and Contexts*, Edward Elgar, Cheltenham, pp. 228–245.
[12] Sen, P. (2007), "Ashoka's big idea: Transforming the world through social entrepreneurship", in *Futures*, vol. 39, pp. 534–553.
[13] Yunus, M. (2007), *Creating a World Without Poverty: Social Business and the Future of Capitalism*, Public Affairs, New York.
[14] Yunus, M. (2010), *Building Social Business: The New Kind of Capitalism that Serves Humanity's Most Pressing Needs*, Public Affairs, New York.

13 Critical Reflections on Social Entrepreneurship

Pascal Dey & Chris Steyaert
University of St. Gallen

Learning goals

Upon completing this chapter, you should be able to accomplish the following:

- Understand that the euphoria surrounding social entrepreneurship marks a severe hindrance for the advancement of knowledge.

- Comprehend that critique represents an affirmative means for extending the knowledge of social entrepreneurship beyond the confines imposed by common sense and ideology.

- Recognize the difference inherent in critical approaches of social entrepreneurship.

- Understand the distinct paradigmatic and theoretical contribution each type of critique makes to the field of social entrepreneurship.

- Acknowledge that the critique of social entrepreneurship is never completed and that retaining the imaginative and radical potential of social entrepreneurship presupposes institutionalising critique as an on-going task.

- Draw from linguistic approaches to get immersed in critically reflecting iconic texts of social entrepreneurship.

13.1   Introduction

Critique of Social Entrepreneurship: An Impossible Act?
On the face of it, 'social entrepreneurship' represents a concept whose meaning cannot be exhausted by a single definition. Where its various interpretations have been conceived by some as a hindrance to the unfolding of its full potential (e.g. Martin and Osberg, 2007), the worrying point, in our estimate, is not that 'social entrepreneurship' encompasses too many meanings but that the term's potential richness, inventiveness and radicalness has been narrowed down by dominant, politically-shaped understandings of the word 'social'. Given that social entrepreneurship has not been properly understood in its relation to power, ideology and the rendition of the social as governable terrain (Carmel and Harlock, 2008), our contribution departs from the conviction that prevailing understandings of social entrepreneurship are limited as a result of being aligned with elites' comprehension of the good life and society *propre*. Many possible understandings of social entrepreneurship become unthinkable, precisely because they are made to appear to be unreasonable, odd or illegitimate by prevailing standards of truth.

We should critically reconsider the limitations to which social entrepreneurship is currently subjected, so as to instigate more imaginative articulations. However, the point is that a critique of the social entrepreneurship canon is highly unlikely. But why exactly is this the case? There are many reasons for the current paucity of critical engagement with social entrepreneurship, however, a case can be made that the widespread belief in the redemptive power of management, combined with an unshakable belief in the market as leverage for 'making a difference', makes social entrepreneurship appear to be good, reasonable, and necessary. Partly due to social entrepreneurship's taintless evaluative reputation, it has, in fact, become easier to celebrate the most far-reaching utopia than to express even the most marginal point of discontent. In other words, any provocative, counter-intuitive or anachronistic enactment of social entrepreneurship is neutralized a priori because this would direct attention away from the ostensible "real-life" pressures of the day, thus delaying the immediate involvement with today's most pressing social problems. Where dominant narratives of social entrepreneurship promote harmonious social change based on instrumental business-case logic (Arthur et al, 2010), this leaves little space for a substantial critique of social entrepreneurship, for the simple reason that the canon suggests that the solution is already there. Anyone who raises concerns is immediately looked at suspiciously, because social entrepreneurship is overwhelmingly perceived to have already passed the test of critical scrutiny.

Whilst the costs related to the current normalisation of social entrepreneurship are manifold, one of the pre-eminent problems is that social entrepreneurship has been envisioned as a de-politicised blueprint for dealing with social problems. In extremis, social entrepreneurship has been appointed the role of tackling the symptoms of the capitalist system rather than its root causes (Edwards, 2008), thus reinforcing a system that has lately revealed its full toxicity (Noys, 2011). Because social entrepreneurship appears to be beyond question, this paper wants to reclaim the space of critique, for, as we will argue, critique is the pivotal quality that must be fostered to overcome social entrepreneurship's current stasis and to unlock its potential. Given that the academic treatment of social entrepreneurship has played a crucial role in mainstreaming logics of problem-fixing, linear progression, and social equilibrium, we will start by analysing academia's immanent critical potential.[30] The first objective of this paper will be to develop a typology of critical approaches that maps how critique of social entrepreneurship is currently being done. As we make clear that scholarly mechanisms of censorship and control are not fully effective in averting critical activity, the second objective of this contribution will be to go beyond current possibilities and to consider ways to expand the range of critical approaches and, in particular, to describe ways for radicalising, both conceptually and pragmatically, the critique of social entrepreneurship. Overall, critique is viewed as a means for problematising 'social entrepreneurship' with the aim of releasing some of its suppressed possibilities (Sandberg and Alvesson, 2011). By implication, critique is never an end in itself, but rather serves as a means for creating solutions (both imaginative and real) which are not possible within the matrix of the present. Thus, by critically examining social entrepreneurship we will, in the end, be able to implement social entrepreneurship differently.

To develop our contributions, we will proceed in the following manner. After a short exposition of the emergence of critical approaches in social entrepreneurship, we will identify, based on a review of the extant academic literature, four types of critique, called 'myth busting', 'critique of power effects', 'normative critique' and 'critique of transgression', all of which will be presented and discussed in terms of how they question and add a different, if not fresh, view to some of social entrepreneurship's most powerful assumptions. Each type of critique is illustrated through a particularly demonstrative study. Thereafter, we will discuss new possibilities by focusing on the kinds of critique that elicit the radical cause of social entrepreneurship. Emphasis will be placed on fostering the view of critique as intervention (Steyaert, 2011), for interventions clearly show that social entrepreneurship, the way we know it, does not exhaust what social entrepreneurship might become. The paper will close with a short introduction to critical thinking, based on the merits of language-based inquiry.

---

[30] As will become evident in this paper, critical research on social entrepreneurship derives primarily from non-profit, voluntary or third-sector scholars. Scholars in this realm have been sceptical towards the logic of the market (which represents an important aspect of social entrepreneurship). Though a more elaborate treatise of why other threads of research in social entrepreneurship have not engaged in critical reflection exceeds our ambitions, we believe that the maturity of critical thinking in the realm of non-profit, voluntary or third-sector research justifies rendering it an explicit focus of this present contribution.

13.2   Problematising Social Entrepreneurship: Typology of Critical Endeavours

To critique is a research area that is slowly gaining legitimacy in entrepreneurship studies. While the field of entrepreneurship is no longer the paradigmatic monolith it used to be, calls for more 'critical' applications to study entrepreneurship have been of more recent date (Ogbor, 2000; Armstrong, 2005, Jones and Spicer, 2010; Weiskopf and Steyaert, 2009). These critical approaches are not homogeneous, as they draw from quite different understandings of critique. What these various approaches have in common is that they question the representation of entrepreneurship as dominantly being 'treated', as always stimulating and worth being pursued, as not requiring any reflection or change of established ways of research and method (Steyaert, 2011). Critical approaches thus emphasise practices of problematisation which impact the research questions we want to ask. Problematisation consists of examining and challenging assumptions that guide a certain way of doing research (Sandberg & Alvesson, 2011), with the aim to confront the particular logics a field uses to formulate research questions, to legitimise certain methods and to claim theoretical or practical implications. Critical research of entrepreneurship thus focuses on "what the scholar is doing, for whom, and for what as he or she does entrepreneurship theory and research" (Calás et al., 2009, p. 554).

As pleas for a more critical engagement with social entrepreneurship have been growing (e.g. Cho, 2006; Steyaert and Hjorth, 2006; Steyaert and Dey, 2010), we will start by addressing and endorsing some critical issues which scholars have stipulated as urgent. While considering the conundrums and voids of social entrepreneurship research, we will analyse current critical research and create different concepts to capture their critical potential. This will lead into a typology that provides a variety of possible anchor points to engage with critique, rather than a neat plan of strict categorisations. Though our selection is not exhaustive, it gives some direction for how critical research can be employed to advance our understanding of social entrepreneurship.

The first issue, 'myth busting', concerns the paucity of empirical knowledge and the problem of truth. This concept will be used to deliberate how empirical 'reality tests' can put our understanding of social entrepreneurship on a more solid knowledge basis. The second issue, 'critique of power effects', concerns the fact that social entrepreneurship research has mainly ignored the political effects it creates and of which it is a part. Such critique of power effects, as practiced in 'critical sociology', is thus suggested as a way to raise awareness that social entrepreneurship is invested with particular political worldviews that shape reality according to an image of "goodness". The third issue, 'normative critique', addresses the fact that very few studies have reflected social entrepreneurship in terms of its normative foundations. 'Normative critique' is presented as a means for emphasising the moral limitations of those interpretations which envision social entrepreneurship merely from the perspective of market dogmatism and economic self-sufficiency. The fourth issue, 'critique of transgression' deals with the fact that the views of practicing social entrepreneurs have not received enough attention from the research community. 'Critique of transgression' thus inquires how practitioners' narratives differ from academic or political discourse respectively, and how these instances of micro-resistance and -emancipation open up new paths of understanding. In each case, illustrations will be used to demonstrate how critical inquiry reveals the self-evidence of social entrepreneurship and, in doing so, prepares the ground for novel articulations.

13.3   Myth Busting: Testing Popular Ideas and their Assumptions

"So long as an illusion is not recognized as an error, it has a value precisely equivalent to reality." (Jean Baudrillard, 2008, p. 53; quoted in Gilman-Opalsky, 2011, p. 52)

A first form of critique examines how the field is based on unchallenged assumptions which might take mythological form as they become naturalised as established truths. Many ideas in the field of social entrepreneurship, developed in other disciplines (notably management and business entrepreneurship studies) seem to be applied to social entrepreneurship in a rather flippant manner. Such casual, unelaborated associations risk basing social entrepreneurship on false premises (e.g. Cook et al., 2003), and it can be observed that after some time, such assumptions tend to take on an existence of their own. How ideas about social entrepreneurship come to be viewed as knowledge or truth may have little to do with their actual truthfulness. That is, much of what is said and known about social entrepreneurship is mythological in the sense of being perceived as true rather than being effectively true. As a result of myths' self-reinforcing and -reifying tendencies, social entrepreneurship scholarship has in many areas come to rely on untested assumptions pertaining to, for instance, the nature of the social entrepreneur, the reasons for social entrepreneurship's emergence or the prevalence of social entrepreneurship. Because the theorising on social entrepreneurship often relies on impression or instinct rather than on empirical evidence, this makes it necessary to inquire whether statements about social entrepreneurship actually correspond with reality. A first task of critique would hence entail demystifying social entrepreneurship by subjecting its unchallenged assumptions to empirical scrutiny. What we henceforth refer to as 'myth busting' encompasses empirical endeavours that inquire as to whether popular ideas about social entrepreneurship are actually true or merely tall tales.

To illustrate the critique of myth busting, an academic article written by Janelle Kerlin and Tom Pollak (2010) will be analysed. It examines one of the most popular and powerful myths of the third sector: resource dependency theory (RDT). Briefly, RDT implies a causal relationship between the emergence of social entrepreneurship in the nonprofit sector and cutbacks in public spending. As the authors state, a "number of nonprofit scholars have held that nonprofit commercial activity increased significantly during the 1980s and 1990s. [...] they suggest that nonprofits use commercial income as a replacement for lost government grant [...]" (p. 1). RDT explores the idea that traditional nonprofit organisations were experiencing financial pressure as governments became less able to finance their services.

As a result, nonprofits had no other option than to accept that "they must increasingly depend on themselves to ensure their survival [...] and that has led them naturally to the world of entrepreneurship" (Boschee and McClurg, 2003, p. 3). Evidently, RDT positions nonprofit organisations in a Darwinistic scenario, as only the most flexible and entrepreneurial organisations are deemed fit enough to evolve into social entrepreneurship, thus averting their looming demise. One of the most pervasive assumptions of RDT is that nonprofits immediately and rationally adapt to changing financial circumstances. Commercial activity becomes something which nonprofits can willingly and spontaneously switch on and off, depending on the availability of public money (and private donations). If the theory is correct, nonprofits' economic behaviour is purely opportunistic: during prosperous years, they rely on public grants (and public donations); in less prosperous ones, they look for earned-income possibilities to fill the financial gap.

Though RDT is in no way absurd (indeed, it appears reasonable to assume that nonprofit organisations turn towards commercial activities to become self-sufficient), its claims were often not tested or its tests were based on weak empirical data. As Kerlin and Pollak (2010) explain, "scholars have largely lacked the data to substantiate claims that government cuts directly resulted in increased nonprofit commercialization" (p. 2).

Kerlin and Pollak's inquiry represents one of the first tests of RDT that meets the standards of academic rigour. Using the IRS Statistics of Income (which provide reliable financial information on charitable organisations in the United States) allowed for an unambiguous identification of nonprofits' revenue streams over an extended period of time. Kerlin and Pollak thus analyse their data, containing financial information between 1982 and 2002, in two ways. First, they carry out a trend analysis to check whether nonprofits' "commercial revenue rises in response to declines in private contributions and government grants" (p. 5). Second, they perform a panel analysis to see if "growth in commercial revenue is a function of gain or loss in government grants and private contributions over six-year periods" (ibid.). On an aggregate level, the results indicate that the rise of commercial revenue of nonprofits, though more or less steady throughout the investigated period, has actually been smaller than assumed: "commercial income as a percentage of total nonprofit revenue rose from 48.1% in 1982 to 57.6% in 2002" (pp. 7-8). Additionally, and more importantly, the results suggest that "commercial revenue was not a factor in "filling in" for losses in government grants and private contributions" (p. 8). Bluntly expressed, Kerlin and Pollak disqualify RDT's assumption that increases in nonprofit commercial revenue is causally linked with cuts in government grants (as well as private contributions). Even though Kerlin and Pollak's inquiry cannot be imputed to established traditions of critical thought, nor do they claim so, their work can, nevertheless, be regarded as a highly critical contribution, as it creates a sense that something is fundamentally wrong with how social entrepreneurship had previously been understood. Kerlin and Pollak's contribution should thus be conceived as affirmative, as it impels scholars and practitioners alike to find better explanations for the reality of social entrepreneurship. Kerlin and Pollak themselves take the dismantling of RDT as myth as a point of departure to probe alternative theoretical explanations.

Kerlin and Pollak end their contribution by discussing whether institutional theory might not offer a better frame for explaining changes in nonprofits' commercial activities. In doing so, they conclude that their results support such a theoretical shift as the increase in non-profit commercial activity can be interpreted as a passive acceptance of the broader environment and a response to outside pressures "rather than a deliberate effort to subsidise declining revenue from discreet sources" (p. 3). Kerlin and Pollak, whose study epitomises a strong scepticism vis-à-vis over-confident truth claims, are willing to sacrifice beloved myths for a clearer understanding of social entrepreneurship. In alignment with the enlightenment ideal, they open up social construction to its own flaws and errors, so as to create space for whatever lies behind the myth (read: the truth).

In the following section, we will deal with a form of critique that is interested not so much in the truthfulness of given statements than in its relationship to power, knowledge and ideology.

13.4   Critique of Power Effects: Denormalising Discourses, Ideologies and Symbols

"[...] we should try to discover how it is that subjects are gradually, progressively, really and materially constituted through a multiplicity of organisms, forces, energies, materials, desires, thoughts, etc." (Michel Foucault, 1978, p. 97)

In many instances, the validity of a given statement might be less a function of its correspondence with reality than of its normalisation through dominant discourses and technologies of power. This imposes limitations on myth busting, for prevailing systems of power are not necessarily alterable through objective truths. Hence, where myth busting's main opportunity lies in opposing prejudice and established errors vis-à-vis an audience which acknowledges its flaws while being willing to endorse the truth (Gasché, 2007), what we refer to here as 'critique of power effects' takes a more political stance towards knowledge. In particular, such inquiry into power effects has been undertaken in the realm of 'critical sociology' (Boltanski, 2011), which encompasses accounts that are interested in understanding power in its relationship with shaping, controlling and even dominating individuals, groups, and organisations. As an umbrella term that captures a broad array of theoretical perspectives on the making of political effects, critical sociology might take the form of governmental studies (Foucault, 1991) which investigate how people rely on expert knowledge (e.g. guidebooks on nonprofit management) to govern themselves according to the stipulations of post-welfare societies, and how such a process implies a transformation of untaught/non-responsible into responsible subjects. Alternatively, it would be possible to use Boltanski and Chiapello's (2005) theory of ideology to inquire how entrepreneurial reforms in the third sector are justified as necessary, and how social entrepreneurship is presented to the individual as offering "attractive, exciting life prospects, while supplying guarantees of security and moral reasons for people to do what they do" (Boltanski and Chiapello, 2005, pp. 24-25). Or, one might look at social entrepreneurship as an indication of symbolic violence (Žižek, 2008) so as to inquire how it preserves the social order, including instances of inequality, domination or suppression. The pre-eminent aim of these approaches is to develop an understanding of how power conditions the contours of truth, which in turn, renders individuals (and organisations) amenable to political forms of (self-)control. The essential difference between myth busting and critique of power effects is that the former inquires if popular (but untested) ideas stand the test of reality, whereas the latter approaches such ideas as political truths which enable processes of cultural reproduction or self-imposed control to occur. The shift of perspective entailed in the analyses of power along the approaches of critical sociology is that given statements are not examined in terms of "right or wrong", but in terms of the kind of political reality the respective statement prioritises or normalises (including the consequences which derive from this normalisation). The critical inquiry of social entrepreneurship requires a meticulous analysis of the material, historical, economic, discursive or linguistic structures and practices that constitute the conditions of possibility of social entrepreneurship and of which social entrepreneurship is an effect.

Using the above as a starting point, we shall deepen our engagement with the critique of power effects through a revealing study by Sarah Dempsey and Matthew Sanders (2010). There the authors show how iconic representations of social entrepreneurship normalise a particular understanding of meaningful work. Analysing autobiographies of famous US-based social entrepreneurs John Wood, Greg Mortenson and Wendy Kopp, Dempsey and Sanders demonstrate that those accounts provide people in the nonprofit sector with a deeply moralised style of existence which engenders a rather problematic understanding of work-life balance. For instance, the autobiographies instigate a "complete dissolution of a work-life boundary" (Dempsey and Sanders, 2010, p. 449), promoting a standard of meaningful work based on self-sacrifice. Showing that the autobiographies are replete with notions of sleep deprivation, lack of spare time, inexistent personal life, long working hours, in short, frail emotional, social and physical well-being, Dempsey and Sanders conclude that social entrepreneurship is a double-edged sword as it, on the one hand, offers "alternatives to traditional corporate career paths" (p. 438) while, on the other hand, delineating meaningful work as presupposing "stressful working conditions, significant personal sacrifice and low wages" (ibid.).

The important point to note here is that the downsides and exploitative nature of nonprofit careers is not ideologically concealed. Rather, the autobiographies normalise the idea that meaningful work in the nonprofit sector must necessarily be arduous, which is evidenced from the authors portraying "themselves as willingly trading a work/life boundary in return for being able to engage in work that they find truly meaningful" (p. 451). Arguably one of the most serious problems with such representations of social entrepreneurship is, as Dempsey and Sanders rightly contend, that people accept that a higher calling, and social and moral meaning at large, presupposes significant personal sacrifices. The further consequences of this normalisation is that people who are involved in social entrepreneurship might not even try to protect their private lives as popular images of social entrepreneurship propagate that the sense of satisfaction and meaningfulness one gains from working in the nonprofit sector will (or indeed must) compensate for the social and personal costs related with this kind of work.

On the other hand, it has also been suggested that ideas such as the ones discussed by Dempsey and Sanders might weaken the cause of social entrepreneurship by making it less likely that people will identify with a professional career in the nonprofit sector. Once people are fully able to grasp the inevitable disenchantment associated with social entrepreneurship, they might, as Dempsey and Sanders warn us, conclude that the entry barriers for working in the nonprofit sector are simply too high. Though the autobiographies analysed might fuel "lack of understanding, conflict, misallocation of resources and loss to the sector" (Parkinson and Howorth, 2008, p. 286), we should not ignore the possibility that people submit to a career in social entrepreneurship despite full awareness of the high social costs related with such a move. The reason why people might be willing to tolerate being exploited, to the point where they actively endorse their own subjection, is that they have come to accept that there will be no remedy without sacrifice. Practicing individuals should thus be seen not merely as ideologically misguided subjects, but as reflective beings who more or less willingly sacrifice their personal desires for a higher cause. In any case, the question remains as to whether people who are subjected to or subject themselves to dominant conditions of power or knowledge actually reproduce or resist, respectively, the ideological climate of which they are part (Jones et al., 2009).

13.5   Normative Critique: Marking Moral Foundations

"Justice is the first virtue of social institutions, as truth is of systems of thought. A theory however elegant and economical must be rejected or revised if it is untrue; likewise laws and institutions no matter how efficient and well-arranged must be reformed or abolished if they are unjust." (John Rawls, 1999, p. 3)

What myth busting and critiques of power effects from critical sociology have in common is that they both reveal the problems of social entrepreneurship without giving clear indications as to what it should be instead. In contrast, normative critique is explicit about the kind of trajectory social entrepreneurship must endorse. Such an investigation might begin with a thorough survey of mainstream accounts of social entrepreneurship, however, the ultimate objective is to perform a moral judgement of social entrepreneurship, not least pertaining to its role in society. This might sound easy. Contrary to traditional business entrepreneurship, whose normative foundations mark a highly debated issue, social entrepreneurs and enterprises are usually regarded as a priori good. Though the meaning of 'social entrepreneurship' varies from author to author, it is usually said to alleviate social problems, to catalyse social transformation, or to make conventional businesses more socially responsible (Mair and Marti, 2006). Yet, where scholars have mostly remained positive about the redemptive qualities of social entrepreneurship (Yunus, 2008), seeing the market as the means for solving the problems which neither the state nor the nonprofit sector were able to solve, a normative check is worthwhile, as the assumed synergies between the social and the economic aspects might be more controversial than the literature suggests.

As a cursory look into scholarly texts reveals, one of the most pressing domains of normative reflection concerns the idea that the link-up of the two terms 'social' and 'entrepreneurship' necessarily engenders a uncontested win-win situation. Initially seen by many as an oxymoron (e.g. Hervieux et al., 2010), more normatively inclined objections held that social entrepreneurship forms a euphemism for undermining the social mission, heritage or identity of nonprofit or voluntary sector organisations. Instead of taking the 'social' for granted, including suggestions that it is easy to balance social and economic objectives, scholars quickly raised the question of social entrepreneurship's antidemocratic trends. Trading or earned-income strategies were thus less regarded as merely technical or instrumental-rational matters than as organising metaphors that exert a distinct influence on social entrepreneurship's normative foundation.

One of the main concerns was related to the belief that markets would be able to tackle social and environmental problems (Humphries and Grant, 2005), a view which becomes questionable as it suggests that the single best way of solving the ills of the market is through the market. Such a proposal is not just contestable logically (e.g. circularity), it also raises normative issues related with the potential totalitarianism of economic thinking. Dey and Steyaert (2010) have touched upon this problem, using academic texts to probe the normative foundation of the 'social' of social entrepreneurship. The authors' analysis thus revealed that social entrepreneurship is often embedded in discourses stressing rationality, utility, progress and individualism. These discursive significations delineate social entrepreneurship as a "societal actor that confirms the modernist, Western notion of order and control, while contributing to the impression that social change can be achieved without causing debate, tensions or social disharmony" (p. 88). Dey and Steyaert point out that such alignments are problematic because social entrepreneurship is conceived as worthwhile if (and only if) it bears immediately measurable, economic results. Seeing social entrepreneurship primarily as a means for compensating for ostensible state and market failures hence transforms the subject matter into a de-politicised, quasi-economic entity. Dey and Steyaert's reflection takes issue with the view that social entrepreneurship is univocally good, for it is often embedded in functionalist, instrumental and economic logics.

Where normative critique generally calls for elaborating precisely the sort of common good social entrepreneurship seeks to offer, we would like to illustrate this point based on an eloquent treatise by Angela Eikenberry (2009). In her article, Eikenberry contends that the nonprofit and voluntary sector is currently witnessing a shift towards "a normative ideology surrounding market-based solutions and business-like models" (p. 586; cf. also Eikenberry & Kluver, 2004). Social entrepreneurship is conceived to be an inherent part of this normative shift, as it propounds that nonprofit organisations should take on more market-based approaches to gain funding. In Eikenberry's estimate, what is problematic about social entrepreneurship from a normative perspective is that by creating earned-income strategies to meet their financial needs, nonprofits risk weakening "their appeal to donors because individuals think their donations are not needed" (p. 587). Apart from obscuring the validity of their nonprofit status, there is also evidence that social entrepreneurial nonprofits draw attention and resources away from their social mission: "marketisation is problematic for the potential democratic contributions of nonprofit and voluntary organisations. Although these institutions have long been admired for their democratic effects, a market discourse appears to compromise the contributions that nonprofit and voluntary organisations might make to democracy" (p. 588). As a way of counteracting the "colonialisation" of nonprofits by the market logic in general and social entrepreneurial funding strategies specifically , Eikenberry recommends setting "up spaces for citizen participation and deliberation" (p. 583). Such participatory spaces are construed as a corrective for dealing with the antisocial effects of the market. In particular, involving diverse stakeholders of nonprofit organisations in organisational and societal governance, agenda setting, deliberation and decision making will allow for "a more just, humane, and socially cooperative future", Eikenberry believes (p. 593).

To conclude, Eikenberry's (2009) treatise is testament to the urgency of further investigating the moral role of social entrepreneurship in today's society. In a very important way, it offers an analytical perspective for disentangling social entrepreneurship from its economic and managerial over-codification, and for rendering it a matter of society once again (Hjorth, 2009). In the next chapter, we will present a fourth type of critique that focuses on the perspective of practitioners.

13.6   Critique of Transgression: Resisting and Re-appropriating Prescribed Routes

"[…] to attempt explanations without reference to the meanings […] held by actors, and without regard to their underpinning symbolic codes, is to provide a very thin account of reality." (Richard Freeman and Michael Rustin, 1999, p. 18)

To flesh out the intention and merits of the critique of transgression, we would like to begin by pointing out the immanent limits of both normative critique and critical analysis of power. As discussed above, normative critique is mainly about analysing and taking issue with moral justifications of social entrepreneurship and, if expedient, about prescribing a more worthwhile moral foundation. The innate danger of such a gesture is that the critic might replace one ideology (e.g., marketisation) with another (e.g., participative democratisation). Though Eikenberry (2009) seems aware of this trap, writing that she does not "intend to create another hegemonic discourse" (p. 593), it is hardly possible to repudiate that her decision reflects her own perspective. Normative critique will always be ideological, for the simple reason that there is no space beyond ideology (Boje et al., 2001). There is a second, related limitation associated with normative critique: it reflects the views of social scientists over, for instance, those of the subjects being researched. This objection also holds true for critical approaches from critical sociology, which has been accused of denying the people being studied any critical competences with regard to their own situation. As Boltanski and Thévenot (1999) have argued in this respect, if "we want to take seriously the claims of actors when they denounce social injustice, criticise power relationships or unveil their foes' hidden motives, we must conceive of them as endowed with an ability to differentiate legitimate and illegitimate ways of rendering criticisms and justifications" (p. 364).

By extension, unlike both these forms of critique which maintain a certain distance towards their subject of inquiry, the critique of transgression takes people's perspectives, utterances and stories into account. People, less than being construed as ideologically blinded or dominated by intangible forces, are treated as reflexive beings who are very well able to reflect on and criticise the social reality they live in. Where the main task deriving from the critique of transgression is to concentrate on what people say and do, this is largely in accordance with recent pleas to better understand how social entrepreneurs themselves perceive and experience their everyday work, including the motives and ideologies they endorse (Boddice, 2009). Revealing what practitioners do and say offers fresh insights into how they resist their potential domination (e.g., by the market discourse; cf. Eikenberry, 2009), and "how they navigate the resulting work/life tensions" (Dempsey and Sanders, 2010, p. 454). In regard to resistance, this term does not imply a space beyond power (i.e., a sacred space of the authentic individual). Instead, and in accordance with Foucault (1978), critique of transgression concedes that "resistance is never in a position of exteriority in relation to power", (p. 95). The concept 'transgression' hence entails "emancipatory" practices through which individuals appropriate authoritative discourses and technologies of power to their own ends (Foucault, 1998). Though individuals are never beyond power, they might punctuate, breach and creatively reassemble that which is given and taken for granted, thus creating the conditions of possibility of 'becoming other'.

Such transgressive moves can be illustrated through empirical inquiries which investigate how social entrepreneurs react in and towards the ideological climate in which they operate. Caroline Parkinson and Carole Howorth's (2008) study appears particular fitting, as it was conducted in the United Kingdom, a context in which social enterprise has "been heavily promoted and supported as a site of policy intervention" (Teasdale, 2011, p. 1), and thus has been used to promote an efficiency logic of "more for less" (Hogg and Baines, 2011). Addressing how social entrepreneurs view the dominant understanding of social enterprise (as produced and disseminated by UK policy-makers, funders and support agencies), Parkinson and Howorth use a linguistic approach to study the disjuncture between official reasoning and practitioners' ability to make sense of their work. Where the analysis reveals that official discourse of social enterprise places great emphasis on individual capabilities as well as on a managerially defined model of community service delivery, the authors used discourse analysis to probe the extent to which social entrepreneurs' language mimics or transgresses respectively, notions of problem fixing, individualism and managerialism. The analysis revealed that business terms were, in fact, used by social entrepreneurs, though mostly in conjunction with negative attributes such "as 'dirty', 'ruthless', 'ogres', 'exploiting the black economy', 'wealth and empire building' and 'treating people as second class'" (pp. 300-301). Importantly, being asked whether they saw themselves as social entrepreneurs, interviewees often dismissed the concept, claiming that "'it's amusing!', 'it's ridiculous!', 'too posh [...] I'm working class'" (p. 301). Parkinson and Howorth provide ample evidence that social entrepreneurs' articulations are at odds with UK social enterprise policies, which chiefly promote efficiency, business discipline and financial independence. At the same time, however, their analysis also indicates that social entrepreneurs' talk does partially echo the ideological context in which they work (notably what concerns the framing of local problems and their respective solutions).

As follows from Parkinson and Howorth, critique of transgression acknowledges that resistance is often transient and partial, as social entrepreneurs are never fully outside the influence of power (though never completely infiltrated by it, either). The obvious merit of such a view is that it offers a more nuanced understanding of how prevailing ideologies are contested at the level of practice, while raising awareness that this contestation must not necessarily take the form of rational, deliberate, or even conscious opposition.

To sum up, putting a spotlight on social entrepreneurial practitioners is important as this offers "a better understanding of how social entrepreneurs define themselves" while shedding light on "whether the discourses of social entrepreneurs are consistent with those of the actors that study, fund and teach them" (Hervieux et al., 2010, p. 61). The ideological voids and disjuncture which necessarily emanate from such empirical journeys might in turn be used not only for opposing dominant formations of knowledge but also, importantly, for redefining the conditions under which something new can be produced.

13.7   Interventionist Critique: Opening More Radical Trajectories

In view of the seemingly infinite possibility of critique, it must be borne in mind that there is a danger that critique remains an intellectual undertaking which has no real effects on the level of practice. It is for this reason that we will deepen our initial elaboration (cf. Chapter 13.1) on the social dynamics that might diminish critique, in order to suggest 'interventionist critique' as a promising way forward.

Regarding the relationship between critique and change, there are insightful theoretical and empirical studies which have pointed out how ruling systems of power are able to absorb, incarnate and neutralise critique (e.g. Boltanski and Chiapello, 2005). Instead of overthrowing its object or adversary, critique itself often is instrumentalised in such a way as to maintain prevailing hierarchies, relations of domination and social segregation (Willig, 2009). Concerning social entrepreneurship, there are rather clear indications that the more critical potentials of the concepts are being sidelined by political, business, and academic discourses. Instead of conceiving social entrepreneurship as an instrument for unsettling ruling conventions, paradigms or dominant (economic) systems (Edwards, 2008), it is mostly envisioned as a pragmatic instrument for expanding entrepreneurial forms to the social, for saving tax-money or simply for rendering people and organisations in the nonprofit sector more responsible and accountable. The integration of social entrepreneurship into business schools seems to have accelerated this diminishment, as dominant approaches mainly envision social and ecological problems and solutions in line with conservative images of 'progress'. Using Cukier et al.'s (2011) study as an example, we understand that the academic representation of social entrepreneurs strongly relies on well-known cases such as Bill Drayton, Fazle Abed, Herry Greenfield and Ben Cohen, Muhammad Yunus or Ibrahim Abouleish. Though these references are not problematic per se, they become problematic once they prevent us from understanding that this group of iconic individuals, including the societal blueprints they produce, and the institutions that award and support them, collectively produce a rather selective understanding of what is good for society as a whole. If this is taken to its logical conclusion, we must address whether the kind of critique previously discussed has any chance of changing the 'standard language' of social entrepreneurship.

Where it might be true that spectacular representations have already normalised a biased understanding of social entrepreneurship, this makes it even more urgent to create the conditions of critique under which new scenarios (both ideologically and materially) become possible. This entails uncovering and confronting the conservatism inherent in the everyday activities of policy-makers, academics, think thanks and incubators. In addition, it entails 'tuning into' the work of conservative imagination and actively producing the space in which the unexpected can take flight. According to Nealon (2008), the task is to find ways to intensify the sort of tensions and struggles discussed in conjunction with the critique of transgression. This makes it necessary to conceptualise the nexus between critical thinking and intervention (Steyaert, 2011).

To begin with, we would like to use the concept 'intervention' to signal a rethinking of the conventional, academic understandings of critical research. Interventionist research sees the researcher not in a state of external reflection to the research objects, but in a state of active and internal alliance with them. Being allied is conceived by interventionist research as a precondition for re-modelling social entrepreneurship in inventive ways. Interventionist research relies on participatory modes of interaction to co-produce new knowledge while simultaneously enacting new realities (Steyaert and Dey, 2010). Writing with social entrepreneurs and not about them, interventionist research represents a political stance, as it is primarily interested in acts of world-making (Beyes and Steyaert, 2011). Such ontological processes cannot be but critical as they bring new issues to our attention (i.e. those which are not imaginable in the parameters of academic reason) and clearly question shared assumptions (Beaulieu and Wouters, 2009). Characterised by an interest in intervening in the enactment of societal and community issues, interventionist critique's yardstick is less representation and understanding (though this might play a role) but the extent to which research is able to "reconfigure what is sayable and visible in a specific social space" (Beyes and Steyaert, 2011, p. 112). Fostering dissensus and antagonism instead of consensus and agreement, interventionist research disrupts the taken-for-granted knowledge about social entrepreneurship by mobilising the immanence of the people on the ground (Willig, 2009; cf. also part 6). Shaking up the self-content of elitist imagination, interventionist research becomes, as Steyaert (2011) tells us, parrhesia: an event that speaks out against authority and creates reality in the name of another truth. For such a novel critique of social entrepreneurship, which intervenes in order to invent (Steyaert, 2011), the task is to try to change the canonical organisation of experience by sensing and amplifying the "not-yet" (Bloch, 1986) that manifests itself in ephemeral pulses of the social. Therefore, by reflecting and amplifying practitioners' spontaneous ideas and inspirations, interventionist critique might support social entrepreneurs in releasing society's always present (yet thoroughly contained) emancipatory promises.

Granted, it might have been helpful for the reader to have had an illustration of what inter-ventionist critique looks like exactly, and what the inventive intervention into societal or community issues actually means. Yet, telling readers precisely what is expected from them would have run counter to our conviction that any overtly prescriptive account can hamper instead of enable the re-invention of social entrepreneurship critique. Consequently, the void being produced here is deemed instrumental for calling upon scholars' curiosity and imagination, and to enlist them as inventive and interventionist participants in tomorrow's critical research agenda of social entrepreneurship.

13.8   Introduction to Critical Reflection

The following remarks are primarily directed towards readers who are new to critical thinking and who are keen to engage critically with the subject of social entrepreneurship. As an entry point into critiquing social entrepreneurship, we recommend being immersed in "deep readings"[31] of popular social entrepreneurship texts. The first step towards this end comprises gathering adequate textual material. As a rule of thumb, the more well-known and socially authorised the texts being analysed are, the more likely it is that the analysis will yield significant results, not least by raising questions about social entrepreneurship's dominant modes of signification. One could start by collecting definitions of social entrepreneurship as produced by promotion agencies such as Ashoka (cf. www.ashoka.org/social_entrepreneur) or the Schwab Foundation (cf. www.schwabfound.org/sf/SocialEntrepreneurs/Whatisasocialentrepreneur/index.htm). Alternatively, texts comprising political speeches and programmes on social entrepreneurship could be analysed (e.g. www.socialenterprise.org.uk/pages/quotes-about-social-enterprises.html). Lastly, it might be useful to study practitioner guidebooks which seek to equip nonprofit managers with knowledge that enables them to become more effective and efficient as social entrepreneurs (e.g. Dees, Emerson and Economy, 2001; 2002).

Once the analytic material has been collected, the next step is to analyse how a particular text is set up to make social entrepreneurship appear in a determinate way (e.g. useful, necessary, non-ideological, spectacular, etc.). At the most elementary level, the textual analysis, which might broadly be defined as iconoclastic, aims at raising awareness that there is nothing inherently 'natural' about social entrepreneurship and that what we commonly accept as its very essence is, in fact, contingent on language. We thus recommend reading texts in two steps. In the first reading, texts should be approached in a casual manner (e.g., as one would read the newspaper). In the second reading, which is unfaithful to the texts' surface logic, the critic takes a step back from the texts, cultivating the view that all we can know about social entrepreneurship, its promises, dreams, and utopias, ultimately depends on the use of language. Hence, acknowledging that the "truth" of social entrepreneurship depends on how the latter is dealt with through language, the critic approaches the texts by asking who is talking, based on what language conventions, to what audience, and with what intention. A good way to reveal how the dominant meaning of a text on social entrepreneurship is linguistically constructed, and how it depends on what the text excludes, is to imagine what the text emphasises and what it ignores, or how it could have been shaped differently altogether. As linguistic readings are anything but trivial, we have put together some guiding questions (cf. below).

---

[31]   Though the kind of readings I am promoting here are not inspired by one particular school of critical thinking, probably the most accurate way of describing their analytic heritage is linguistics.

The list is not exhaustive and the questions should support nascent critical analysts in becoming acquainted with the basic principles of language-based analysis.

■ **Genre:** what is the function/purpose of the text (e.g., to persuade, to inform, to explain, to prescribe, to sell, to compare, etc.)?

■ **Audience:** who is the imagined audience of the text?

■ **Framing:** how is the issue of social entrepreneurship presented, from which perspective (theoretical angle, discipline, world-view) is it depicted?

■ **Foregrounding/backgrounding:** which parts of social entrepreneurship are emphasised, marginalised or even omitted (in other words, what is said and what is not said)?

■ **Style:** what sort of language is used (e.g., objective, scientific language versus colourful, expressive, emotional language)?

■ **Lexicon:** does the text make frequent use of particular words, concepts?

■ **Ideological dimension:** how does the text try to convince the reader that social entrepreneurship is attractive, necessary, even representing a potential career option for her/him?

13.9   Further Reading

[1] Baines, S., Bull, M. and Woolrych, R. (2010), "A more entrepreneurial mindset? Engaging third sector suppliers to the NHS", in: *Social Enterprise Journal*, vol. 6, no. 1, pp. 49-58.

[2] Bull, M. (2008), "Challenging tensions: Critical, theoretical and empirical perspectives on social enterprise', in: *International Journal of Entrepreneurial Behaviour & Research*, vol. 14, no. 5, pp. 268-275.

[3] Chand, V.S. (2009), "Beyond nongovernmental development action into social entrepreneurship", in: *Journal of Entrepreneurship*, vol. 18, no. 2, pp. 139-166.

[4] Curtis, T. (2008), "Finding that grit makes a pearl: A critical re-reading of research into social enterprise", in: *International Journal of Entrepreneurial and Behaviour & Research*, vol. 14, no. 5, pp. 276-290.

[5] Froggett, L. and Chamberlayne, P. (2004), "Narratives of social enterprise: From biography to practice and policy critique", in: *Qualitative Social Work*, vol. 3, no. 1, pp. 61-77.

[6] Goss, D., Jones, R., Betta, M. and Latham, J. (2011), "Power as practice: A micro-sociological analysis of the dynamics of emancipatory entrepreneurship", in: *Organization Studies*, vol. 32, no. 2, pp. 211-229.

[7] Jones, R., Latham, J. and Betta, M. (2008), "Narrative construction of the social entrepreneurial identity", in: *International Journal of Entrepreneurial Behaviour & Research*, vol. 14, no. 5, pp. 330-345.

[8] Latham, J., Jones, R. and Betta, M. (2009), "Critical social entrepreneurship: An alternative discourse analysis", in: J. Wolfram-Cox, T.G. LeTrent-Jones, M. Voronov and D. Weir (eds.), *Critical management studies at work: Negotiating tensions between theory and practice*, pp. 285-298, Cheltenham, UK, Edward Elgar.

[9] Levander, U. (2010), "Social enterprise: Implication of emerging institutionalized constructions", in: *Journal of Social Entrepreneurship*, vol. 1, no. 2, pp. 213-230.

[10] Lounsbury, M. and Strang, D. (2009), "Social entrepreneurship: Success stories and logic construction", in: D. Hammack and S. Heydemann (eds.), *Globalization, philanthropy and civil society: Projecting philanthropic logics abroad*, pp. 71-94, Indiana University Press, Bloomington, IN.

[11] Peredo, A.M. and McLean, M. (2006), "Social entrepreneurship: A critical review of the concept", in: *Journal of World Business*, vol. 41, no. 1, pp. 56-65.

[12] Sud, M., VanSandt, C.V. and Baugous, A.M. (2008), "Social entrepreneurship: The role of institutions", in: *Journal of Business Ethics*, vol. 85, no. 1, pp. 201-216.

[13] Ziegler, R. (ed.) (2009), *An introduction to social entrepreneurship: Voices, preconditions, contexts*, Edward Elgar, Cheltenham, UK.

[14] Zografos, C. (2006), "Rurality discourses and the role of the social enterprise in regenerating rural Scotland", in: *Journal of Rural Studies*, vol. 23, pp. 38-51.

13.10   Bibliography

[1]   Armstrong, P. (2005), *Critique of entrepreneurship: People and policy*, Palgrave Macmillan, Basing-stoke.

[2]   Arthur, L., Cato, M.S., Keenoy, T. and Smith, R. (2009), "Where is the 'social' in social enterprise?", in: D. Fuller, A.E.F. Jonas and R. Lee (eds.), *Interrogating alterity: Alternative economic and political spaces*, pp. 207-222, Ashgate , Aldershot.

[3]   Baudrillard, J. (2008), *The perfect crime*, Verso, New York.

[4]   Beaulieu, A. and Wouters, P. (2009), "e-research as intervention", in: N. Jankowski (ed.), *e-Research, Transformation in Scholarly Practice*, pp. 54-69, Routledge, London.

[5]   Beyes, T. and Steyaert, C. (2011), "The ontological politics of artistic interventions: implications for performing action research", in: *Action Research*, vol. 9, no. 1, pp. 100-115.

[6]   Bloch, E. (1986), *The principle of hope*, MIT Press, Cambridge, Mass.

[7]   Boddice, R. (2009), "Forgotten antecedents: Entrepreneurship, ideology and history", in: R. Ziegler (ed.), *An introduction to social entrepreneurship: Voices, preconditions, contexts*, pp. 133-152, Edward Elgar, Cheltenham, UK.

[8]   Boje, D., Böhm, S.G., Casey, C., Clegg, S., Contu, A., Costea, B., Gherardi, S., Jones, C., Knights, D., Reed, M., Spicer, A. and Willmott, H. (2001), "Radicalising Organisation Studies and the meaning of critique", in: *Ephemera: Critical dialogues on organization*, vol. 1, no. 3, pp. 303-313.

[9]   Boltanski, L. (2011), *On critique: A sociology of emancipation*, Polity Press, London.

[10] Boltanski, L. and Chiapello, E. (2005), *The new spirit of capitalism*, Verso, London.

[11] Boltanski, L. and Thévenot, L. (1999), "The sociology of critical capacity", in: *European Journal of Social Theory*, vol. 2, no. 3, pp. 359-377.

[12] Boschee, J. and McClurg, J. (1), "Towards a better understanding of social entrepreneurship: Some important distinctions", online: http://www.setoolbelt.org/resources/180.

[13] Calas, M.B., Smircich, L. and Bourne, K.A. (2009), "Extending the boundaries: reframing "entre-preneurship as social change" through feminist perspectives", in: *Academy of Management Review*, vol. 34, no. 3, pp. 552-569.

[14] Carmel, E. and Harlock, J. (2008), "Instituting the 'third sector' as a governable terrain: Partner-ship, procurement and performance in the UK", in: *Policy & Politics*, vol. 36, no. 2, pp. 155-171.

[15] Cho, A. (2006), "Politics, values and social entrepreneurship: a critical appraisal", in: J. Mair, J. Robinson and K. Hockerts (eds.), *Social entrepreneurship*, pp. 34-56, Palgrave Macmillan, Basing-stoke.

[16] Cook, B., Dodds, C. and Mitchell, W. (2003), "Social entrepreneurship: false premises and danger-ous forebodings", in: *Australian Journal of Social Issues*, vol. 38, 57-71.

[17] Cukier, W., Trenholm, S., Carl, D. and Gekas, G. (2011), "Social entrepreneurship: A content anal-ysis", in: *Journal of Strategic Innovation and Sustainability*, vol. 7, no. 1, pp. 99-119.

[18] Dees, G.J., Emerson, J. and Economy, P. (2001), *Enterprising nonprofits: A toolkit for social entrepre-neurs*, John Wiley & Sons, New York.

[19] Dees, G.J., Emerson, J. and Economy, P. (2002), *Strategic tools for social entrepreneurs: Enhancing the performance of your enterprising nonprofit*, John Wiley & Sons, New York.

[20] Dempsey, S.E. and Sanders, M.L. (2010), "Meaningful work? Nonprofit marketisation and work/life balance in popular autobiographies of social entrepreneurship", in: *Organization*, vol. 17, no. 4, pp. 437-459.

[21] Dey, P. and Steyaert, C. (2010), "The politics of narrating social entrepreneurship", in: *Journal of Enterprising Communities*, vol. 4, no. 1, pp. 85-108.

[22] Edwards, M. (2008), *Just another emperor? The myths and realities of philanthrocapitalism*, Demos, New York.

[23] Eikenberry, A.M. (2009), "Refusing the market: A democratic discourse for voluntary and non-profit organizations", in: *Nonprofit and Voluntary Sector Quarterly*, vol. 38, no. 4, pp. 582-596.

[24] Eikenberry, A.M. and Kluver, J.D. (2004), "The marketization of the nonprofit sector: Civil society at risk?", in: *Public Administration Review*, vol. 64, no. 2, pp. 132-140.

[25] Foucault, M. (1978), *The history of sexuality, Vol. I: An introduction*, Random House, New York.
[26] Foucault, M. (1991), "Governmentality", in: G. Burchell, C. Gordon and P. Miller (eds.), *The Foucault effect: Studies in governmentality*, Harvester Wheatsheaf, Hemel Hempstead.
[27] Foucault, M. (1998), "A preface to transgression", in: L.D. Faubion (ed.), *Michel Foucault: Aesthetic, method and epistemology*, pp. 69-87, The Penguin Press, Harmondsworth.
[28] Freeman, R. and Rustin, M. (1999), "Introduction: welfare, culture and Europe", in: P. Chamberlayne, A. Cooper, R. Freeman and M. Rustin (eds.), *Welfare and culture in Europe: Towards a new paradigm in social policy*, pp. 9-20, Jessica Kingsley, London.
[29] Friedman, V.J. and Desivilya, H. (2010), "Integrating social entrepreneurship and conflict engagement for regional development in divided societies", in: *Entrepreneurship & Regional Development*, vol. 22, no. 6, pp. 495-514.
[30] Gasché, R. (2007), *The honor of thinking: Critique, theory, philosophy*, Stanford University Press, Stanford.
[31] Gilman-Opalsky, R. (2011), *Spectacular capitalism: Guy Debord & the practice of radical philosophy*, Minor Compositions, London.
[32] Hervieux, C., Gedajlovic, E. and Turcotte, M.F.B. (2010), "The legitimization of social entrepreneurship", in: *Journal of Enterprising Communities*, vol. 4, no. 1, pp. 37-67.
[33] Hjorth, D. (2009), "Entrepreneurship, sociality and art: Re-imagining the public", in: R. Ziegler (ed.), *An introduction to social entrepreneurship: Voices, preconditions, contexts*, pp. 207-227, Edward Elgar, Cheltenham, UK.
[34] Hogg, E. and Baines, S. (2011), "Changing responsibilities and roles of the voluntary and community sector in the welfare mix: A review", in: *Social Policy and Society*, vol. 10, no. 3, pp. 341-352.
[35] Jones, C. and Spicer, A. (2010), *Unmasking the entrepreneur*, Cheltenham, Edward Elgar.
[36] Jones, R., Betta, M., Latham, J. & Gross, D. (2009), "Female social entrepreneurship as a discursive struggle", in: *AGSE*, pp. 871-885.
[37] Kerlin, J.A. and Pollak, T.H. (2010), "Nonprofit commercial revenue: A replacement for declining government grants and contributions?", in: *American Review of Public Administration*, November 17, 2010, 0275074010387293.
[38] Mair, J. and Marti, I. (2006), "Social entrepreneurship research: a source of explanation, prediction, and delight", in: *Journal of World Business*, vol. 41, pp. 36-44.
[39] Martin, R.L. and Osberg, S. (2007), "Social entrepreneurship: The case for definition", in: *Stanford Social Innovation Review*, pp. 28-39.
[40] Nealon, J.T. (2008), *Foucault beyond Foucault: Power and its intensifications since 1984*, Stanford University Press, Stanford.
[41] Nicholls, A. and Young, R. (2008), "Preface to the paperback edition", in: A. Nicholls (ed.), *Social entrepreneurship: New models of sustainable social change*, pp.vii-xxiii, Oxford University Press, Oxford.
[42] Noys, B. (2011). "The fabric of struggles", in: B. Noys (ed.), *Communization and its discontents: Contestation, critique, and contemporary struggle*, pp. 7-22, Minor Compositions, London.
[43] Ogbor, J. O. (2000), "Mythicising and reification in entrepreneurial discourse: Ideology-critique of entrepreneurial studies", in: *Journal of Management Studies*, vol. 37, no. 5, pp. 605-635.
[44] Parkinson, C. and Howorth, C. (2008), "The language of social entrepreneurs", in: *Entrepreneurship & Regional Development*, vol. 20, no. 3, pp. 285-309.
[45] Rawls, J. (1999), *A theory of justice*, Oxford University Press, Oxford.
[46] Sandberg, J. and Alvesson, M. (2011), "Ways of construction research questions: Gap-spotting or problematization?", in: *Organization*, vol. 18, no. 1, pp. 23-44.
[47] Steyaert, C. (2011), "Entrepreneurship as in(ter)vention: reconsidering the conceptual politics of method in entrepreneurship studies", *Entrepreneurship & Regional Development*, vol. 23, no. 1-2, pp. 77-88.
[48] Steyaert, C. and Hjorth, D. (2006), "What is social in social entrepreneurship?", in: C. Steyaert and D. Hjorth (eds.), *Entrepreneurship as social change: A third movements in entrepreneurship book*, pp. 1-18, Edward Elgar, Cheltenham.
[49] Steyaert, C. and Dey, P. (2010), "Nine verbs to keep the research agenda of social entrepreneurship

'dangerous'", in: *Journal of Social Entrepreneurship*, vol. 1, no. 2, pp. 231-254.

[50] Teasdale, S. (2011), "What's in a name? Making sense of social enterprise discourses", in *Public Policy and Administration*, vol. 25, doi: 10.1177/0952076711401466

[51] Weiskopf, R. and Steyaert, C. (2009), "Metamorphoses in entrepreneurship studies: towards an affirmative politics of entrepreneuring", in: D. Hjorth and C. Steyaert, (eds.), *The politics and aesthetics of entrepreneurship. A fourth movements in entrepreneurship book*, pp. 183-201, Edward Elgar, Cheltenham, UK.

[52] Willig, R. (2009), "Critique with anthropological authority: a programmatic outline for a critical sociology", in: *Critical Sociology*, vol. 35, no. 4, pp. 509-519.

[53] Yunus, M. (2008), *Creating a world without poverty: Social business and the future of capitalism*, PubliAffairs, New York.

[54] Žižek, S. (2008), *Violence: Six sideways reflections*, Picador, New York.

The Authors

Prof. Dr. Dr. **Ann-Kristin Achleitner**
Technische Universität München

Ann-Kristin Achleitner holds the Chair in Entrepreneurial Finance (supported by KfW Bankengruppe) and is Scientific Co-Director at the Center for Entrepreneurial and Financial Studies (CEFS) at Technische Universität München (TUM). Her research focus is in the areas of venture capital, private equity, family firms and social entrepreneurship.

E-Mail: ann-kristin.achleitner@wi.tum.de
Web: www.ef.wi.tum.de

Prof. Dr. **Markus Beckmann**
Leuphana University Lüneburg

Markus Beckmann is Assistant Professor of Social Entrepreneurship at the Centre for Sustainability Management as well as director of the Social Change Hub (SCHub) at Leuphana University Lüneburg, Germany. His research and teaching interests are in the areas of social business and entrepreneurship, sustainability, corporate social responsibility as well as business ethics.

E-Mail: markus.beckmann@leuphana.de
Web: www.leuphana.de/markus-beckmann

Dr. **Holger Berg**
University of Wuppertal

Holger Berg is managing director at the Institute of Entrepreneurship and Innovations Research (IENTIRE) at the Bergische University of Wuppertal. He is visiting lecturer at Academia de Studii Economice (ASE), Bucharest, and the Technical University of Kosice, Slovakia. His research interests concern Entrepreneurship Policy, Regional Development, Renewable Energies and Evolutionary Economics.

E-Mail: berg@wiwi.uni-wuppertal.de
Web: www.igif.de

Christiane Blank, *MBA*
University of Wuppertal

Christiane Blank is a postgraduate research associate at the Chair of Entrepreneurship and Economic Development at University of Wuppertal since January 2009. Her special research interests lie in the fields of Social Entrepreneurship, Nonprofit Management and Corporate Social Responsibility.

E-Mail: blank@wiwi.uni-wuppertal.de
Web: volkmann.wiwi.uni-wuppertal.de/index.php?id=508

Prof. Dr. **Heather Cameron**
Freie Universität Berlin

Heather Cameron is Professor of Inclusive Education at the Freie Universität Berlin, a honorary professor at the University of the Western Cape in South Africa, and a social entrepreneur. As the founder and director of Boxgirls International, a girls rights through sports organization operating in Germany, South Africa and Kenya, Heather Cameron has been awarded an Ashoka fellowship in 2010. Her research concerns organizational development, impact assessment, gender inclusion, and innovative program design.

E-Mail: cameron@zedat.fu-berlin.de
Web: www.ewi-psy.fu-berlin.de/einrichtungen/arbeitsbereiche/integrationspaedagogik, www.boxgirls.org

Dr. **Pascal Dey**
University of St. Gallen

Pascal Dey is a senior research fellow at the Institute for Business Ethics at the University of St. Gallen. His research interest lies in investigating phenomena such as social entrepreneurship, social innovation and change from the perspective of discourse, power, flows or critical thinking.

E-Mail: pascal.dey@unisg.ch
Web: www.iwe.unisg.ch/en/Ueber+uns/Team/Dey.aspx

Dr. **Kati Ernst**
University of Wuppertal

Kati Ernst was a former doctoral student at the Schumpeter School of Business and Economics, University of Wuppertal. Her research is on the formation of social entrepreneurial intentions, in which she applies the theory of planned behaviour. Kati Ernst has also been a management consultant at McKinsey & Co., Inc. since 2006. She belongs to the Berlin Office.

Dr. **Marc Grünhagen**
University of Wuppertal

Marc Grünhagen is a lecturer and researcher in entrepreneurship at the Schumpeter School of Business and Economics, Wuppertal University, Germany. His teaching portfolio includes entrepreneurial management and economics courses at the undergraduate and postgraduate level. Marc's current research focus is on university entrepreneurship, entrepreneurial growth, and entrepreneurial intentions.

E-Mail: gruenhagen@wiwi.uni-wuppertal.de
Web: volkmann.wiwi.uni-wuppertal.de

Prof. Dr. **Andreas Heinecke**
European Business School

Andreas Heinecke is founder and CEO of Dialogue Social Enterprise. Andreas currently holds the position of an honorary professor at Danone Chair of Social Business at EBS Business School. He was the first Ashoka Fellow in Western Europe and is a Global Fellow from the Schwab Foundation of Social Entrepreneurship. He focuses his research on topics of social innovation, investment and learning as well as on emotional intelligence, aging and poverty.

E-Mail: andreas.heinecke@ebs.edu
Web: www.ebs.edu/fakultaet.html?id=11582

Prof. Dr. **Benjamin Huybrechts**
University of Liege

Benjamin Huybrechts is Assistant Professor in Social Enterprise Management at HEC Management School, University of Liege. His research and teaching interests are in the areas of social enterprise and social entrepreneurship, fair trade, renewable energy, governance, legitimacy and institutional theory.

E-Mail: b.huybrechts@ulg.ac.be
Web: www.ces.ulg.ac.be/fr_FR/a-propos-du-ces/equipe/benjamin-huybrechts-2

Prof. Dr. **Johanna Mair**
Hertie School of Governance

Johanna Mair is the academic editor of Stanford Social Innovation Review and the Hewlett Foundation Scholar at the Stanford Center on Philanthropy and Civil Society. Her research focuses on how novel organizational and institutional arrangements generate economic and social development and the role of entrepreneurs in this process. She received her Ph.D in strategy at INSEAD.

E-Mail: jmair@stanford.edu
Web: johannamair.com; ssireview.org or pacscenter.stanford.edu

Judith Mayer, *M.Sc.*
Technische Universität München

Judith Mayer is research assistant at the chair in Entrepreneurial Finance of Prof. Dr. Dr. Ann-Kristin Achleitner at Technische Universität München. Her research interests refer to relationship of social investors and social entrepreneurs, protection of the double bottom line of social enterprises and corporate governance of social enterprises.

E-Mail: judith.mayer@wi.tum.de
Web: www.ef.wi.tum.de

Dr. **Susan Müller**
University of St. Gallen

Susan Müller is a senior research associate at the Swiss Research Institute of Small Business and Entrepreneurship at the University of St. Gallen. Her research interests are in social entrepreneurship, entrepreneurship education, and business models.

E-Mail: susan.mueller@unisg.ch
Web: www.kmu.unisg.ch

Prof. Dr. **Alex Nicholls**
University of Oxford

Alex Nicholls is University Lecturer in Social Entrepreneurship at the University of Oxford. His research and teaching interests are in the areas of social entrepreneurship, organizational legitimacy and governance, social finance, fair trade, impact measurement and innovation.

E-Mail: alex.nicholls@sbs.ox.ac.uk
Web: www.sbs.ox.ac.uk/research/people/Pages/AlexNicholls.aspx

Dr. **Wiebke Rasmussen**
Ruhr-University of Bochum

Wiebke Rasmussen has worked as a research and teaching assistant at the Marketing Department of the Ruhr-University of Bochum. Her main research interests comprised for nonprofit and foundation marketing, whereas she also covers commercial marketing topics and topics at the interface between for nonprofit and commercial marketing, such as corporate social responsibility and cause-related marketing.

Dipl.-Phys. **Heike Schirmer**
Freie Universität Berlin

Heike Schirmer is a doctoral candidate at the Freie Universität Berlin. Her research focuses on partnerships between social entrepreneurs and corporations. Heike Schirmer holds a Master in Physics from the Technical University Munich and has worked as a management consultant before starting her PhD.

E-Mail: heike.schirmer@fu-berlin.de

Shuchi Sharma, *MBA*
Bennett Day School Chicago

Shuchi Sharma is an entrepreneur and the Director of Operations at the Bennett Day School in Chicago. Her research focuses on assessing impact in double bottom line ventures. She received her MBA from IESE Business School.

E-Mail: shuchisharma@gmail.com

Dipl.-Ing. **Wolfgang Spiess-Knafl**
Technische Universität München

Wolfgang Spiess-Knafl is Scientific Assistant at the Chair in Entrepreneurial Finance (supported by KfW Bankengruppe) at Technische Universität München (TUM). His research interests are in the field of social entrepreneurship.

E-Mail: wolfgang.spiess-knafl@wi.tum.de
Web: www.ef.wi.tum.de

Prof. Dr. **Chris Steyaert**
University of St. Gallen

Chris Steyaert is Professor of Organizational Psychology at the University of St. Gallen, Switzerland. Professor Steyaert's research and teaching focus on creativity and newness, diversity management and difference, language and translation, and aesthetic and political implications of organizational life. His work has been published in leading academic journals such as Human Relations, Organization, Journal of Management Studies, European Journal of Work and Organizational Psychology, Journal of World Business and International Studies of Management and Organization.

E-Mail: chris.steyaert@unisg.ch
Web: www.opsy.unisg.ch

Prof. Dr. **Kim Oliver Tokarski**
Bern University of Applied Sciences

Kim Oliver Tokarski is Professor of Business Management and Entrepreneurship as well as head of the Competence Centre on Corporate Business Development at the Bern University of Applied Sciences, Switzerland. He is a visiting professor at Academia de Studii Economice (ASE), Bucharest. His research and teaching interests are in the areas of entrepreneurship in general, social entrepreneurship, as well as business ethics, and corporate social responsibility.

E-Mail: kim.tokarski@bfh.ch
Web: www.wirtschaft.bfh.ch/tokarski

Prof. Dr. **Christine K. Volkmann**
University of Wuppertal

Christine Volkmann is Chair of Entrepreneurship and Economic Development, Director of the Institute for Entrepreneurship and Innovations Research and visiting professor at the Academia de Studii Economice (ASE), Bucharest. She also holds the UNESCO Chair of Entrepreneurship and Intercultural Management and is board member of the Dr. Werner Jackstädt Center for Interdisciplinary Entrepreneurship and Innovation Research. Social/Responsible and Sustainable Entrepreneurship are among her major fields of research.

E-Mail: volkmann@wiwi.uni-wuppertal.de
Web: volkmann.wiwi.uni-wuppertal.de

Index

Management / Unternehmensführung / Organisation
↗

Rico Baldegger / Pierre-André Julien
Regionales Unternehmertum
Ein interdisziplinärer Ansatz
2011. 350 S., Br. € (D) 39,95
ISBN 978-3-8349-2630-2

Jörg Fischer / Florian Pfeffel
**Systematische Problemlösung
in Unternehmen**
Ein Ansatz zur strukturierten Analyse
und Lösungsentwicklung
2010. 341 S., Br. € (D) 34,95
ISBN 978-3-8349-0776-9

Swetlana Franken
Verhaltensorientierte Führung
Handeln, Lernen und Diversity
in Unternehmen
3. überarb. u. erw. Aufl. 2010. XII, 355 S.,
Br. € (D) 32,95 ISBN 978-3-8349-2232-8

Rolf Franken / Swetlana Franken
**Integriertes Wissens- und Innovations-
management**
Mit Fallstudien und Beispielen aus der
Unternehmenspraxis
2011. 320 S. mit 78 Abb. Br. € (D) 32,95
ISBN 978-3-8349-2599-2

Jörg Freiling / Martin Reckenfelderbäumer
Markt und Unternehmung
Eine marktorientierte Einführung
in die Betriebswirtschaftslehre
3., überarb. u. erw. Aufl. 2010. XXVIII, 492 S.,
Br. € (D) 36,90 ISBN 978-3-8349-1710-2

Erich Frese / Matthias Graumann /
Ludwig Theuvsen
Grundlagen der Organisation
Entscheidungsorientiertes Konzept der
Organisationsgestaltung
10., überarb. u. erw. Aufl. 2012. XVIII, 711 S. mit
120 Abb. u. 4 Tab. Br. € (D) 49,95
ISBN 978-3-8349-3029-3

Urs Fueglistaller / Christoph Müller /
Thierry Volery
Entrepreneurship
Modelle - Umsetzung - Perspektiven
Mit Fallbeispielen aus Deutschland,
Österreich und der Schweiz
2. überarb. u. erw. Aufl. 2008. XXVI, 512 S.,
Br. € (D) 39,90 ISBN 978-3-8349-0729-5

Asmus J. Hintz
**Erfolgreiche Mitarbeiterführung
durch soziale Kompetenz**
Eine praxisbezogene Anleitung
2011. 373 S., Br. € (D) 39,95
ISBN 978-3-8349-2441-4

Harald Hungenberg
Strategisches Management in Unternehmen
Ziele - Prozesse - Verfahren
6., überarb. u. erw. Aufl. 2010. XXVI, 605 S.,
Br. € (D) 46,95 ISBN 978-3-8349-2546-6

Hartmut Kreikebaum / Dirk Ulrich Gilbert /
Glenn O. Reinhardt
**Organisationsmanagement
internationaler Unternehmen**
Grundlagen und moderne Netzwerkstrukturen
2., vollst. überarb. u. erw. Aufl. 2002. XVI, 243 S.,
Br. € (D) 34,95 ISBN 978-3-409-23147-3

Stand: Januar 2012. Änderungen vorbehalten.
Erhältlich im Buchhandel oder beim Verlag.

Abraham-Lincoln-Straße 46. D-65189 Wiesbaden
Tel. +49 (0)6221 / 345 - 4301. springer-gabler.de

⚘ Springer Gabler

Klaus Macharzina / Joachim Wolf

Unternehmensführung

Das internationale Managementwissen
Konzepte – Methoden – Praxis
7., vollst. überarb. u. erw. Aufl. 2010.
XXXIX, 1.181 S., Geb. € (D) 59,95
ISBN 978-3-8349-2214-4

Klaus North

Wissensorientierte Unternehmensführung

Wertschöpfung durch Wissen
5., akt. u. erw. Aufl. 2010. XII, 378 S.,
Br. € (D) 49,95 ISBN 978-3-8349-2538-1

Marc Oliver Opresnik / Carsten Rennhak

**Grundlagen der Allgemeinen
Betriebswirtschaftslehre**

Eine Einführung aus marketingorientierter Sicht
2012. XII, 478 S. mit 92 Abb. u. 33 Tab. Br.
€ (D) 39,95 ISBN 978-3-8349-1562-7

Georg Schreyögg

Organisation

Grundlagen moderner Organisationsgestaltung
Mit Fallstudien
5., vollst. überarb. u. erw. Aufl. 2008.
XII, 516 S., Br. € (D) 36,90
ISBN 978-3-8349-0703-5

Georg Schreyögg / Jochen Koch

Grundlagen des Managements

Basiswissen für Studium und Praxis
2., überarb. u. erw. Aufl. 2010. XIV, 496 S.,
Br. € (D) 26,95 ISBN 978-3-8349-1589-4

Albrecht Söllner

**Einführung in das Internationale
Management**

Eine institutionenökonomische Perspektive
2008. XXII, 487 S., Br. € (D) 42,95
ISBN 978-3-8349-0404-1

Horst Steinmann / Georg Schreyögg

Management

Grundlagen der Unternehmensführung
Konzepte – Funktionen – Fallstudien
6., vollst. überarb. Aufl. 2005.
XX, 952 S., Geb. € (D) 44,90
ISBN 978-3-409-63312-3

Martin K. Welge / Andreas Al-Laham

Strategisches Management

Grundlagen – Prozess –
Implementierung
6., akt. Aufl. 2012. XXII, 1028 S., Geb.
€ (D) 57,95 ISBN 978-3-8349-2476-6

Martin Welge / Marc Eulerich

Corporate-Governance-Management

Theorie und Praxis der guten
Unternehmensführung
2012. XX, 250 S. mit 79 Abb. Br. € (D) 32,95
ISBN 978-3-8349-3003-3

Axel v. Werder

Führungsorganisation

Grundlagen der Corporate Governance,
Spitzen- und Leitungsorganisation
2., akt. u. erw. Aufl. 2008. XXVIII, 445 S.,
Br. € (D) 47,95
ISBN 978-3-8349-0678-6

Joachim Wolf

**Organisation, Management,
Unternehmensführung**

Theorien, Praxisbeispiele und Kritik
4., vollst. überarb. u. erw. Aufl. 2010.
XXVIII, 712 S., Br. € (D) 46,95
ISBN 978-3-8349-2628-9

Stand: Januar 2012. Änderungen vorbehalten.
Erhältlich im Buchhandel oder beim Verlag.

Abraham-Lincoln-Straße 46 . D-65189 Wiesbaden
Tel. +49 (0)6221 / 3 45 - 4301 . springer-gabler.de

⚉ Springer Gabler

CPSIA information can be obtained
at www.ICGtesting.com
Printed in the USA
LVHW110833030122
707670LV00011B/640